"Don't let the fun of reading th[...] profound explanation of the ro[...]

—Max O. De Pree,
author of *Leadership Is an Art*
and *Dear Zoe*

"With wit, humor, and occasional disarming directness, Donald McCullough brings sight to a culture that is often blind to the wonder of being and to the simple respect we owe each other. A delightful book, which delivers what it promises: healing, laughter, and grace."

—Alan Jones,
dean of Grace Cathedral, San Francisco,
and author of *Soul Making* and
The Soul's Journey

"A sensible handbook . . . [written] with sprightly humor."

—*Publishers Weekly*

"A gently humorous voice."

—*Kirkus Reviews*

"This is more than instructions to behave yourself! It's a charmingly honest account of applying common courtesy in everyday situations. *Say Please, Say Thank You* should be mandatory reading for everybody."

—Luci Swindoll,
featured speaker for the
"Women of Faith" national tour and
author of *Celebrating Life*

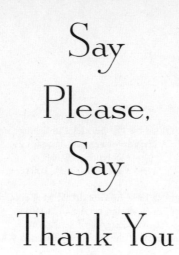

Say Please, Say Thank You

The Respect We Owe
One Another

Donald McCullough

Perigee Books

A Perigee Book
Published by The Berkley Publishing Group
A division of Penguin Putnam Inc.
375 Hudson Street
New York, New York 10014

G. P. Putnam's Sons edition: September 1998
First Perigee edition: October 1999

Perigee ISBN 0-399-52538-6

Published simultaneously in Canada.

The Penguin Putnam Inc. World Wide Web site address is
http://www.penguinputnam.com

The Library of Congress has catalogued the G. P. Putnam's Sons edition
as follows:

McCullough, Donald W., date.
Say please, say thank you: the respect we owe one another /
Donald W. McCullough.
p.   cm.
ISBN 0-399-14439-0 (alk. paper)
1. Etiquette.   2. Respect for persons.   I. Title.
BJ1853.M44   1998   98-22401 CIP
395—dc21

Printed in the United States of America

10   9   8   7   6   5   4   3

To my sister,
Patti Blue,
in gratitude for her love

Acknowledgments

To fail to thank those who helped produce a book on courtesy would be an act of egregious discourtesy. Not wanting to be guilty of this, I'm eager to mention the contributions of several people for whom I have deep, deep gratitude. Kathy Yanni, my agent, went far beyond the call of duty by providing support not simply at the initial stages of this project but also in the long process of bringing the idea to fruition; her considerable skills in the making of a book were immensely helpful. John Duff, my editor at Putnam, was a joy to work with, offering, as needed, the crack of a whip, a sharp and wise editorial pencil, and energizing encouragement. Kathleen Stahl, as copy editor, helped strengthen the text. Betty Waggoner provided invaluable secretarial help, keeping organized both this manuscript and my life in general. I did most of my writing on a computer, which means I frequently called upon the assistance of Gussie Manigluck; more than once she rescued me from the breakdowns of thingamajigs that will forever be a mystery to this technologically challenged writer. San Francisco Theological Seminary—trustees, faculty, and students—provided a thumbs-up signal to keep writing when other responsibilities pressed upon me. Scott Schaefer read a number of chapters, offering helpful suggestions, as did my daughters, Jennifer and Joy, along with Jennifer's husband, my wonderful new son-in-law, Geoff Ziegler. My parents, John and Ione McCullough, made insightful comments and continue to be the nurturing presence they have always been for me. If I've forgotten anyone, call me, and we'll sail San Francisco Bay as restitution for my oversight.

Finally, a personal word to my sister. Thanks, Patti, for your love through a difficult season of my life. You're the best sister a brother could have. Had I known this when we were kids, maybe I wouldn't have made you walk behind me on the way to school and left you lying in the middle of Twenty-fourth Avenue the day you fell. Sorry. I dedicate this book to you as an expression of my love.

Contents

Say
Please,
Say
Thank You

Mind Your Manner

Treating People with Respect

On a recent trip out of town I was hurrying to the terminal gate before my plane left without me. I calculated I had a few seconds to spare, so I stopped at the newsstand to pick up the morning paper and a box of mints to avoid arriving at my destination with an uninformed mind and bad breath. The cashier silently mouthed the amount I owed, punched buttons on her computer, and handed me change—all while carrying on a telephone conversation. I was a little irritated at her rudeness but wouldn't have thought much about it if she hadn't given me back a couple of dollars less than I had coming.

I was ticked off. I'm not usually short fused, at least not unless seriously provoked. But I had been thinking about the distressing loss of courtesy in American life, and all my frustration about this—my annoyance at people who don't RSVP or who telephone during dinner or who freely flip the bird in traffic or who can't seem to throw a baseball without spitting prodigious amounts of tobacco juice through the television camera onto my living room floor—rose up into my throat. I did my own sort of spitting as I threw her a look of complete disgust.

She said, "I'm sorry." And then continued talking on the telephone.

Which was probably what pushed me over the edge, provoking me to launch into a lecture about how she wouldn't have shortchanged me had she not been distracted by her telephone call. My outburst wasn't all that bad (not as bad as my daughters sometimes got); I wasn't ranting or raving or making a complete fool of myself. But what I said did have a sharp edge to it.

"Look, I told you, I'm sorry." And then she continued talking on the telephone.

This was probably what made me start my second speech that began with "I'm sorry" but didn't have a single sorrowful syllable in it.

Whereupon she lowered the telephone receiver, carefully put her hand over it, and laser-beamed me with eyes of intense anger. She said, "*You listen to me.* I'm talking to my elderly mother, a shut-in who lives out of town. We can talk only once a week, and she really needs me. Now you apologize to me right now. I'm waiting, mister. You tell me you're sorry."

At that moment I felt something like the embarrassment of a preacher who, halfway through his sermon, discovers he has forgotten to put his pants on. I felt exposed. My own lack of courtesy was showing.

I mumbled an apology and slithered down the concourse toward gate 78. The sour feeling in my stomach during the flight had nothing to do with airline food. I told myself she *had* been rude, and yet I beat up myself for having been rude in response; back and forth it went, self-justification and self-incrimination. What I felt most of all was dirty, as though I had gotten down in the mud of incivility that seems to cover our world.

Because this mud is getting pretty deep, the subject of civility has suddenly become a hot topic in our national conversation. The cover story of a recent issue of *USA Today* was titled, "Excuse Me, But . . . Whatever Happened to Manners?" The article noted how impossible it is "to ignore the growing rudeness, even harshness, of American life. . . . An overwhelming majority of Americans—89% in a *U.S. News & World Report* poll last April—think incivility is a serious problem. More than three in four said it's gotten worse in the past 10 years."[1]

So I decided to write this book about courtesy. Let me be clear at the outset that you will find very little about etiquette in these pages. If you want to know how to seat ex-spouses at a wedding, or if you need guidance on which fork to use first at a formal dinner, you would do better to consult Amy Vanderbilt or Emily Post or Judith Martin. To tell the truth, I never have. I would no doubt be a classier guy had I taken the time to read their books, but my family and friends have watched over me and kept me from making a social jackass of myself (at least most of the time).

My concern has to do with something more basic: the respect we owe one another. Without this, there isn't much point in talking of manners or etiquette. Without a proper foundation, the most elaborate house of rules will come tumbling down in the slightest breeze of rudeness, let alone the tornado of crudity now assaulting us.

Simply put, *the neglect of courtesy leads to the collapse of community.* Does this sound melodramatic? Think about it. The heart of courtesy is respect for persons; it has less to do with manners than with a manner of relating, a manner that acknowledges the worth of human beings. At the heart of discourtesy is disrespect for people; it has less to do with breaking rules of etiquette than with breaking the tie that binds us together.

The one who neglects to say "please" cradles within his or her soul an infant dictator who thinks it's all right to bark orders and who just may grow up to become a cruel despot. The one who flips the bird when cut off in traffic indulges an inner violence that, unchecked, can lead to assault or even murder. The one who tells jokes at the expense of others panders to a prejudice not unrelated to the diabolical impulse that sets fire to African-American churches.

Not every kid who forgets to say "please" when asking for candy grows up to be Saddam Hussein, of course. We can thank God that most of the time we keep the demon of discourtesy under control. We may put our feet up on our neighbor's coffee table, but our disrespect for property doesn't extend to throwing a rock through their picture window just because we're mad that their kid practices the drums until two in the morning. We might sorely *long* to chuck a big one into their living room with a note tied to it threatening far worse, but we check that impulse before it gets out of hand. Not always, though, and that's one reason the world sometimes seems headed downhill faster than the stomach-turning plunge of a first-class roller coaster. If much modern life seems not simply rude but torn apart by conflict, it's because too often we've allowed our baser inclinations and selfish desires to run over the dignity of other persons.

Here's my basic assumption: *people deserve to be treated with respect,* not because they have earned it, not because they are always kind or easy to get along with, but because they are part of something bigger than themselves. They partake of humanity—and that means they occupy a pretty important place in the scheme of things.

The great religions teach this. Hindus greet one another with folded hands and bowed head, a symbol of reverence for the sacredness of that person's life. Buddhists believe that humans, though enmeshed in the karma of cause and effect, are capable of transcending suffering and eventually reaching the state of nirvana, the transformed mode of human consciousness, the eternal realm that is utterly true and dependable. Muslims teach that humans have been created by God and thus have the dignity of being responsible for adoration and obedience. Jews call one another to live with righteousness and justice, believing that humans have been created in the very image of God.

The festivals of my Christian tradition begin with Advent, the season of longing for God's intervention in the mess of this world, and move into Christmas, the celebration of God's appearance in Jesus. In Jesus, Christians believe, God has become one with us—fully human—and thus humanity itself has been lifted to a place of immense significance. Humans are the beloved of God, claimed by a holy love that summons us to respond in gratitude with love for God and love for one another.

Now, I can't speak for other religions, but I can admit

we Christians aren't always faithful to our deepest convictions. In our best moments, though, and on our best days, we know that God delights not just in people like us, not just in those who, at least from outward appearances, seem more or less to have their ducks in a row, but that God loves everyone—old Clyde, sleeping in a urine-reeking stairwell with a half-empty bottle of muscatel; terrified Maria, hiding in the hills under a cardboard shelter and hoping to find work; hardened Sam, making his way "up the river" for whatever life he has left on death row. We know that all people, whatever their condition and whatever their achievements or failures, have an eternal worth, a value beyond our ability to calculate. If only we could see others the way God sees them!

Did you see the stage version of the story of Don Quixote, *The Man of La Mancha*? Aldonza serves drunken camel drivers as a waitress by day and in other ways at night. The man of La Mancha sees this whore and yet sees something more, something no one else sees. "My Lady," he says.

She looks at him incomprehensibly and exclaims, "Lady?!"

"Yes, you are my Lady, and I shall give you a new name. I shall call you Dulcinea."

Later Aldonza suffers the ultimate insult. She is raped. Don Quixote finds her hysterical and disheveled; her blouse has been pulled off and her skirt ripped. He says compassionately, "My Lady, Dulcinea, Oh, my Lady, my Lady."

"Don't call me a lady," she cries. "Oh God, don't call me a lady. Can't you see me for what I am? I was born in a ditch by a mother who left me there naked and cold—too hungry to cry. I never blamed her. She left me there hoping I'd have the good sense to die. Don't call me a lady. I'm only Aldonza. I'm nothing at all."

As she runs into the night he calls out, "But you are my Lady."

The man of La Mancha, a knight serving his beloved Lady, seeks his adventure. But at the end he is alone, dying from a broken heart, despised and rejected. To his deathbed comes a Spanish queen with a mantilla of lace. Quietly she kneels beside him and prays. He opens his weak eyes and says, "Who are you?"

"My Lord, don't you remember? You sang a song, don't you remember? 'To dream the impossible dream, to fight the unbeatable foe, to bear the unbearable sorrow, to run where the brave dare not go.' My Lord, don't you remember? You gave me a new name, you called me Dulcinea." She stands proudly. "I am your Lady."[2]

Aldonza is transformed because Don Quixote sees something in her she doesn't see in herself: a dignity befitting royalty. He treats her with the manners of the court, as though she were a queen.

The word *courtesy* actually comes from the word *court.* My dictionary defines courteous as "marked by polished manners, gallantry, or ceremonial usage of a court . . . marked by respect and consideration of others."[3] To be courteous is to adopt the manners of the court, to treat one another like royalty.

C. S. Lewis, reflecting on the Christian teaching that humans are eternal beings, said, "It is a serious thing to live in a society of possible gods and goddesses, to remember that the dullest and most uninteresting person you talk to may one day be a creature which, if you saw it now, you would be strongly tempted to worship, or else a horror and a corruption such as you now meet, if at all, only in a nightmare. All day long we are, in some degree, helping each other to one or other of these destinations. It is in the light of these overwhelming possibilities, it is with the awe and the circumspection proper to them, that we should conduct all our dealings with one another, all friendships, all loves, all play, all politics. There are no *ordinary* people."[4]

Because every person deserves to be treated with respect, we ought to consider the way we treat one another. When pondering patterns of behavior, the big ethical questions may first spring to mind: What is justice? How can a capitalist society engender compassion? Where do we draw the line between economic growth and environmental stewardship? What about abortion and euthanasia and capital punishment? We should give much thought to these things. In this book, though, I'm more interested in the little things, such as remembering to say "thank you" and to call your mom on Mother's Day. These things may not seem very important when compared with the major problems facing our culture. Yet they may be the best place to begin; they may be the only honest place to begin. If a person can't remember to say thank you to her housekeeper, it probably won't matter much if she writes a major philosophical treatise on kindness; if a person is rude to his family, the angels probably won't give a holy rip if he preaches soaring sermons on the nature of love.

Our lives are built one small brick at a time, ordinary day by ordinary day. With each little expression of thoughtfulness we create something of immense significance—character, both our own and that of others. The big things will eventually confront us; there's no evading life's tough stuff. But by then we just might have become the kind of people who will more likely know, and be able to do, what is right.

In the following chapters I prescribe and proscribe, indulging myself at times in what may be my own crotchets. They may not all be your crotchets. Fair enough. I encourage you to make your own list and write your own special book. Better yet, send your ideas to me, and maybe I'll write a sequel. But at least join with me in thinking about how little acts of courtesy can have a big role in creating a more *humane* humanity.

One

---•◦•---

Say Please

Respecting the Freedom of Others

"GIVE ME CANDY, MOMMY."

"What do you say?"

"Thank you."

"No, before that . . ."

"*Pees,* Mommy, *pees.*"

Most of us have been in a conversation like this, and many of us have been on both sides of it. We were taught to say please, and we teach our children to do the same. It's in the core curriculum of Courtesy 101; it's as rudimentary to politeness as the alphabet is to reading. Even if we sometimes neglect the word because we're too irritated or too busy or think we're too important, we know we should preface a request with it. The most imperious jerk, barking out orders like a royal pain in the backside has, I suspect, a little voice within that sounds a lot like his mother asking, "Didn't you forget to say something?"

Why is this word so important? Simply put, it acknowledges the freedom of others. If you say to your spouse, "Get me a cup of coffee," you deserve a night on the sofa, if not a session with the marriage counselor; your spouse is not a slave, not an object of your control. But if you say, "Would you please get me a cup of coffee?" you will likely get coffee and perhaps even more. The word "please" changes the tone completely. It's really an abbreviated way of saying, "If you please, if it gives you pleasure, get me a cup of coffee." Don't even think about going to the kitchen, in other words, unless you *want* to do this for me.

Personal freedom is part of the joy and responsibility of being human. The extent of freedom varies, of course, depending on the context: we have obligations to others and we have commitments to moral and spiritual and national laws. But no matter how constricted our choices might seem in a given circumstance, we still have something within that resists being captive. Even prisoners retain a freedom of spirit, as so clearly seen in reading Dietrich Bonhoeffer's letters from a Nazi prison or Nelson Mandela's autobiographical account of life in a South African jail.

This freedom creates both joy and misery. When used wisely—selecting the right Cabernet, say, or marrying the right person—it leads to delight. When used unwisely—getting drunk with the Cabernet or abusing your spouse—it leads to suffering. But no matter how we use freedom, whether for good or for ill, it's part of the dignity of being human, and therefore something we ought to acknowledge in our relationships. Saying "please" erects a little castle to protect the inherent royalty of other persons.

When I don't say "please," I'm not intending to be a dictator, but that's essentially the result; I might as well strut around with self-congratulatory medals pinned to my chest, expecting everyone to salute when I get near. To be sure, I always have excuses to explain my behavior, at least to my mind: I'm in a hurry and need to get things done; I'm really bushed; I'm under a lot of stress. But no matter how much cheap cologne you spread over a stinky body, you still have a stinky body. The truth is, if I can't take half a second to say "please," I don't deserve to have anyone do anything for me, except perhaps have a judge lock me up for reckless use of a dangerous ego.

The problem is that very freedom we were just thinking about: I enjoy my freedom and I like to exercise it at all times—even over other people. I like to be in control; I like to be in the driver's seat, or I'm a little edgy, ramming my foot through the floor board and having to restrain myself from grabbing the steering wheel. (I'm speaking metaphorically, but my family would tell you this is also literally true. The only time I was completely willing to have someone else drive was when I had to get to the hospital because of a kidney stone kicking the living daylights out of my urethra and I thought I was going to die anyway. But that's another story.) It's not that I don't trust other people; I simply trust myself more.

You know what's scary about this? I'm beginning to sound like G. Gordon Liddy. Because of patriotic service rendered at Watergate he was sent to prison, and this apparently gave him time to think about what was important in life. So after being released, he said, "I have found within myself all I need and all I ever shall need. I am a man of great faith, but my faith is in George Gordon Liddy. I have never doubted me."[1]

Well, I *have* doubted myself and I'm not planning any political burglaries, but I have to confess I prefer being in charge. I'm spilling my guts about this because I'm pretty sure I'm not alone in this compulsion to control. I'm not pointing any fingers, but is anyone reading this who hasn't, at one time or another, wanted to *guarantee* the outcome of a situation, who has wanted to *ensure* another person's response? Let's admit it: we've all wanted to play God. We haven't necessarily wanted to *be* God (too much responsibility and too little respect nowadays), but we have wanted to assume God's role in certain instances. Not more than once or twice a day maybe, but enough to complicate life for those around us, who, it should be pointed out, want the same thing, and all these conflicted egos slugging it out is one good reason why the evening news should be followed with a Mylanta chaser.

If I order my secretary to get a folder without the courtesy of a "please," I chip away a little piece of her freedom, and she resents it and, being in a foul mood, orders her husband to clean up the kitchen, and he knows he shouldn't be treated like this and reacts by barking a command at one of his employees . . . and on it goes, until we've all been demeaned.

The Golden Rule tells us to do unto others as we would have them do unto us. Because this is in the form of an imperative, we might have the wrong impression: we might imagine we can choose to put this rule into effect or not, depending on whether we obey it. Actually, it's closer to the Tall Buildings Rule—step off the top of a tall building and you will be squished on the sidewalk. We're talking law here, a statement of what happens in the universe of relationships. Whatever you do unto others they will do back to you. Call it the Law of Reciprocal Action.

I know: sometimes the law is broken. Thank God the chain of events gets interrupted when someone turns the other cheek and chooses not to see something, or having seen it chooses to forget it, or not able to forget it chooses to forgive it. Grace happens, and when you receive it, you know it's what makes life worth living. But grace always comes as a gift not as law. You can't count on it. The only grace you can trust is God's, but as for grace from others, don't bet your pension on its inevitability. Act as though the Law will be operative, because it probably will.

Treat one another with a lack of respect, and that lack of respect will spread, not only back to you but toward others. Treat one another with the dignity befitting human beings, and that dignity will in turn multiply. Attitudes and actions are as infectious as a mean virus.

I recently came across a story about Billy Martin, the irrepressible baseball manager and player. Back in the days when he and Mickey Mantle were playing for the New York Yankees, they wanted to go hunting during the off-season. Mickey had a friend down in Texas where he was allowed to hunt, so he drove Billy out to the ranch.

When they arrived, Mickey suggested that Billy stay in the truck while he went into the ranch house to check with the owner. Mickey was given immediate approval. But the owner asked a favor: his mule was going blind and he didn't have the heart to kill it. The rancher wondered if Mickey would do it for him. Mickey agreed and saw an opportunity to play a joke on Billy.

He sulked back to the truck, got in, and slammed the door. Billy asked what was wrong. Mantle replied that the rancher wouldn't let them hunt. He said, "In fact, I'm so mad that I'm going over to that barn and shoot one of his mules." Martin protested that he couldn't do that. But Mantle was determined. "Just watch me. He wouldn't let me hunt, and I'll show him!" Mantle marched over to the barn, went inside, and shot the mule.

When he came out he was shocked to see Billy Martin standing near the barn with a smoking rifle, shouting, "That no good son of a gun; I just shot two of his cows."

The contagion of attitudes and actions. But thank God it works in reverse, too. In the Greek myth, Pygmalion sculpted a statue of a beautiful woman and fell in love with it. Through the power of his love and expectations he brought the statue to life. Eliza Doolittle becomes My Fair Lady. Aldonza becomes Dulcinea. Our stories reflect a truth about human relationships: we can fan the hidden spark of goodness in another person until it bursts into flame. A boy grows into a man of character through a mother's undying love; a girl blossoms into a woman of great achievement through the nurturing imagination of a lover; a fumbling, bumbling employee becomes a department head through the unflagging confidence of a boss.

So we treat one another with courtesy, with respect, because others always carry within themselves more than meets the eye. What's at the core of their being, of course, is humanity, a great mystery theologians and philosophers and psychologists struggle to define, but never will. Some mysteries will not surrender to the control of explanation; some mysteries can only be received on their own terms. "Mystery withers at the touch of force," Diogenes Allen has written. "This is a law, a truth that governs us as firmly as any law we have met so far, and as firmly as exists in all the permutations of matter and energy. When we treat other people as objects subordinate to our goals, their mystery has no effect on us. The larger mystery into which genuine personal encounter can lead us never becomes open to us."[2]

And thus, to protect the mystery, we don't run roughshod over the freedom of others, but we pause for a split second to say "please," to create a buffer zone that acknowledges the dignity of being human.

Two

Say Thank You

Acknowledging Dependence on Others

WHEN JIM THORPE WON THE DECATHLON AND PEN-
tathlon events at the 1912 Olympics in Stockholm, King
Gustav V of Sweden presented him with a bronze bust and
told him, "You, sir, are the greatest athlete in the world."

Thorpe responded, "Thanks, King."[1]

Brief, but to the point. Had he failed to say at least this
much our country would have been embarrassed and people
would have commented on his lack of manners. From the
time we were children and our mothers grabbed us by the
collar, not letting us escape until we mumbled a "Thank you,"
we have known that some situations call for an expression of
gratitude.

After receiving a birthday gift or having a colleague side
with us in a losing battle, we write a thank you note. At least

we intend to do this. Sometimes we don't quite get around to it, do we? Or am I the only one who always has exactly 137 things that are more important to do? Procrastination is one thing I never put off. So I often wait until the next day to say thanks, and then the next day after that, and then by the next day the whole idea gets swept under the carpet of far more pressing and important demands upon my time.

But if I'm too busy to take five minutes to acknowledge a gift—a friend shopping for groceries, say, and preparing a delightful dinner—I'm not simply in danger of Miss Manners hauling me before the court of public opinion and throwing the book of etiquette at me, I'm just too busy for my own good and the world's too. If I always move forward to the next task on my agenda without pausing to look back in gratitude to the good things I have been given, I allow my almighty self-importance to blind me to the truth of things: I am completely dependent on others, and every achievement of "mine" has been won through a team effort.

From the moment we were conceived in our mother's womb to when we are given the last shot of morphine as life slips away amid tubes and monitors in the intensive care unit, we depend on others.

Can you think of anything you have accomplished completely on your own? Did you have the highest gross sales this month? Congratulations, but don't forget your secretary's tireless efforts to make you look a whole lot better than you really are. Did you win a Nobel Prize in literature? Congratulations, but don't forget the junior high teacher who endured your adolescent nonsense long enough to instill within you a love of good books. Did you win a marathon? Congratulations, but don't forget your parents' fine genes, not to mention the people who design increasingly efficient and expensive running shoes. No one does it alone!

And there is another reason why we should say thanks: it helps us. When we express gratitude, we experience, however fleeting and brief, a moment of contentment. When we say thank you, we heave a sigh of satisfaction in a world of grasping. Instead of reaching out toward more, we pause to enjoy what we have.

This is why gratitude has a hard time surviving. We live in a culture of consumption that constantly tells us we need more. The *New York Times* estimated that the average American is exposed to thirty-five hundred commercial messages each day[2], and from billboards and television and newspapers and magazines and the sides of buses they're all saying, "You don't have enough! Keep striving to achieve more and acquire more!" A thankful spirit gets run over in the ensuing stampede, often left a flattened wreck along the road of our ambitions. We pause occasionally to try to resuscitate the corpse, such as on Thanksgiving Day, but we're not about to slow down for fear of losing the race.

But even if you win the rat race, you're still a rat. Maybe even a discourteous rat, which is of course the worst kind. On the other hand, when you look back long enough to say thank you, acknowledging your dependence on others, an inner transformation happens—a kind of turning upside down of your perspective—that enables you to rejoin the human race.

Years ago, as a pastor struggling to find ways to comfort people whose lives had exploded because of the missiles of suffering that life can launch our way, I came across a little book by John Claypool, *Tracks of a Fellow Struggler*, in which he tells of the horror of losing his ten-year-old daughter to leukemia. A couple years after her death, when he was able to look back from a little distance, he said, "At least it makes things bearable when I remember that Laura Lue was a gift, pure and simple, something I neither earned nor deserved nor had a right to. And when I remember that the appropriate response to a gift, even when it is taken away, is gratitude, then I am better able to try and thank God that I was given her in the first place. . . . The way of gratitude does not alleviate the pain, but it somehow puts some light around the darkness and builds strength to begin to move on."[3]

Here is the revolutionary truth revealed through the eyes of gratitude: *nothing has to be.* The proverbial cup may be half empty, but it could be completely empty. Ten years isn't much, and it's easy to wail against the injustice of a child's death. But it occurred to John Claypool that even ten years of his daughter's life didn't have to be, and therefore they should be received with gratitude.

Part of the problem, I think, is our sense of entitlement. We feel we deserve the good things of life, that blessings have a kind of inevitability about them. If something wonderful happens, we need hardly pause to give thanks. We had it coming to us, after all; we deserved it. And when something doesn't work out the way we had expected, we feel robbed, cheated.

If we understand that nothing has to be, that all life is a gift, it revolutionizes our perspective. Our view of things gets topsy-turvy. This is what happened to St. Francis of Assisi, according to G. K. Chesterton. He saw the world upside down, hanging in complete dependence: "Instead of being merely proud of his strong city because it could not be moved, he would be thankful to God almighty that it had not been dropped; he would be thankful to God for not dropping the whole cosmos like a vast crystal to be shattered into falling stars."[4]

Consider all the ways you are dependent on others, all the ways you move through your days at the mercy of others. The Latin word for dependence, as Chesterton reminds us, literally means hanging. When you walk into your office and see framed degrees and certificates displaying the splendor of your achievements to the world and you actually begin believing your own press notices, imagine everything suddenly turned upside down and hanging. By what? The goodness of others, that's what. And if you're a person of faith, you will also say the goodness of God.

Why not pause long enough to acknowledge this dependence? It can make a profound difference in the deep-down places. Instead of a fevered grasping after the next thing, you just might feel something like peace.

For a long time I've tried to begin each day with a prayer of thanksgiving. To be strictly accurate, I first get a cup of coffee and then I thank God. Starting to pray this way isn't easy, because my first instinct is to confess my failures. It feels as though I ought to clear up certain uncomfortable matters between me and the Almighty before moving on to higher ground. But that usually doesn't work. If you've screwed up as much as I, there never seems enough time left for other subjects; self-absorption has a kind of gravitational force, and the larger I let it grow, the harder it is to escape its pull. So against all instinct, I start by expressing gratitude as things come to mind—a good night's sleep, my daughter calling from college the day before simply to say hi and not to ask for more money, the fact that I like my other daughter's new husband, the view of redwoods out my window, the miracle of Mozart on the stereo, the blessedness of coffee in the morning and wine in the evening—everyday things, perhaps, but good things that ought never to be taken for granted.

I've noticed that when I do this an inner shift takes place: the problems that seemed so heavy, that started assaulting me in the first minutes of consciousness, suddenly seem less threatening. They're still there, to be sure, but it's as though my interior furniture was re-arranged and the ugly sofa was taken out of the living room and stored in the basement. Everything seems brighter, too, as though a new light shines through the windows of my soul. I recall that my faith has given a name to this light—Grace—and my faith tells me it is a manifestation of divine love. As I continue my prayer, I go on to ask for help with problems, listing my worries and needs and even my selfish desires. After thanksgiving, however, I do so not in fearful desperation, but more as a child in the arms of a loving parent.

Just try it. You might be surprised.

I know. There are times when things can go so badly you need pretty sharp eyes to see flowers in the desert of your misery. Sometimes it takes serious creativity to view things in a positive way. I'm reminded of the time General Creighton Abrams once found himself and his men completely surrounded by the enemy. Not a good situation. But he said, "Men, now for the first time in the history of this campaign, we are in a position to attack the enemy in any direction!"[5] That's what I call a creative angle of vision. No matter how awful the circumstances there is at least something for which to give thanks.

Your son comes home with purple hair, three rings in his nose, and more aimlessness than you thought possible in one human. At least he's home, and it's good to hear his laughter, even if he's on the phone with his girlfriend. You've been notified that you're about to be audited by the I.R.S. At least you have enough money to pay your house payment and maybe even your credit card bill this month. Your mother has been offering entirely too much advice on how to raise children, and her little maxims are starting to make you want to suck your own thumb and cry in helpless frustration. At least she will be available next weekend to baby-sit so you and your spouse can get away for a few days. There is always *something* for which to give thanks.

Acknowledging dependence on others becomes a kind of gift to yourself. Do it, and contentment will follow. The feeling may be fleeting, but I promise it will be there. If it doesn't last long, try saying thanks again, and then again. As gratitude becomes a habit, peace will begin to feel at home.

Three

---·◆·---

Tell White Lies (Occasionally)

Protecting from Unnecessary Hurt

VERNA CLAIMS THAT I SAID HER BABY WAS UGLY. I
can't imagine being that insensitive, though it was a long time
ago and my memory isn't exact in these matters. I do recall
Verna holding up her newborn and saying, "Isn't she cute?"
And I, seeing a splotchy, scrunched little face and being committed to complete honesty, must have said something like,
"Well, she really is . . . a baby." Or maybe, "It takes an infant
a few months before she can really be considered cute." Or I
suppose there is a teensy-weensy possibility I said, "Strictly
speaking, she is kind of ugly at the moment but will undoubtedly become a ravishing beauty."

Nearly thirty years have passed, but whenever I run into
Verna she reminds me that I called her baby ugly. I don't
know her daughter; for all I know she became Miss Universe,

or perhaps my words lodged in her tiny subconscious and she has spent the last fifteen years in psychoanalysis working on low self-esteem. In any event, I now wish I had lied. It would have saved all of us a lot of grief.

Occasionally, courtesy calls for a lie. Let me hasten to stress I'm talking about *white* lies, not black or gray or even off-white lies. Snow-white lies. But even so, I realize I've just launched this chapter into very dangerous waters, with rocks and riptides of tough ethical questions all around us. We had better navigate through this subject very carefully, with a firm grip on the tiller.

It's difficult to be truthful about the importance of lying, because we're so used to liars claiming the high ground of truth. Politicians lie to get elected, doctors lie on Medicare reports, universities lie about athletes, advertisers lie to sell products, ordinary citizens lie on income tax returns, and yes, even preachers lie. In the words of a *Time* magazine essay, ours is "a huckstering, show-bizzy world, jangling with hype, hullabaloo, hooey, bull, baloney, and bamboozlement."[1] We live in a market-driven society, and to make the sale—whether it be a car or a candidate or a beer—the truth gets pulled and stretched past anything resembling reality.

And yet, strangely, we also live in a tell-all culture. We have elevated the personal confession to an art form: supermodels confess insecurity about their bodies, movie stars confess shyness, politicians confess frustration, and preachers confess sexual indiscretions. It's the AA approach run amok—"Hi, my name is Bill, and I'm a recovering alcoholic/gambler/overeater/sex addict/couch potato." I have nothing against AA, mind you. The twelve-step program provides an excellent way to overcome a variety of addictions. But there is a time and place for psychological stripping; call me uptight and closed down, but I don't think it should be in front of just anyone who will listen, not to mention on national television or in supermarket tabloids. Howard Stern, the apotheosis of *anything goes,* has let the whole world in on his anxieties over—as Dave Barry would say, I'm not making this up!—his small . . . uhm . . . how shall I say it in a family book? . . . "male member." Do we really need this sort of "honesty"?

This sharing, unfortunately, has a way of spreading outward toward others, as if my openness gives me the right to pull you out of whatever closet you're in. It's the aren't-you-glad-we're-so-psychologically-mature-that-we-can-be-completely-honest manner of relating to others: "Theresa, really, you have too much of an inferiority complex about your figure; it's not as bad as you think." We did the same thing in junior high school ("Break out the gas masks! Bobby just let one!"), but now that we're more mature we practice psychobabble hit-and-run as we sit in the hot tub and sip Chardonnay. Frankly, I would just as soon go back to the good old days when a put-down was a put-down. (My all-time favorite, by the way, took place at a dinner party at the end of a heated exchange between Winston Churchill and a female MP. The woman scornfully remarked, "Mr. Churchill, you are drunk." Churchill replied, "And you, madam, are ugly. But I shall be sober tomorrow." That was not courteous, I know, and so forget I mentioned it.)

Back to the problem before us: How can we speak truthfully about lying in a schizoid environment torn between deceitful hype and compulsive confession? The ancient philosopher Aristotle may be of help to us. He said that honesty was more than unloading everything to everyone. Rather, it is speaking *the right truth to the right person at the right time in the right way for the right reason.*[2]

Not every truth is mine to tell: a truth shared in confidence and a truth that would needlessly hurt another is not mine to tell. Not every person has a right to know the truth: some willfully distort what they hear; some use facts to bludgeon the life out of a larger, more important truth; some have blabbermouths with unrelenting and indiscriminating tongues. Not every time is appropriate for the truth: some seasons call for tactful silence; the day your friend's daughter dropped out of school is not the day to tell her about your daughter making the honor roll. Not every way of communication honors the truth: sometimes the manner in which something gets conveyed subverts reality, as when a preacher says all the right words about God's love but through a tone of voice and a concluding string of "oughts" (therefore we *ought* to do this and we *ought* to do that) that makes you feel guiltier than ever. Not every reason deserves the use of truth: some motives for telling the truth are simply too destructive to deserve the respectability of being clothed in the truth; some expressions of "honesty" are really attempts to demean and belittle another person.

When it's the wrong truth or the wrong person or the wrong time or the wrong way or the wrong reason, a white lie may have more integrity than a facile, insensitive "honesty." But when does a white lie begin to turn a slight shade of gray? When does it crossover and become an immoral act of dishonesty?

Perhaps a good test would be to ask, Does this lie protect the other person or does it protect me? Let's waste no time in admitting that it's not easy to tell the difference. On the surface, a lie may appear to protect another from unnecessary pain; on closer examination, however, it's actually an attempt to save me from uncomfortable exposure. In Graham Greene's *The Heart of the Matter,* a police officer in a West African colony during the war has an affair, and in an effort to "protect" his wife from the pain of the truth, walks down a road of falsehood that leads to disaster. Greene's story may be fiction but it's a profound truth reenacted everyday. It's easy to convince ourselves we're guarding the feelings of another when we're only trying to protect our own hides— and this sort of deception often ends in more complication and more lying and more pain than we could have ever imagined.

But just because it's difficult to tell the difference between an appropriate lie and a morally unacceptable lie does not mean we give up the attempt to make the distinction. Life, after all, is difficult. So we press on, doing our best, knowing we're not God, and counting on the grace of God when we blow it. Though committed to honesty, we know that sometimes courtesy calls for creative stretching of the truth.

The telephone rings and when you answer it you hear the voice of your wife's best friend. She speaks in a perky, over-friendly way that's a dead giveaway she thinks you're a first-class horse's heinie. And the feelings are mutual. But your wife likes her a lot, so you return the banter. She asks to speak to your wife, but she's out for the evening. "Well, I guess I can mention it to you," your wife's friend says. "I'm calling to invite you two to dinner next Friday evening. Yesterday your wife said she thought you were free, and I told her I'd get back to her. What do you think?"

What you really think is that you've already seen more than enough of that woman and her boring husband, and that even if next Friday evening wasn't the opening game of the NBA championship series you still wouldn't want to be with them, not for any reason, not under any circumstances, not if they were the last people on earth, not in a million years. So you say, "Well, I suppose that would be just fine. We'll look forward to being with you. Thanks for the invitation." You lie! Yes, but it's not a bad lie, as lies go. It's the sort of white lie that helps lubricate the inevitable friction in social relationships. And though it hides some of your true feelings, it also protects a larger truth—the truth that your wife, at least, will look forward to the evening and really does love her friend, who happens to be going through a very difficult time, and that you love your wife and want to make her happy. In the interests of this larger truth you told a white lie, and it was the courteous thing to do.

At this point some of you may be uncomfortable reading a book by a Presbyterian clergyman who has just advocated lying. If so, may I suggest you turn immediately to chapter 33 ("Tell Your Buddy His Fly Is Open: Speaking the Truth in Love") for a rousing defense of the importance of speaking honestly.

Four

———•·•———

Don't Let Your Fingers Do the Talking

Curbing the Violence Within

ONE DAY, HEADING HOME FROM SOME PASTORAL duty, I turned the corner to drive up my street. Close in front of me was another car, with a driver who apparently had had an abrupt change of mind. He suddenly stopped in order to make a U-turn.

I honked at him, of course. I would like to report that I was simply offering a friendly warning of his impending danger. Actually, to continue the honesty you've already come to appreciate in this book, I have to admit I was irritated. A little honk seemed perfectly justified, if not positively required. (Why else do they put horns on cars if not to communicate with idiots who do stupid things?)

Completing his dangerous, illegal, and altogether jerky maneuver, he waved as he passed by me. At first I thought it was a friendly gesture and felt a pang of guilt for honking. Then I noticed it was a specialized sort of wave, the one with the middle finger standing by itself in obscene isolation, what is commonly called "flipping the bird." (If you're one of the three people left in the world who doesn't know what this means, do two things: first, get down on your knees and thank God for your innocence; second, ask your kids to explain it— their reaction will help you understand, if not the exact details, at least the general idea.)

I noticed his gesture first, but then looking beyond the finger I saw his face—a face belonging to a member of my congregation.

Instinctively, I laughed: here was a guy who flipped off his pastor! I pictured him trying to get up the courage to tell his wife. But then I began to wonder whether it really was a mistake. Perhaps he had recognized me *before* expressing himself. Was it something I had said in a recent sermon? All I can tell you is that I did not see him in church the following Sunday, or, come to think of it, ever again.

He need not have been all that embarrassed. I know we all get angry at times and react in ways we later regret. I have not personally flipped the bird, mind you—unless you count the time I broke my middle finger, as a consequence of my wife washing the kitchen floor and neglecting to tell me, and I had a gargantuan cast that was very conspicuous whenever I lifted my hand (after one especially energetic sermon, my associates gently but firmly suggested I refrain from so many gestures—but I have wanted to. And when really provoked I have felt like doing far worse.

Getting through life with other people who never seem to have sufficient sensitivity and good sense can be like running through an obstacle course of constant provocation. And unless you're Mother Teresa, the frustration of this can build up until you want to beat the hell out of someone. The problem is, if you give way to these feelings, you're more likely to beat the hell *into* someone, and that someone may very well be yourself. If we've learned anything at the end of this bloody century, we should have learned that conflict leads to more conflict, violence leads to more violence, and the escalating whirlpool sucks all down into an ugly darkness.

Before the psychologists jump all over me, let me acknowledge that anger is a natural human emotion. We all experience it in one degree of intensity or another. And yes, anger seeks and perhaps should always find some outlet. But the way it expresses itself makes all the difference. It's one thing to beat the pavement in a five-mile run after a fight with your boss; it's something else to beat your boss. Indulging anger to the point of running over the dignity of other people threatens the fragile bonds of human community.

Unrepressed emotions have created an express-yourself-and-let-it-all-hang-out culture, leaving few boundaries of respect still in place. To make my case, I set before you exhibit A: the present state of organized sports. Rewarding Dennis Rodman for being as bad as he wants to be (cursing, butting, and kicking his way through NBA games) with celebrity status and a stratospheric salary may be questionable, but this probably shouldn't trouble us greatly. We have always made a place in our society for the entertainment of oddities, finding pleasure, presumably, not simply in seeing something unusual but also in consoling ourselves with our comparative normality. But we ought to be unable to sleep at night when a guy like Rodman is turned into a role model. How else do you account for the increasing violence in sports? The *New York Times* recently reported on the difficulties faced by today's referees: a high school wrestler in Spokane head-butted a referee so hard he was knocked unconscious; a group of teenage baseball players in Texas, ejected from a game, took out their unhappiness on the ribs and face of the sixteen-year-old umpire; halfway through the 1996–97 school season, one hundred "adult" coaches in Texas had already been ejected from games, twice the number of the year before; 333 players in Florida were thrown out of high school football games in 1996, up from 227 in 1995 and 212 in 1994.[1] The way things are going, it makes one long for the mild-mannered restraint of Dick Butkus, former Chicago Bears football player, who commented on his reputation for dirty playing, "I never set out to hurt anybody deliberately unless it was, you know, important. Like a league game or something."

I could go on to mention exhibit B: celluloid violence, strewing mayhem from Saturday morning cartoons to Saturday evening movies. Or I could point to exhibit C: gang warfare, turning our streets into battle zones. Or I could really get on a roll and set before you exhibit D: the awful bloodshed in places like Rwanda and Bosnia and Northern Ireland. But you would accuse me of getting carried away by my own anger at the anger of others.

Am I really suggesting that flipping the bird when cut off in traffic leads to hundreds of thousands slaughtered in "ethnic cleansing"? Well, yes, sort of. And I'm not exaggerating, at least not very much. Once the tiger of violence is let out, it's not easy getting him back in the cage; he enjoys the freedom. The expression of anger feels pretty good. Actually, it feels *very* good—good enough to do it again and then again. Each outburst of self-justified anger makes it easier for the next one and creates an addicting rush of adrenaline. But as with any addiction, greater hits are required to produce the same effect, like an alcoholic needing more booze to get the same punch. A person who flips the bird when cut off in traffic more readily spits in the face of an umpire and, I have to believe, if the circumstances are right, aims a gun at another human guilty of being the wrong race or nationality or religion. And thus an angry action provokes an angrier reaction, until we find ourselves in a sorry mess.

Violence never stays put. You can never count on it to stop with those who richly deserve it. It always bounces back with overinflated energy to hit you in your own face. As the boy said when he was caught fighting with his brother, "Mom, it all started when he hit me back!"

A story from the Middle Ages tells of two warriors who happened upon each other at a particularly dark spot in the road. The startled knights misinterpreted each other's movements, each believing he was under attack. Lances were lowered, shields were raised, a conflict ensued. Finally, one succeeded in unhorsing the other and, with a mighty thrust, drove his lance through the fallen man's heart. The victor dismounted, limped over to the motionless pile of armor, and lifted his adversary's mask. To his horror, the pale moonlight revealed the face of his own brother.

There are really no strangers in the human community, only unrecognized family members.

The good news is that if conflict begets conflict, the reverse is also true: kindness begets kindness. If you feel the urge to flip the bird, quickly dispatch your other fingers to join the middle one, making a friendly wave, and you just might get a friendly wave in return.

An article in *Princeton Living* tells the story of Cantor Michael Weisser, who had just moved with his wife and family to Lincoln, Nebraska, to serve as the spiritual leader for Congregation B'nai Jeshurun. "The first phone call came on a Sunday morning, amid the banter at the breakfast table . . . 'You will be sorry you ever moved into 5810 Randolph Street, Jew boy,' a voice hissed from the other end. The line went dead.

"A few days later, the mail began to arrive—hateful diatribes calling for the extermination of Jews—and blacks and Catholics and Asians. For residents of Lincoln, the bitter provocations could lead to only one person: Larry Trapp, the Grand Dragon of the White Knights of the Ku Klux Klan in Nebraska. Poster boy for the local police and the FBI, Trapp, forty-two, had terrorized and organized physical attacks on many others, operating from his cramped apartment, jammed with guns and hate literature and even a dog-eared copy of Adolf Hitler's *Mein Kampf*. Michael Weisser was simply his latest target."

Surely the only way to deal with that sort of hate is to hate back, right? To sustain a blow to your humanity like that demands a blow in return, doesn't it? You get hit in the face, you hit back. So fight fire with fire, and call in the FBI and the ATF and maybe even the CIA; surround his house and issue warnings and, if all else fails, burn him out.

But Michael Weisser took a different approach. "Instead of calling the authorities and unwilling to return the volley of hate, Weisser began his own campaign: intimidation by love.

For four months, the cantor left phone messages on Trapp's answering machine. Finally, an exasperated Trapp picked up the phone one day in midmessage and demanded that Weisser stop bothering him. The cantor replied by offering to bring Trapp some groceries. A long silence ensued. Then, the sound of Trapp's voice saying, 'I've got that taken care of, but thanks for asking.'

"So began the chain of events that transformed a hate-filled bigot to a man of love and humanity, a moving tale of redemption that concluded with former KKK leader Larry Trapp actually living in the home of the very people whom he once stalked, and converting to Judaism."[2]

Flip the bird and you will likely get the finger—if not a fist—back at you. But if you turn an obscene gesture into a friendly one, if you offer a wave or even extend an embrace, you will very likely help to build the human community, and so make this world a far better place to live.

———·•·———

Five

Don't Show Up at the Wedding in a Baseball Cap

Showing Respect with What You Wear

FOR YEARS I HAD A SATURDAY AFTERNOON ROU-
tine, part of my preparations for Sunday morning pastoral
duties. I would spread newspapers over the kitchen counter
and carefully arrange my equipment—bottles and tins and
brushes and rags—with the precise care of a cardiologist
about to perform open heart surgery. It was time to polish
my shoes, and I never took the task lightly. I confess a certain
neurotic fastidiousness about footwear; it would take a psychiatrist to explain it all, I'm sure, but whether it has to do
with my potty training or that I worked briefly as a shoe sales-
man in college, I like shoes to be well tended. When I see a
well-dressed man my eyes automatically drop to his feet. It's
a major disappointment to see a fine suit with a distinctive tie
set against a neatly starched white shirt, and then discover at

the foundation a pair of shoes that seem not to have been touched by polish since they walked out of the store in 1962. There's a man, I say to myself, who has no follow-through, who can't be trusted with the details.

Knowing my prejudices in this matter, my daughters would actually warn their boyfriends before they were introduced to me. This created serious anxiety for the poor guys—an anxiety, I admit, that provided me a type of perverse pleasure any father of daughters will understand. But there is only so much you can do with sneakers and sandals, and it was interesting to watch the lads trying to make their feet look inconspicuous.

"Dad," my daughters would say, "we could bring home *drug dealers* and you wouldn't care so long as their shoes were polished!" Well, not quite, though they had a point. Perhaps I was too much of a stickler on this matter, but I think what we wear matters.

Clothes count. If you doubt this, visit a nudist camp. Not that I ever have, let me hasten to make clear. But I once found myself running along a beach, not paying much attention to where I was, until I saw a couple frolicking in the surf as naked as the moment they emerged from their mother's womb. And then I noticed they were not alone: on a strip of beach about a mile long, I was the only person wearing anything at all! All around me was a good deal of flesh, bouncing and flopping in the midday sun. Sun bathers and surfers and volleyball players and frisbee throwers were all carrying on with concerted nonchalance.

No, I did not strip off my running shorts. But neither did I immediately turn back. I have always felt it important to take advantage of every sort of educational opportunity, and so I embarked upon a sociocultural study of the situation. I learned at least two things. First, the bright red patches on otherwise brown bodies indicated that newcomers ought at least to wear sunscreen; I can't imagine the kind of very personal pain some of them had to deal with. And second, most people look much better in clothes.

But clothes do more than provide covering for our private parts and protection from sun and cold. The clothes we choose to wear make a statement about us. When Edgar Allan Poe was a cadet at West Point in 1831 he received instructions for a public parade calling for "white belt and gloves, under arms." He took this literally, appearing with rifle over his bare shoulder and wearing belt and gloves — and nothing else. He was expelled for "gross neglect of duty." Whether it was gross or not — I suppose you would've had to be there to say for sure — I'm certain it was some sort of statement about Poe, either a witness to his literal-mindedness or his feelings about the military.

After the alarm goes off and you haul yourself out of bed and do a tour of duty in the bathroom and get a cup of coffee in you, then what? Decision time! You must decide what to put on and the choice will say something about you. The paralysis you sometimes feel is not simply because it's the time of day when your brain feels about as solid as the dust balls behind the turquoise pumps that haven't been worn since your sister's wedding, but because you must now find a delicate balance: you want to wear clothes that are socially acceptable, appropriate to what others will be wearing, and yet you don't want to blend in with the crowd but reveal your true distinctiveness. This makes it hard to plan your day, doesn't it? Anxiety about what to wear, whether great or small, testifies that clothes will make some sort of statement about you.

I am more concerned, though, about something else: the clothes we wear reveal an attitude about others. A woman spends half the afternoon in Victoria's Secret, selecting a gown, the total material of which could fit in a sewing thimble. Before meeting his father for lunch, a man searches through the back of the closet for an out-of-style tie that years ago was sewn by his now deceased mother. At the funeral of a ten-year-old boy, a minister proudly wears a stole made by the fifth grade Sunday school class. A doctor gets out of her dress and into a flannel shirt before making a house call on a shut-in farmer. Clothes enable us to show affection and respect for others.

Cecil Rhodes, the South African statesman and financier, was a stickler for correct dress. One evening he was hosting a formal dinner and as he was about to welcome his guests, who were all wearing full evening dress, he was told about a young man who had arrived by train without the opportunity to change from his travel-stained clothes. Rhodes disappeared, leaving the guests to wonder what had happened to him. Eventually he returned wearing a shabby old blue suit so his young guest would not feel uncomfortable.

Going from evening dress to shabby suit is something our contemporary culture would appreciate. The rate at which we are "dressing down" will lead us, if my calculations are correct, to complete aboriginal freedom by the year 2007. Doctors show up at the bedside in jeans; pastors visit parishioners in polo shirts; teachers wear sweats to class; many businesses designate Friday as "casual day." Now that Microsoft is taking over the world, the necktie industry may be headed for a major recession. I'm from California, and therefore I accept my share of the responsibility for this state of affairs. Our laid-back beach culture has fallen on the country like ten-foot waves at high tide.

This is not all bad. Casual clothes generally mean an increase in comfort, and comfort, though not necessarily one of the highest virtues, has its charm. But I would simply raise a small cautionary flag: casual clothes can indicate a casual disregard for people or situations.

For example, consider what we wear to services of public worship. I cannot speak for other religious traditions but I can tell you that the Sunday-go-to-meetin' clothes of the Christian church are getting about as dressy as a bowling alley on Friday nights. Before going any further let me clearly affirm some things: *of course* much sartorial parading and other forms of nonsense have obscured the true meaning of worship; *of course* clothes have sometimes widened the lines of class distinctions; *of course* you can worship God in whatever you are wearing. After all, the Bible tells us that Jonah prayed from the belly of a whale, and you don't even want to think about what a whale's gastric juices will do to a white shirt. But with this acknowledged, I still believe dressing casually runs the risk of subtly conveying, to others and ourselves, that what we are doing can be taken casually. When an elder serves communion dressed in shorts and sandals, as I have seen, what does that say? Someone might protest, "Well, it's not *that* big a deal!" And that's my point. Some things *are* a big deal and worthy of a respect that attends to even small, seemingly insignificant things.

What is true about corporate worship is also true of other situations in which we find ourselves. Don't show up at a wedding wearing a baseball cap; don't attend your sister's funeral in shorts, even if she was a free spirit; don't celebrate your anniversary by wearing the obscene T-shirt given to you at the bachelor party the night before your wedding. Take a little common sense and sensitivity into the closet when you make a decision about clothes. Besides worrying about the statement you will make about yourself, give some thought to what you will be saying about your esteem for others.

Fashions change, to be sure, and what is casual today may be considered dressy tomorrow. But whatever the current style, there always exists a range in which we express ourselves. If nostril rings ever become a standardized fashion, then there will be times calling for dressy gold rings as well as other times in which the funky orange plastic will work.

It is certainly possible to give too much attention to what we wear, to spend too much money on clothes, to have too much of our ego tied up in threads. Moderation may be the most important accessory in our wardrobe. It doesn't take much to show our respect for others.

Not long ago my oldest daughter was married. As I dressed that morning, my mind raced, my hands shook, and my eyes welled up with tears. I was filled with profound happiness and also a nostalgic longing, a tender love for my little baby. After the studs had been gingerly eased through the hard-pleated shirt front and the bow tie straightened for the sixteenth time and my shoes rubbed one last time with a sock worn the day before, I started walking toward the church. I had a nagging disquiet within me, but that wasn't surprising given the fact that I was on my way to be the father of the bride and the minister performing the ceremony. It was a long walk on a hot, muggy midwestern day. I walked slowly, with methodical care to keep the streams running down my back from becoming cataracts. When I arrived at the church I still felt a nagging in my spirit, as though there were a stuck key in the middle of an organ concert that was ruining the whole thing. Just an insignificant note, but enough to cause discord.

A few minutes after my arrival one of the groomsmen came up to me in a panic. The tux shop had forgotten to include his cuff links, and the poor lad was in a lather over his unfastened, floppy white cuffs. Then it suddenly occurred to me what I must do. I said, "Here, take mine." He looked at me in utter disbelief. "Are you sure?" "Yes, I'm sure. *Really.*" He provided the reminder I needed, and I bolted out the door and down the street, surrendering to the inevitability of sweat. A man has to do what a man has to do. Once I got back to my room I rooted around in a corner of my suitcase until I found what I was looking for—the little black cuff links my father had given me some time ago. They were the only material remembrance he had of his father, who had died when my father was ten years old and after whom I had been named. I would not be dressed for Jennifer's wedding, I knew, until I had them on. With all the activities of the day I wasn't sure anyone would notice them. But I hoped my father would; I wanted him to see that on one of the most important days of my life I was remembering his father and that I was filled with gratitude for the gift of life given to me and passed on to my daughter. And I hoped my daughter would see them, though I realized it was unlikely they would mean much to her next to the sight of her new husband; I wanted her to know that what was happening was not just between her and Geoff but was a rite of passage involving all of us, with her parents and grandparents and even her great-grandparents, surrounding her like a great cloud of witnesses.

Did I invest too much meaning in a small item of clothing? Maybe, I don't know. I do know the gesture, at least, meant something to me and played a small part in adding dignity to the occasion and showing my esteem for those whom I love.

Six

---·•·---

Don't Be Late

Guarding the Time of Others

ONE OF THE NICE THINGS ABOUT THIS BOOK, PER-
haps you've noticed, is how it enables me to vent frustrations
about the behavior of certain people. Psychologists testify to
the danger of repressing negative thoughts, so I'm occasionally letting myself get carried away in the interests of mental
health. But in this chapter we come to a human failing for
which I have such disdain that I must cautiously restrain
myself lest I go *too* far. My irritation with people who are late
inclines me to spew forth on them a particularly nasty impre-
cation, such as the fervent wish that fleas of a thousand camels
will infest their underwear for a hundred years. So I need to
breathe deeply and go back and re-read chapter 4 ("Don't
Let Your Fingers Do the Talking").

This subject exposes a raw, infected nerve of mine: not long

ago I moved from being a pastor to becoming a seminary president, and it felt as though I had moved through a time warp
in which the usual standards of punctuality suddenly disappeared. In my congregation things started on time but here
things start whenever enough people happen to show up,
which usually bears no resemblance to the stated time of the
meeting. I have fussed and fumed, ranted and raved, but to no
avail: I am only the president, after all, and faculty and students
love nothing better than proving how powerless a president
really is. They have pretty much won; I am nearly ready to surrender to SST (Seminary Standard Time).

Perhaps I'm overly sensitive in this matter, but hear me out.
If we have an appointment to meet at 2:00 P.M. and you do
not arrive until 2:15 P.M., you have said, in effect, that you
consider your time more valuable than mine, that what you
are doing is more important than what I'm doing, and that
you do not mind stealing fifteen minutes of my day to squander on your own purposes.

A friend told me his doctor's appointment hadn't gone very
well. "He said my blood pressure was up. Can you imagine that?
I said to him, 'Of course my blood pressure is up! What else do
you expect? I'm having a very busy day, and you have kept me
sitting in your waiting room for over an hour!'" Being forced
to wait for others can cause a good deal of stress.

Emergencies happen, certainly, which make it impossible to
be on time. The flight is delayed, an accident turns the freeway
into a parking lot, your kid starts throwing up just before you're
ready to go out for the evening, your spouse gets rushed to the
emergency room—things like these cause everyone to be late
at one time or another. But my concern is with people who
make a *habit* of being late. Why do these people choose—and

I do mean *choose*—to be late? It's one of the mysteries of life, along with the mystery of socks (how can one of them get lost so frequently between washing machine and bedroom drawer?) and the mystery of hangers (what do they do in the closet to multiply at such a fantastic rate?). If somebody is always ten minutes late, why can't he or she learn to arrive ten minutes earlier? An act of will is involved; choices are made, for whatever reason. It's a free country, you might protest, and if someone wants to be late, well, so what? I suppose it makes no difference, unless other people are involved. In that case the latecomer may very well be guilty of stealing time. And time is something I'm not eager to lose.

One day Albert Einstein and Philipp Frank were to visit the Berlin Astrophysical Observatory, and they agreed to rendezvous on a certain bridge at Potsdam. Frank was worried that he might be late. Einstein said not to worry, that he would wait on the bridge. Frank protested that this would waste Einstein's time. But Einstein said, "The kind of work I do can be done anywhere. Why should I be less capable of reflecting about my problems on the Potsdam Bridge than at home?"[1]

This might be a fine attitude if you're Einstein, but the rest of us probably need to be sitting at a desk to come up with equations explaining the universe. Thus most of us need to worry about being stood up by others and to pay attention to the ticking of the clock. Did you know that in a lifetime, the average American will spend six months sitting at stop lights, eight months opening junk mail, one year looking for misplaced objects, two years unsuccessfully returning phone calls, and five years waiting in line? That leaves precious little time for meditating on God, drinking a beer with a friend, going to the circus with the grandkids, and other truly important matters.

A Hebrew poet prayed, "So teach us to count our days / that we may gain a wise heart" (Psalms 90:12). In my work as a pastor I have participated in many funerals and memorial services, and on such occasions I have almost always had those words go through my mind. It often takes the death of a loved one to sober us to the reality of life's swift transience. We seem often to be racing toward the future, worrying and planning and fussing our way into tomorrow, and we lose the treasure of the present moment. Count our days, indeed. And our minutes, for that matter. Reckon them. Savor them. Guard them.

Courtesy calls us to do this for others, too. Even as you don't let your dog chew up the neighbor's geraniums, you try to keep a leash on your own behavior so it doesn't chew up another's time. So if you have scheduled a breakfast for 7:00 A.M., you get yourself up and moving, whether you feel like it or not, in order to arrive before your friend has been served his first cup of coffee. If you're scheduled to teach a class at 10:00 A.M., you get there in time to set up so you can begin promptly, because you know starting even five minutes late means, in a class of thirty students, a waste of two-and-a-half human hours. It you have a meeting scheduled for 2:00 P.M., you don't sneak in one last telephone call at 1:59 P.M. If you have a committee meeting at 7:30 P.M., you show up by 7:30 P.M. so as not to thumb your nose at the whole group. Even as you wouldn't slip your hand into another person's wallet to steal money, you don't slip your self-centered agenda into another person's life in order to rob valuable minutes.

When we're late it's tempting to make excuses by stretching the truth a bit. "I didn't think I would *ever* find a parking place!" "My elderly mother called just as I was walking out the door." "My secretary had the wrong time down on the calendar." We feel tempted to offer excuses like these, because we know we've taken something that doesn't belong to us.

But be careful with excuses: they can backfire. During my seminary years I spent one summer as an interim pastor. Things were going well until I got ready for church one Sunday and discovered that the week before I had left my suit trousers at my parents' house across town. I had no option but to race over to get them before heading to the church, which made me late for the service. I began my sermon by apologizing, saying, "I'm sorry I was late this morning, but I got messed up in my pants . . ." This was not a good thing to say. A very proper woman in the front row waited approximately 1.3 seconds before exploding in laughter, which was all it took for the rest of the congregation to disintegrate into complete chaos. Instead of trying to carry on as though nothing had happened, I should have dismissed them and put us all out of our misery; I should have acknowledged that maybe even God was laughing and had lost interest in spiritual matters that morning.

As I went home that day I thought about what I had done. I multiplied the number of people present times the number of minutes I was late, which equaled a huge amount of time I had wasted. The guilt formed a resolution within me to guard as carefully as possible the time of others, to treat it like a delicate wildflower that lives only a short while and must neither be overlooked nor stepped on.

Simply put, don't be late. Unless of course you happen to be reading these sentences standing in the aisle of a bookstore and you're still undecided about buying this book. In that case it wouldn't hurt to take a few extra minutes . . .

Seven

Repondez, S'il Vous Plait

Being Considerate of Others' Plans

ON YOUR WAY TO THE MAILBOX YOU FEEL HOPE raise its attractive head above the routine of an ordinary day. Repressing your fear of bills, you choose to imagine possible treasures awaiting you. A letter from your daughter at college perhaps? Or the income tax refund? Or a newsletter from the club announcing your victory in last week's golf tournament? Or an invitation to someone's party? Yes, under a stack of advertisements and coupons the size of a small child, you discover an invitation to a friend's birthday party. In the lower left-hand corner are four letters—RSVP. A small—*very* little—voice from somewhere inside your conscience says you should respond one way or the other to the invitation. You ignore this, naturally, because as everyone knows RSVP is a fancy foreign phrase that means, "Don't trouble yourself with responding unless you have *absolutely* nothing else to do." And so, because you have other things to do, you don't bother to indicate whether you're planning to attend.

Actually, RSVP means something else: *repondez, s'il vous plait,* which those of you who haven't forgotten high school French know means "Reply, if you please." If my experience as a host can be generalized, not many these days seem pleased to reply. In my various roles as family man, pastor, seminary president, father of the bride, and friend, I have had many occasions through the years to send invitations, and the number of people who respond seems to have declined to the last 2.6 percent of the population who are still in psychotherapy because they can't escape the domineering influence of mothers who pounded manners and a lot of other things into them. Once they graduate from counseling, the uncertainty in planning events will be perfectly complete.

All right, I'm exaggerating. But not by much. When was the last time you conscientiously sent a card or picked up a telephone to indicate whether you were planning to attend something? Your silence proves my point.

I spent many years as a pastor, and this means I presided over the planning of numerous events. All-church dinners, family camps, youth parties, bridge groups, women's teas, men's breakfasts, Bible studies, lectures, every twelve-step program known to the human race—we offered just about everything this side of *Fanny La Boom Boom's* workshop on striptease. These things often required a good deal of preparation, so inevitably the conversations in our staff meetings would go something like this:

"We must ask people to send in a pre-registration form," an associate pastor would say.

"Why?" I would ask.

"Because we don't know whether fifty or two hundred people will show up, and how can we be sure to have enough food if we don't have at least a rough estimate of how many to expect?"

"But you know they won't respond."

"But we need to know how many to expect!"

"Can you remember an occasion in which anyone actually notified us of their intentions?"

"No. But I still think we should ask for pre-registration."

At which point I would want either to fall on the floor into a fetal position and suck my thumb or jump up on the table and scream, "But you are assuming that people are rational and your own way of thinking proves how stupid that is!" Neither of these options seemed pastorally sensitive to me, so I limited myself to a heavy sigh and, as all good leaders do, tried to stay with my team to appear in control even as they marched off in another direction.

Since I raised the issue of rationality, let's stay with that idea a bit. If your daughter is getting married, for example, and you're taking out a second mortgage on your home to put on a reception featuring a sit-down dinner, at fifty five dollars per person not counting drinks and cake, you would certainly want to know how many people to expect before signing the contract with the hotel caterers. Right? But now let's suppose that you're not, God be praised, the parent of the bride but merely a guest invited to enjoy a wonderful meal and dance the night away in happy exhaustion. Surely you would agree that it's only reasonable to reply to the invitation whether you're pleased or not. All of this seems patently obvious.

But then why, when the invitation arrives, do you set it on the corner of your desk to deal with later? And we all know what happens when later comes, don't we? You're still busy, so you put it off until even later, and when even later comes, you assume it's too late to respond, but not to worry because they have probably figured in a certain number of extra settings and it probably won't matter all that much. Another victory for procrastination.

What causes this procrastination? Here is a problem we all have, to one degree or another, and we're all intending to do something about it—perhaps tomorrow. But what sits underneath procrastination, providing its support?

The real problem, it seems to me, is self-centeredness—and when I say *real* problem I mean *the* problem, the problem at the heart of discourtesy, and for that matter, most other problems. We're back to the issue of control I mentioned in chapter 1. I want *my* will to prevail; I want *my* desires satisfied; I want people to fit into *my* plans. This is the basic law of human nature, a fifth law of the universe that should be added to the laws of gravitation, electromagnetism, and weak and strong atomic particles. Not quite, perhaps, because we can occasionally rise above self-centeredness to perform acts of self-sacrifice. But even then, even in acts of apparent self-surrender, our motives are always mixed and the thread of self-centeredness continues to weave its way through everything we do. The major religions have identified this as the disruptive element between God and humanity and the cause of discord in human community. In the Christian tradition, it's considered a manifestation of the S-word (sin).

Donald Baillie, a Scottish theologian writing in the middle of this century, offers a helpful image as he tells "a tale of

God calling His human children to form a great circle for the playing of His game":"In that circle we ought all to be standing, linked together with lovingly joined hands, facing towards the Light in the centre, which is God ('The Love that moves the sun and the other stars'); seeing our fellow creatures all round the circle in the light of that central Love, which shines on them and beautifies their faces; and joining with them in the dance of God's great game, the rhythm of love universal. But instead of that, we have, each one, turned our backs on God and the circle of our fellows, and faced the other way, so that we can see neither the Light at the centre nor the faces on the circumference. And indeed in that position it is difficult even to join hands with our fellows! Therefore instead of playing God's game we play, each one, our own selfish little game. . . . Each one of us wishes to be the centre, and there is blind confusion, and not even any true *knowledge* of God or of our neighbors. This is what is wrong. . . ."[1]

The Love at the center of reality intends for us a great dance, a joyous game. But we each want to do our own dance, play our own game. And so we turn away from the Light, and as a consequence we see only frightening shadows before us. To calm our anxieties we dance ever more furiously, but the shadows mock us ever more menacingly. It's a hell of a way to live, as I think we sometimes know at 3:00 A.M. when from the depths of our being there rises the weariness and ultimate emptiness of our frantic pursuit of distracting pleasures. At a time like that the despair can be awful, but it can also be blessed; it can be a call turning us around so we once again face the Light.

You may be wondering what this has to do with failing to

RSVP. Good question. Here's my answer: the self-centeredness in me, which creates more trouble than it's worth, makes me insensitive to another person's need to plan and make preparations for an event. If I don't take time to communicate my intentions, it's because I don't want to be bothered with an interruption in *my* plans for *my* day in *my* life. Besides, why get committed to something when I might get a better invitation to a more interesting event with more interesting people? To keep *my* options open in order to maximize *my* happiness, I make it difficult for someone else.

So the next time the mailbox yields an invitation, you know what to do. You will "reply, if you please" and even if you don't please; you will treat others' plans as carefully as your own. It may seem a little thing, but it's the accumulation of little things that make a big pattern of life. And anyhow, one day you will be planning an event yourself and need people to return the courtesy.

Eight

Wait Until Everyone Is Served
Before You Pick Up a Fork
Observing the Social Significance of Meals

MY OLDEST DAUGHTER RECENTLY CELEBRATED HER twenty-third birthday, and for me the day brought forth many memories of her growing from childhood through adolescence into young adulthood. As it turns out, she was also reminiscing that day. When we spoke on the telephone she said she had been thinking about her most memorable birthday. I assumed it was her sixteenth. On that day all the anxieties of parenthood reached a brutal climax as she did the unthinkable, the outrageously insane, the thing for which I was completely unprepared: she drove off in the family car. By herself. And she left me standing on the curb in a state of nervous meltdown. Surely that had to be her most memorable birthday.

But no, what stood out in her mind was the ladybug cake

her mother made on her sixth birthday. "There was just something about that cake," she said, "that made it so special." Well, it doesn't surprise me that her recollection of a favorite celebration had to do with food. For most people, meals are like mountains on the landscape of memory; food and drink and conversation have formed peak experiences, summits standing tall against the terrain of the ordinary.

I could probably write an accurate memoir of my life in which all the action takes place around tables laden with food. The meals with my father and mother and sister were the day-by-day enactment of being a family; they were sometimes filled with tension (I had a sister, after all, which created its own difficulties), and sometimes great hilarity (my father and I would sometimes get laughing so hard we couldn't catch our breath and I came to believe it was literally possible "to die laughing"). I remember meals with my own children, with so much of our lives shared at that time; I learned what my wife did at work and heard the girls tell about great teachers and awful teachers and, as they got older, cute boys and jerky boys. I remember lunches at which big decisions were made and breakfasts at which reconciliations were attempted. I remember meals of lavish abundance set before me in warm hospitality by Africans and Koreans. I remember meals to celebrate the union of a man and woman in marriage, and I remember meals that in the midst of death offered not only physical strength for the grieving but a kind of spiritual solace in the practicality of their preparation and consumption.

I mention these experiences not because they're unique, but because I hope they will trigger your own memory of meals in your life. Of all the wonderful gifts of the Creator, near the top of the list is the joy of eating. God, I presume, could have made us with neither the biological necessity nor the aesthetic pleasure of consuming nourishment. But I don't think it's entirely metaphorical when the psalmist says, "Taste and see that the Lord is good." Take a bite of a well-made pizza, covered with sausage and artichoke hearts and mushrooms, and follow it with a swallow of fine Cabernet, with hints of blackberry and spice and vanilla, and meditate on the exquisite explosion of sensations on your palate. *Taste* that the Lord is good, indeed. If you're of the reductionist "food is fuel" school, such as the British, who have only recently begun to discover that food can be fun, you're to be pitied for your lamentable poverty of imagination. It's never too late for repentance, though, and I beg you to return from the far country of ingratitude to enjoy the full feast of life.

As with any good gift, we can and do abuse it. Because eating is so central to our humanity, it often becomes the arena for acting out our various neuroses. Thus our culture has often had an uneasy relationship with food, swinging between gluttonous consumption and bulimic purging, stuffing ourselves into obesity and starving ourselves into anorexic thinness. This leaves us torn between desire and guilt, not to mention more than a little concerned about our health.

To get through this maze and find a better balance, we would do well to recover the *social* dimension of eating. Sharing meals serves a very important purpose in helping us become more fully human: it helps strengthen the bonds of community. In an almost mysterious way, food and relationships are intimately connected. Remember the last serious argument you had with someone; if you eventually worked your way through to a reconciliation, it probably involved a meal along the way. Sure, you could have apologized and resolved to put the unpleasantness behind you without eating together, but didn't it feel right—even *necessary*—to have lunch together?

There are at least two reasons why eating establishes community: it makes possible both sacrifice and delight. In sharing a meal something is given, often with great labor or cost, and something is received, often with great pleasure. The giving and receiving, the sacrifice and delight, are two essential movements in the dance of human community.

The image of pelicans can occasionally be seen in religious art. An old legend has it that a mother pelican will, if her young are starving, peck out her own heart to feed them. Thus the pelican became a symbol of self-sacrificing love. I don't mean to suggest that you're expected to peck out your heart when you have your boss for dinner, but it seems to me there is an element of self-sacrifice when we take it upon ourselves to feed others. We spend money to buy proper ingredients, and we give time and attention to preparing them in a pleasing manner. There are simple meals, of course, when you simply throw burgers on the barbecue; even in these meals, though, there is sharing, giving to another.

And in response to giving comes receiving, in response to sacrifice comes delight. So if you prepare a meal for me, it's my responsibility—my solemn *duty*—to enjoy it. Admittedly, this is becoming difficult to do, what with our obsessive worries about calories and cholesterol and fat grams and sodium and the growing list of evils waiting to ambush us in every bite. But moderation is called for in all things, including zealotry in diet. Robert Capon, an Episcopal priest who loves good cooking almost as much as he loves God, puts it this way: "Food these days is often identified as the enemy. Butter, salt, sugar, eggs are all out to get you. And yet at our best we know better. Butter is . . . well, butter: it glorifies almost everything it touches. Salt is the sovereign of all flavors. Eggs are, pure and simple, one of the wonders of the world. And if you put them all together, you get not sudden death, but hollandaise—which in its own way is not one less bit a marvel than the Gothic arch, the computer chip, or a Bach fugue. Food, like all the other triumphs of human nature, is evidence of civilization—of the priestly gift by which we lift the whole world into the exchanges of the Ultimate City which even God himself longs to see it become."[1]

This delight in good food was memorably portrayed in the movie *Babette's Feast,* based on a story by Isak Dinesen. An exiled French woman mysteriously enters the lives of the members of a small religious community. The people of this community have a very narrow view of God's creation, believing we should "cleanse our tongues of all taste and purify them of all delight or disgust of the senses, keeping and preserving them for the higher things of praise and thanksgiving."[2]

But Babette cooks for them a magnificent banquet that challenges their severe resolve not to enjoy themselves. Throughout the feast, they valiantly try not to have pleasure; they say not a word to Babette about the meal, as though by not speaking they can deny what they feel. But they can't help themselves. They get swept away by the taste and beauty of the meal, and in that delight old walls begin to crumble. Ancient arguments get resolved, and forgiveness is expressed around the table. Something happens during the meal that the diners do not fully understand, something almost transcendent. The meal reestablishes their community.

Because eating with others makes possible self-giving and

delight, and because it helps create community and therefore is central to our humanity, meals have an honored place in our most important rituals. The liturgies of some religions come to high expression in a common meal. Hinduism's *prasada* features fruits and vegetables offered to the Gods and then eaten together by the worshipers. Zen Buddhism, particularly in its Japanese form, has an elaborate tea ceremony, with the ceremony being far more important than the tea. Islam calls for fasting during Ramadan, in part to remember hungry people in the world and to be grateful for the gift of food. Judaism has its Passover *seder,* recalling the deliverance of the Israelites from slavery in Egypt. And Christianity, growing out of Judaism, continues to uphold the significance of community meals. In fact, the story of Jesus as we read it in the Gospels seems to take place in one dinner party after another, and theologians tell us this witnesses to the joy of the reign of God. At the heart of Christian worship is the Lord's Supper, a simple fare of bread and wine, which Christians believe they eat in the presence of the resurrected Christ; this meal is sometimes called Communion, referring to the renewed fellowship with God and other believers.

But if the rituals of faith lead to meals, it's also true that meals give rise to certain rituals. Nowadays the word "ritual" carries negative connotations, and it usually follows a damning adjective, such as *boring* ritual or *dull* ritual or *dead* ritual. We have a drunken infatuation with things new and spontaneous; as with all inebriation, though, there is more than a little stupidity and madness in this. For the most important things ought not to be left to the vicissitudes of impulse. We instinctively know this, I think, and that's why we create rituals—predictable patterns of behavior—to safeguard our deepest humanity. Our relationship with God calls for rituals of worship, our relationship with a spouse calls for rituals of affection and sex, our relationship with children calls for rituals of family life, our relationship with a body calls for rituals of grooming—and our relationship with other people around a table calls for certain rituals of behavior.

A list of table manners will readily come to your mind: wait until all are seated before beginning to eat, don't talk with your mouth full, pass food to others, don't belch out loud, and so forth. These are culturally conditioned, certainly, and the list differs in other parts of the world. I have no interest in reviewing the fine points of table etiquette in this chapter; Amy or Emily or Judith eagerly wait to be consulted on these matters. I am simply pleading that we be attentive to the cultivation of manners around the table. We ought to do this not out of obsessive fastidiousness and not out of elite stuffiness, but because of the sanctity of shared meals.

The pace of modern life has made, for some families, sitting down to a meal as extinct as a brontosaurus barbecue. Barely edible food gets grabbed at drive-through windows to be gulped down in the car on the way to the kids' soccer game. And for some households, a rare evening in which everyone happens to be home and eating at the same time becomes an occasion to break out the TV trays to dine with Peter Jennings.

But if we lose the art of sharing a meal with others, we will deprive ourselves of the self-giving and delight that are central for the creation of human community. If food is simply fuel, a pit stop at the golden arches will do just fine. But if it's more, then we need to make space in our lives for eating that is neither cheap nor quick, an eating that not only fills our stomach but ennobles our souls.

Nine

Keep Your Feet
Off the Coffee Table

Valuing the Property of Others

As I BEGIN THIS CHAPTER, I FEEL LIKE A DOCTOR ready to address a group of alcoholics on the health benefits of moderate drinking. When it comes to property, by which I mean our material possessions, most of us are about as balanced as a teeter-totter with a hummingbird on one end and a rhinoceros on the other. We like things and we spend a good deal of time accumulating them.

So let me immediately draw your attention to the subtitle of this chapter. Notice the subject is valuing the property *of others*. Most of us need no encouragement to value our own property; when it comes to our possessions, we have an evangelical passion for their sanctity. And with the economy doing well, with the Dow Jones average continuing to climb, and inflation negligible and interest rates low and unemployment falling, we're in a revivalistic fervor over the blessings of our material prosperity.

At the risk of sounding like an atheist in the temple of the dollar, I wish to raise a few concerns about our relationship with possessions. First, we should remember that material things have a very limited capacity to make us happy. Statistics suggest there may even be an inverse relationship between wealth and happiness. Between 1957 and 1990, per capita income in America more than doubled in real terms. Are we happier? David Meyers, in *Society in the Balance,* says, "We are not. Since 1957, the number telling the University of Chicago's National Opinion Research Center that they are 'very happy' has declined from 35 to 29 percent. In fact, between 1956 and 1988, the percentage of Americans saying they were 'pretty well satisfied with your present financial situation' dropped from 42 to 30 percent."[1]

Many years ago, as I struggled to balance the needs of a young family with a limited income, I thought to myself, If only I made $10,000 a year more, my problems would be solved. Then I made $10,000 a year more, and what did I think? If only I made $10,000 a year more, then things would be easier and we would be happier. But now I make as much in one month as I made in one year, and do you know what I'm thinking? If only I made $10,000 a year more . . . Wealth tends to create a desire for more wealth. Money is like saltwater for a person dying of thirst; far from bringing satisfaction, it makes matters worse. One thinks of George Bernard Shaw's famous comment: "There are two tragedies in life. One is to lose your heart's desire. The other is to gain it."[2]

My second concern about material possessions has to do with the enormous power they exert over us. In an article in the *Atlantic Monthly,* Mark Sagoff observed that "as we work harder and consume more, we seem to enjoy our lives less. We are always in a rush—a 'Saint Vitus' Dance,' as Thoreau called it. Idleness is suspect. Americans today spend less time with their families, neighbors, and friends than they did in the 1950's. Juliet B. Schor, an economist at Harvard University, argues that 'Americans are literally working themselves to death.' A fancy car, video equipment, or a complex computer program can exact a powerful cost in the form of maintenance, upgrading, and repair. We are possessed by our possessions: they are often harder to get rid of than to acquire."[3]

Victor Hugo's novel *The Toilers of the Sea* tells the story of Claubert, an evil man who wishes to rob a whole shipload of people. He steers the ship onto a sandbar and then, playing the part of a hero, puts all the passengers in a lifeboat, sending them off to an island where he says they will be rescued. He remains behind, and as soon as they are out of sight, cleans out the safes on the ship and goes through the staterooms, gathering all the money he can. He plans to leap off the far side of the ship and swim a short distance to a nearby island, where he knows ships pass regularly. He will be rescued with all the money, while the others will be lost.

So, loaded with cash, he jumps into the water, goes down, touches bottom, and then shoves off, surging toward the surface. But just as he starts up, something grabs him. It's a great octopus. The icy tentacles cling and wrap around him. He tries to tear away from the creature that has a hold of him, but even as he tears away from one tentacle, another grabs him, until they are wrapped about his neck and waist and legs, pulling him down to death.

Clinging to possessions, we may very well find ourselves wrapped by more problems than we could have imagined. Because I just mentioned the sea, I'll stick with that general motif and confess that my materialism has manifested itself in the ownership of a sailboat. When I left my congregation they expressed gratitude for my ministry (or their happiness in seeing me go!) by giving me money to buy a sailboat. It was a generous and a wonderful gift, but it was not quite enough to buy a new boat. So I bought a used one and along with it an accumulation of fifteen years of maintenance problems. As soon as I got the water out of the diesel engine, my boom vang broke; as soon as I fixed the boom vang, my standing rigging needed to be replaced; as soon as I had new standing rigging, I needed new lines; as soon as I got new lines, my batteries went out. Thus the well-known definition of a boat as "a hole in the water through which one pours money"! And to complete the tale of woe, I'm writing this chapter by dictating into a little recorder, instead of using a computer, because my right arm is broken. This unfortunate situation came about on my boat; it was a beautiful evening on San Francisco Bay, until the wind suddenly shifted and, sparing you the details, I did a stupid landlubber move that resulted in the fracture of my upper arm. All this investment of time and money and pain might well lead a reasonable person to ask whether I own my boat or my boat owns me.

But my boat illustrates another side of this issue of personal property. Though my boat is at times a power *over* me, it is also an expression *of* me—a concrete representation of part of my personality. From the time I was a boy growing up near Puget Sound, I have loved the beauty of sailboats; I enjoy the sight of wind filling the sail, the feel of a boat heeling on a close hauled tack, the pull of the tiller in my hands, the sound of halyards slapping against the mast, and even the salty, musty smell down in the cabin. My own boat—a Catalina 27 named *Jennifer Lee*—is an outward expression of an inner delight.

And this leads me to affirm the goodness of material things. We are not ethereal creatures but embodied creatures. We *are* material; we are mental and spiritual and emotional, too, but these aspects of our being subsist in bodies. And our flesh and blood move about in a world of other bodies, as well as bump up against trees and stones and other hard objects. Sometimes this encounter with the physical world around us becomes an expression of what is most noble within us, a manifestation of our near God-like capacity for creativity. Rodin's thinker and Van Gogh's sunflowers and Frank Lloyd Wright's buildings reveal not only a personal vision of beauty but witness to a capacity for transcendence within humanity.

Walking through my neighborhood, I'm often over-whelmed by the rather ordinary sight of houses painted, lawns mowed, flowers planted, and hedges trimmed. What is there within human beings that rages toward order and beauty? Why do we bother to grow flowers, for instance? They have no practical value whatsoever, and they demand the labor of watering, fertilizing, and weeding. This impulse toward beauty is evidence, I believe, that we are, as the Good Book says, made in the image of the Creator, that we bear the likeness of One whose love found expression in the making of a physical world.

And this is why you shouldn't put your feet on your neighbor's coffee table. It's an extension of your neighbor himself; for all you know, it was made by your neighbor and his father in the woodshop where he learned woodworking and a good many other things, too, not the least being his father's love. Even if he simply bought it at Macy's, it reflects his aesthetic values, his personal taste. To rest your shoes on the table risks not only scratching the finish but showing disrespect for its owner.

So we don't leave unrepaired a drainage problem in our yard that floods the basement of the house next door; we don't let our dog poop on other people's lawn; we don't borrow a friend's sweater and give it back dirty. You get the idea, I'm sure. But there's one more nearly unforgivable crime against property I should single out for special attention: in a crowded parking lot, we don't open our car door and jump out as though there were a bomb under the hood about ready to explode. *We don't ding one another's doors, do we?* Judging from the chips and dents on the sides of my car, some of you need to be far more careful.

Which brings me back to my boat. Even more than door dings, I hate hull dings. So if you're sailing with me, just remember the first rule of good seamanship: sacrifice your body before you let the boat run into the dock. Why else do you think you'd be invited?

———•◦•———

Ten

Keep Your Bumper Off My Tailpipe

Waiting Your Turn

THERE ARE DAYS WHEN WAITING FOR SERVICE AT my bank feels like a career change. Recently I needed to make a deposit and took my place in a line that stretched from the tellers' counter to fifteen miles south of Bombay, which would have been acceptable if the line had at least moved; as it turned out, the only thing moving was my rising blood pressure. The guy ahead of me didn't help calm me; he was even more agitated than I. The wait finally made him crack, and he exploded in a loud voice, "Hey! Can we get some service in this bank?" The rest of us nearly broke out in applause; had he opened a violin case on the floor, we would have gladly thrown in our dollar bills. It was a bravo performance of frustration, exactly expressing our feelings.

Incidentally, I know why the service is so slow: they're

trying to get us to use the automatic teller machines outside. But I refuse to do this. I have no intention of exchanging a conversation with a live person for sticking a piece of plastic in an impersonal machine. I fully intend to be the last person in America to use my ATM card. But I'm digressing; this is not a chapter about the pernicious influence of technology on human relationships. So, back to my topic.

Waiting is difficult. There are different kinds of waiting, and none is easy. Some waiting annoys: sitting at interminable red lights, for instance, or standing in never-ending lines. A survey published in *U.S. News & World Report* indicates that in a lifetime the average American will spend five years waiting in line. It will probably be at least eight years for me; I have an amazing gift for always picking the wrong line. You want to turn buying a quart of milk into a half-day project? Follow me and watch how I invariably choose the checkout line where the woman in front of me has her credit card numbers take a wrong exit somewhere along the electronic highway, and the man in front of her needs to have a price check on three items, which no one in the store can find, and the checker at the cash register has fingers and wrists bound in a brace because of carpal tunnel syndrome. This sort of waiting is frustrating, but in the grand scheme of things not all that serious.

Other kinds of waiting are more serious, often frightening or even terrifying: waiting for the doctor's report, for instance, or the jury's verdict or the sound of your teenager's steps on the front porch at two o'clock in the morning. This sort of waiting can loosen your bowels, weaken your knees, and toss you about in the middle of the night.

"Hold your horses, young man!" That's what I remember

my father saying when I was in a hurry. I didn't like it, and I still don't. I want to get on with things, and I certainly don't want to be late (see chapter 6). I'm always eager to keep hurrying toward my next destination. And what happens when I reach that destination? I'm eager to get to the next one! I must admit I've spent much of my life wishing I was someplace else. I had barely learned to ride a tricycle before I couldn't wait to learn to ride a bicycle; I had not been riding a bicycle long before I couldn't wait to drive a car; I had not driven a car for more than a day before I couldn't wait to have my *own* car; when I finally bought my own car I couldn't wait to get a better car. And my experience with transportation has been repeated in other areas—schools, jobs, hobbies, relationships.

I may be unusually neurotic, but I would guess you could tell a similar story about yourself. There is a restlessness in the human heart—a longing for something more, for something we may not even be able to name. Pascal claimed that no possession or position or person can satisfy our deepest longing because it comes out of a God-shaped vacuum within us. Whether you agree with Pascal or not, surely you will not deny the restlessness itself. It's something we all experience, and whatever its cause, it propels us forward, often with great impatience.

I'm not saying that when we find ourselves in a traffic jam and we pound the steering wheel in frustration and say, "Oh God," we're consciously praying to the object of our desire. But I do think there's more of a prayer in the cursing than we may realize, that underneath all the minor irritations of life resides an intense hunger for something only God can give. Failing to recognize this, we set our sights on much lesser things, and when our way toward those things gets blocked we can erupt with impatience, if not explode with anger.

So when the car in front of you dawdles along five miles under the speed limit, you'd like to run your bumper up his tailpipe; when the postal clerk works with the speed and personal warmth of a glacier, you'd like to goose him with a cattle prod, or at the very least figure out a good excuse to crowd ahead of your place in line; when God doesn't seem too swift in answering your prayers, you'd like to take a leave of absence from church, if it weren't for the fact that you have just been elected a deacon. Yes, even God can irritate us. The great nineteenth-century preacher Phillips Brooks was renowned for enormous patience, but one day a friend walked into his study and found him pacing back and forth in great agitation. "Dr. Brooks! What on earth is the matter?" he asked. "I'm in a hurry," Brooks said, "but God is not!"[1]

Where does all this hurrying get us? The pace of modern life continues to accelerate as we hustle along freeways and crowded airways, but what have we gained? Not long ago, in a flight across the country, I had a layover at a busy airport that afforded me just enough time to get something to eat. I found myself seated at a counter scarfing down a piece of perfectly awful pizza, trying to eat it quickly before it coagulated, and sitting next to a weary-looking man who was similarly eating a wedged-shaped piece of cholesterol and fat. We spoke not a single word to each other. He was no doubt dashing in one direction and I in another, and neither of us had the time or energy for conversation. I thought to myself, Is this progress? Where am I going with such urgency? To a destination filled with its own pushing and shoving and moving toward the next destination?

Here's the sobering reality: if we push and shove our way through life, we may very well sprint past the very happiness we seek. In our eagerness to get on to the next thing, we may dart through the experiences of the present with complete disregard for their beauty. Much of life is like poetry: it cannot be raced through, but only encountered with a relaxed openness, a humble attentiveness that allows metaphors and rhythms to have their way with us.

In the last chapter I mentioned I broke my right arm in a sailing accident. Believe me, this was not my plan for the summer. I had intended to spend a good deal of time sailing, running, visiting with friends, and working at a word processor to get a good start on this book. But then my humerus snapped in two and so did my spirit. I didn't need an obstacle like this. Eventually my irritation gave way to depression. But what can you do? Life is filled with adjustments, so I did my best to accept my new situation. Instead of typing at a computer, as I said, I have been learning to dictate. I have had to accept other changes as well. After twenty-five years of running, I found I could barely walk without pain in my arm. But with the doctor's permission, I have kept walking, adding blocks and miles until I'm getting a pretty good workout. And do you know what? I've noticed things I've never noticed before. Slowing down to a walk, I've started observing trees in a new way. I've always appreciated them; I just hadn't looked really closely at them. I'm presently in a state of bewildered amazement at the variety of species, and a few days ago I bought my first field guide to help with identification. This discovery wasn't part of my summer plans but it's been a serendipity I treasure.

Compare the movements of an eager high school basketball player with those of Michael Jordan: the novice, propelled by energy and enthusiasm, runs all over the court, like a mosquito searching for flesh on a summer evening; the consummate professional, on the other hand, looks so relaxed, almost lazy, as he saunters down the court waiting for precisely the right opportunity to rocket toward the basket in movements defying gravity and rational comprehension. The one is pure movement, and the other pure attentiveness to the right movement. And in a similar way, some of the best things in life can be seized only when we relax into an observant idleness.

Racing through life and missing trees isn't good, but it's far worse to miss other persons. If the coil of impatience is wound so tightly within me that I elbow my way toward my next goal, I will jab others in the ribs, and though I may be successful in shoving them out of my way, I will also have shoved them out of my life and thus shut myself off from their mystery. The best things in life take time to experience; they cannot be seized with impatience but only received with patience. The best things—whether a Bach cantata or a redwood tree or a human being—have a complexity that can only gradually be revealed. If we're unwilling to wait our turn, we may be unable to receive the revelation of that which is most true and good and beautiful.

The pearl, as someone said, is a garment of patience enclosing an annoyance. There are plenty of irritating grains of sand in most of our shells; but if we learn to wrap them in patience, we may well find ourselves clothed in a new luster.

Eleven

Hold Your Wind

Trying Not to Offend with Bodily Grossness

ONE EVENING I WAS PERFORMING MY PASTORAL
duties by praying with a group of people who had formed a
circle and were holding hands (we were in California), and as
I paused to take a breath the silence was broken by a loud
fart. God knows it's hard enough to keep your mind from
wandering on these occasions without something like this
happening. I did my best to carry on toward the amen, but
it's safe to bet that no one—not even the most resolutely
pious—had anything even resembling a spiritual thought at
that moment. Everyone was thinking, I hope no one thinks
I did this and I hope this won't be a stinker, and everyone
except one person was thinking, Who did this? I have my sus-
picions but I'm not saying.

I'm pretty sure the Almighty wasn't offended, and neither

were the rest of us, at least not in any extreme sense. If we felt a certain discomfort, it was nothing compared with what the guilty party must have felt both before and after this report from the nether regions. But the struggle against embarrassing biological detonations is nothing new; humans have worried about these things for a long time. Erasmus, writing early in the sixteenth century, counsels that it would be good to fol- low "the advice of all doctors, to press your buttocks together and to act according to the suggestions in Aethon's epigrams: Even though he had to be careful not to fart explosively in the holy place, he nevertheless prayed to Zeus, though with com- pressed buttocks. The sound of farting, especially of those who stand on elevated ground, is horrible. One should make sacri- fices with the buttocks firmly pressed together."[1]

Actually, religious professionals ought to exercise caution not only in what they do but in what they say. I heard of a Methodist pastor who wanted to explain why geese fly in for- mation, and she explained that the one in front "breaks the wind" for others. And another pastor, using the same illustra- tion, expressed the hope that church volunteers have heard words of gratitude for "breaking the wind and making it eas- ier for the rest of us."[2] I suppose you could call this full- service leadership.

When it really gets down to it, though, we all have to break our own wind, blow our own noses, liberate our own ascend- ing burps, and manage the sorts of bodily business that can be less than pleasant for others to witness. Courteous people have always tried to protect others from these things. But I think our standards may be shifting. I haven't done any sci- entific research on this, mind you, but lack of hard evidence will not dissuade me from expressing my opinion any more than it has in the rest of this book: I think there has been an increase in the in-your-face candor that says "see how well-adjusted we are in not being puritanical but freely accepting natural bodily functions."

We are so mature these days, so liberated from the Victorian squeamishness of our parents. Aren't you glad that radio airwaves are now filled with Howard Stern wannabes who freely share with us the scatological humor that had hitherto been limited to junior high boys? And aren't you glad we can now get up-to-date information, thanks to TV commercials, on the latest feminine hygiene products brought right into our living rooms, which create wonderful opportunities for family discussions when children are present to ask questions. And speaking of TV, aren't you glad cameramen—perhaps I should say camerapersons—have learned how to focus on baseball players just as they spit gargantuan streams of tobacco juice and zoom in on basketball players as rivers of sweat cascade off nostrils and earlobes and catch football players in the act of grabbing their crotches for reasons we can only guess? Sort of quenches the thirst for another beer, doesn't it? I have just experienced this new openness as I watched a church talent show in which a gifted young man actually burped the entire alphabet. A truly amazing performance. And I understand he is working on being able to burp the Lord's Prayer, but his mother is having a hard time getting him to memorize it. I'm sure God can hardly wait.

Am I being too uptight, too anal retentive (so to speak)? An excessive modesty about physical functions can certainly arise out of puritanical prudishness. Sometimes my own brothers and sisters in the Christian faith have made too sharp a distinction between spirit and body, and thus have given the impression that spirit is good and body is bad. Frankly, this comes more from the dualism of Greek philosophers than from the Bible. Both Old and New Testaments have a far more holistic view of human life, celebrating the glories of both spiritual and physical life. The former teaches that God created the material world, including our bodies, and declared it good; the latter teaches that the Son of God clothed himself in our flesh, becoming completely human. An attentive reading of the Bible itself leads to an appreciation of physical life, in spite of what some of its proponents have occasionally taught. I neither believe nor want to give the impression that bodily realities are a dirty embarrassment.

My conviction that courtesy calls for an appropriate modesty actually arises from a deep love for the body. It's precisely because of the astounding delights of fleshly life that we guard what our bodies do in the presence of other bodies.

First, we should acknowledge the problem of germs. Rules of politeness vary from culture to culture, to be sure. All cultures, though, even the most primitive, have standards of cleanliness; patterns of behavior have evolved to protect humans from diseases. Aesthetic sensibilities are not the only reason for teaching your child not to pick her nose and wipe her acquisition on the tablecloth. We control certain bodily functions out of respect for the health of others' bodies.

And the second reason why we should not gross out others with the sounds and smells and sewage of our bodies is because the most exquisite pleasures of the body come from the senses—seeing, smelling, hearing, tasting, and touching. These are both powerful and delicate; they have the strength to explode with delight and the vulnerability to implode with disgust. The sense of smell, for example, makes it possible to detect the intoxicating aroma of a blooming rose and cinnamon rolls baking in the oven; the sense of smell also enables us to detect the malodorous presence of rotten eggs and deodorant-free underarms. And thus we show respect for others by doing what we can to maximize their bodily pleasures, doing all we can to prevent their senses from being distracted by our personal grossness. So when your guests are about to enjoy the delicate bouquet of fine Cabernet you don't take the chance of farting; you don't punctuate the music of Mozart with loud burps; you don't diminish the pleasure of a kiss with bad breath; you don't distract from the sight of flowers with a pile of your spittle on the sidewalk. Paying attention to these things has nothing to do with puritanical embarrassment of the body; it comes from the highest form of hedonism, from a desire to maximize the pleasures of the body. Our manners in these matters are a kind of contract with one another: I'll hold my wind if you hold yours so that we'll both be able to delight in more pleasing aromas.

This contract is culturally conditioned, of course. In some countries a thunderous belch may be high praise for a cook's artistry. But not here. In some countries it's customary to drive on the left side of the road, but it's not a good idea to try it in Los Angeles. Living with other people without getting run over, either literally or metaphorically, demands that we pay attention to what others do and think and feel. And thus courtesy calls us, on occasion, to hold our wind and hide our burps and do whatever else we can do to avoid offending others with some of our bodily functions. Courtesy is more than a matter of the spirit, in other words; courtesy must get embodied, must show itself in the careful management of our own physical presence.

Twelve

———◆———

Pay What You Owe
Rendering Others Their Due

Roy Bean was both a judge and saloon keeper; he dispensed justice and alcohol, both undoubtedly as rough as you would expect on the American frontier. His establishment, the Jersey Lily in Langtry, Texas, was close to the railroad. One day a train stopped to take on water, and a passenger took advantage of the delay to rush into Bean's bar for a beer. Bean told the man to help himself, but was none too pleased when the man rushed out without paying. Bean grabbed his gun, stopped the train, and found his customer on board. He demanded his money, with the help of a cocked gun. The frightened man handed over a ten-dollar bill. Bean took it and said, "Fifty cents for the beer, nine dollars and fifty for collecting. This squares your account. You can keep the bottle." As he stepped down from the train he told the conductor, "You can go ahead now as soon as you damn well please."[1]

Failing to pay your debts can get you into trouble. Unless you're a drug dealer or a flunky in organized crime who has screwed up badly, you're not likely to find yourself actually staring down the barrel of a gun. But you may sometimes *feel* like the creditor's gun is pointed at your nose. Surviving everyday life, even without extravagance and with only the essentials, creates a mountain of bills on your desk that, when you start to scale it, makes you wonder whether to take an oxygen tank with you. The challenge of trying to pay them all without having $3.82 left in your checkbook for the rest of the month makes you appreciate Rita Hayworth's approach to financial matters. Jack Lemmon once found her working through a pile of mail by tearing up most of the envelopes unopened. "Stop!" he cried. "There may be checks in there." "There are," she replied, shrugging her shoulders, "but there are also bills. I find it evens up."[2]

She was lucky; it doesn't even up for most of us. We're in debt, and in deeply. The average household now has four credit cards with balances of around $4,800, up from two cards and $2,340 in balances five years ago,[3] and the average American has only $83.42 in the bank.[4] No wonder the monthly bill-paying sessions make us feel like circus jugglers on top of a very large elephant. It's hard to keep the balls in the air with a moving mountain of worry under us! But we seem unable to get off. Credit comes at us like water out of a fire hydrant. It used to be different, as some of you will remember. I was awarded my first credit card after I had been married a year and was working full time; I recall the pride I felt that I had been admitted to the select company of the financially trustworthy. Now, unsolicited credit cards arrive in the mailbox about once a week. Even my youngest daughter—in college and not working full time—gets plastic temptation sent to her. And most of us seem to be doing our best to imbibe from this torrent of easy money. Though besotted with credit and falling into the gutter of debt, we keep lurching from one purchase to another as if we had no hangover to meet in the morning.

But alas, the morning arrives and the creditors must be paid. So we do our best to keep them satisfied, stretching paychecks thinner than a microchip to meet our obligations. We have no choice; without paying these bills, one way or another, we'd lose our credit or perhaps even need to file for bankruptcy.

Some debts, though, are easier to avoid paying. Many hire others for help around the house: gardeners, cooks, cleaners. And some who run businesses hire people for low-paying positions: dishwashers, car-wash attendants, fruit pickers. Recent immigrants often get hired for these positions, and often (let's be completely honest) they're not in this country legally. Their vulnerability may tempt us to pay wages far below what our government has determined should be a fair minimum standard. Can this really be wrong, if we're hiring someone for only a few hours work, someone who is more than eager to work for what we're offering? It's fairly easy to justify this by telling ourselves we're not contracting for a long-term job and we're actually providing a bit of cash to survive, and since we're talking to ourselves it's easy to crush the opponent in this debate. Especially when we have so many bills to pay, so many creditors we cannot ignore. I don't intend to argue the legal and ethical case against doing this; I'm neither a lawyer nor professional ethicist. But I do want to stress that paying someone less than he or she deserves is *at the very least* an act of grave disrespect for another human being, and thus a violation of the courtesy we owe one another.

Another form of debt we sometimes neglect is the casual loan from a friend, the generally spur-of-the-moment debt we assume that entails no legally binding obligation. You're on your way to work, say, when you see a friend and suggest meeting for lunch that day. You have a great time together, and when the bill comes, you reach for it, and then suddenly remember the reason you were free at noon: you were planning to visit the bank because your wallet doesn't have enough money even to buy a subway ticket to get home. Embarrassment surges up and joins the onions in the back of your throat, and you nervously explain your problem, going into far more detail than necessary. Your friend says no problemo, he's got plenty of cash. You promise to pay him back and really mean it. But that afternoon at the office things go bonkers, with doo-doo hitting the fan in a big way, so when you get home that evening the last thing to cross your mind is the money you owe your friend. The next few days are spent cleaning doo-doo off the walls and saving your job, and since friends don't send bills, you easily forget about the debt. Something like this has happened to all of us, I'm sure. But courteous people do their best to make sure it doesn't happen again.

During graduate school I developed an unlikely friendship with a bookie. Because he may now have plenty of time on his hands to read this book, thanks to the federal government, not to mention contacts with the sort of people I wouldn't want to visit me, I'll refer to him with the highly fictitious name of

John. For some reason, John decided to entrust me with the details of his business, telling me far more than I cared to know. One of the useful things I learned is how to handle incriminating evidence when the police are breaking down the door of your apartment: John's method was to keep his records—bets placed and money owed—on special paper that disappeared the *millisecond* it touched water, which of course he kept next to a full sink. I can still see him demonstrating the efficiency of this system, flicking paper into the water and *poof!* . . . it was forever obliterated from the face of the earth.

The life span of that paper seems about as long as some of our memories when touched by the little debts we owe friends. Isn't that what friends are for, we might ask, to help out in a pinch? Absolutely, but only for a short-term loan; after that, we violate the covenant of friendship. So we ought to keep short accounts with one another. We each need to develop the system that works for us. Whenever I borrow money from someone, I try to write a note to myself immediately, preferably in my daily calendar or on a scrap of paper I slip into my wallet. I simply can't trust my memory; it's too much like disappearing paper when it comes to money.

Rendering others their due—that's a classic definition of justice. Philosophers have written weighty tomes helping us think about various things we owe fellow human beings. Do we *owe* food and housing? Do we *owe* equal opportunities? Do we *owe* employment? These are complicated questions, for sure. Life is unfair in many ways for many people, and problems can seem overwhelming. But one simple way to make a positive difference in this world is to pay our bills. If we would like to be just persons, the obvious place to begin is to keep our accounts in order and honor our debts.

Thirteen

Keep Your Hands to Yourself
Acknowledging Sexual Boundaries

S<small>EX IS GOOD</small>. (N<small>O, THAT'S TOO TEPID</small>.) S<small>EX IS WON</small>-derful. (Still not right.) Sex is one of the great ecstasies. (Better, but the heavy breathing sounds too earnest.) As you can tell, I'm having difficulty beginning this chapter. How do you describe one of the most powerful forces in human life — a force with potential to provide both abundant pleasure and immense pain?

Alex Comfort titled his best-seller *The Joy of Sex,* and he was at least half right. I can't speak for gerbils or giraffes, but for humans, sex makes possible such physical, emotional, and even spiritual delight that we can speak of the whole event, not just the final orgasm, as a kind of climax. You don't have to be a dyed-in-the-wool Freudian to see that longing for this climax drives much of our thinking and acting. Sex propels toward procreation, thus ensuring continuance of the species; it also consummates love, energizes ambition, embodies spirituality, inspires art, and even stimulates commerce. We call it "the birds and the bees," and that has to be the most inanely anemic euphemism ever invented!

But alas, it's not an unmixed blessing. Sexuality, being at the core of our personality, is like a cord entangling in sometimes messy confusion biology, psychology, and spirituality. Consequently, the act itself can be a screen upon which we project our psychological and spiritual disorder: insecurities, anxieties, guilt, self-centeredness, possessiveness, jealousy— all these get magnified in distressing and even destructive proportions. When we "do it," in other words, we often make not only love but a whole lot of trouble for ourselves and others.

All of which is to say that sex, though a gift to cherish, is mighty complex and powerful. It may not be entirely an exaggeration when, after a vigorous session of romping around in bed, someone uses the cliché about the "earth moving": the act indeed has something of an earthquake about it, something earthy and elemental; it may even feel beyond our control.

And if the biological and emotional forces weren't enough, we must contend with a daily onslaught of erotic images seducing us from billboards, radio, newspapers, magazines, television, and the internet; the media seem dedicated to ensuring that sex never stays out of our minds for more than about forty-five seconds. So it feels like we're nothing but a bundle of ungovernable instincts, nothing but a bunch of cats in heat in an alley full of other cats with the same thing on their minds.

We know better, certainly, and it's worth reminding ourselves that sex is not really beyond our control: we're creatures who, according to the Bible, are made in the image of God, and therefore we have more power of self-control than we sometimes like to admit (especially after we've failed in some way and must contend with a guilty conscience). Most of us choose to limit our sexual expression, circumscribing our behavior according to moral and spiritual commitments. We know we're walking though a minefield, and we want to get through it alive.

But some get careless and forget that others are trying to get through the same minefield. Maybe they think it's funny to tell crude jokes at inappropriate times, or they think it's sexy to flirt in unwelcome ways; worse, maybe they think they're entitled to grab a little thrill on someone's anatomy or even demand sexual favors. Generally speaking, men step across the boundary of propriety far more often than women; whether because of biology or social conditioning, men tend to be more sexually aggressive and thus more often guilty of perpetrating unwanted sexual advances.

To say this is a large problem is like saying the Pacific Ocean is a body of water. Sexual harassment is the most frequent type of discrimination charge filed by workers today; the federal Equal Opportunity Commission reports an increase from 6,883 complaints in 1991 to 15,549 in 1995. Almost every day you hear about another minister or military officer or doctor or politician guilty of crossing the line. This is neither because men in general have gotten randier, nor because the advance guard of the baby boomers are swelling the ranks of "dirty old men." It's because women have taken a stand and said, "Enough is enough!" and the courts are supporting them when they press charges.

So, big fella (women readers, please skip this paragraph), let's talk straight: in case you still think it's your God-given right as a red-blooded male to come on to women like a Mack truck with burned-out brakes on a downhill grade, and in case you still think it's cute to favor coworkers with your amazing sexual wit and wisdom, and in case you still think women are secretly longing for your furtive touch—in case, in other words, you're determined to remain a first-class jackass, let me offer some friendly advice: *knock it off!* We're not simply talking courtesy here; we're talking the possibility of getting yourself hauled into court by an angry woman wanting to sue you into bankruptcy. If the president of the United States isn't immune from big-time trouble in this regard, do you really think your charm will keep you out of this particular pot of hot water?

The most important reason, though, for keeping your hands to yourself has nothing to do with getting caught. It has to do with why sexual boundaries were established in the first place. You may argue, perhaps with justification, that today very few boundaries remain. But the really interesting question is, Why do *any* remain? Why do religions continue to draw lines between appropriate and inappropriate sexual behavior? Why do secular cultures continue to struggle to define acceptable standards and mores? Why do even the most lecherous libertines continue to have at least a few things they wouldn't dream of doing because it would violate an inner ethic?

Here's what I think: sex is far too wonderful to be left to impulsive desires. The best and most important things in life must be guarded from the fickleness of human appetites and moods. Where we want to maximize freedom, we dedicate ourselves to the most demanding disciplines. We protect physical health by denying ourselves short-term pleasures of sweets and sloth, and instead nourishing our bodies by eating balanced meals and taking regular exercise. We protect our most important relationships by refusing to give way to resentments or lust, and instead remaining faithful to promises and commitments. And most of us protect our relationship with God by building a spiritual life not on emotional highs or mystical experiences but on the more solid foundation of time-tested theologies and liturgies.

And we maximize the joy of sex by guarding it, setting barriers around its expression. These "rules" of behavior are like sentries standing at the bedroom door protecting pleasure. The rule of modesty, for example, guards the thrill of seeing your beloved completely naked; if everyone saw him or her in this way, a good deal of the fun would be lost. The rule of fidelity stands watch over the ecstasy of intercourse by preserving its uniqueness; if anyone could have it, the gift would be cheapened, to say the least. Sex that serves only biological impulses of the moment may offer certain physical delights, but it cannot carry with it the emotional and relational cargo that make possible the deepest joys.

An old joke tells of Moses coming down from the mountain and saying, "I've got good news and bad news: the good news is that I got Him down to only ten commandments; the bad news is that adultery is still in." When hormones are raging and you've fallen head over heels in lust, that may *feel* like bad news, but it's actually good news, as anyone who's been cut and left bleeding by the sharp knife of adultery will attest. If God has said "No!" to adultery, and "Yes!" to sex within the covenant of marriage, it's not because God wants to stamp out pleasure, but because God wants to protect it from the staggering stupidity toward which we are prone. God, according to the best theology, is not a killjoy but the ultimate Guarantor of Joy.

All right, I've started preaching and I'll back off. But let me conclude this chapter by asking you to agree with me that sexual pleasure is worth protecting. The only way to do this is to honor sexual boundaries. To run across them by treating others as objects of our impulses undermines the possibility of sexual joy for everyone. It also demeans the dignity of others, and that, as I've been saying, is the reason why we're called to be people of courtesy.

Fourteen

Be Quiet in Church

Cultivating a Sense of Reverence

IT'S HARD TO PREACH WHILE LOOKING AT A NAKED woman. My experience with this particular problem happened on a Sunday in which we had a modern dancer in our worship service. She presented a beautiful offering of praise to God; we were truly blessed. And some of us received a second blessing after she exited. She needed to change out of her leotard, and she thought the "cry room" at the back of the sanctuary would be a good place to do it because it was empty and it had a one-way window (from the congregation's side, it was a mirror). What she didn't know was that if you turn on the lights in this room, the window changes into a normal two-way window, affording an especially complete view of things inasmuch as the room also serves as a changing room for brides, with floor-to-ceiling mirrors all over the back wall. About half-way through the introduction to my sermon I noticed what was happening, and I'm sorry to report that I didn't have the spiritual fortitude to keep my eyes on my notes. Neither did the men in the choir, of course, but they will have to make their own confessions in the appropriate place. I will mention only two of my discoveries that morning: I learned what dancers wear under leotards, and I learned just how hard it is to concentrate on the Jebusites while seeing all the way to Australia. For salacious readers, who got overly worked-up in the last chapter and whose minds are now wondering about the details, I will simply say that the men of the choir felt a bit of Heaven had descended that morning.

Sometimes it's not easy to keep your thoughts centered on God while in church, or for that matter, in synagogue or mosque or any other place of worship. A good many of us try, however. According to opinion polls, about 45 percent of Americans regularly attend public worship services. Which means that about 44.9999 percent of Americans regularly struggle to keep their minds from wandering all over the universe and back between the Call to Worship and the Benediction. The number of possible distractions is roughly equal to the number of dollars owed on the national debt, which I think is currently at about 7.9 gazillion. Rarely do you have to contend with naked women, though I did hear of one *very* liberal church that invited a striptease artist to share her gifts with the congregation. But other diversions abound, such as crying babies, who, trust me, are never as cute as their mothers think, birds in the rafters, sound systems from the twilight zone, ushers fainting, fire alarms set off by truant members of the fifth grade Sunday School class, not to mention all the thoughts flying through your mind like a cloud of locusts ravaging your concentration.

By now you know where I'm heading: courtesy calls us to endeavor not to add to the distractions. So don't whisper to your neighbor in the pew, even if the preacher begins his sermon by saying, "This morning's message has twenty points"; it would probably be a good idea to leave, mind you, but don't hold a discussion before making your escape. And do take out crying babies (you never know who might be in the "cry room"!) and try not to snore too loudly and refrain from crawling over sixteen people when you come in late and when the worst happens — when you get the giggles and can't stop laughing even if the archangel Gabriel should appear and threaten to zap you — leave as inconspicuously as possible. But speaking for clergy of all faiths, I beg you not to leave before the offering is collected.

Not only should courtesy govern our behavior with fellow worshippers, it ought to guide our relationship with God. The assumption of this book is that people deserve to be treated with respect; human beings bear an essential dignity entitling them to receive courtesy. If this is true for the ordinary mortals who cross our paths, what can we say about God?

We Americans are a religious bunch. According to recent Gallup polls, 94 percent say they believe in God; astonishingly, nine out of ten say they have never even doubted the existence of God. Even those who have left formal religion often retain longings for God — longings so palpable they almost feel like the presence of God. In *Life After God,* Douglas Coupland describes the "baby buster" generation: "It was the life of the children of the pioneers — life after God —

a life of earthly salvation on the edge of heaven." But then he confesses, "My secret is that I need God—that I am sick and can no longer make it alone. I need God to help me give, because I no longer seem to be capable of giving. To help me be kind, as I no longer seem capable of kindness. To help me love, as I seem beyond being able to love."[1] Most of us believe in God, or at least we *want* to believe in God.

But which God? Though a majority in our nation still consider themselves Christian, a growing minority have brought a new religious diversity to our communities. Today, your next door neighbor may just as likely be a Muslim or a Buddhist as an Episcopalian. And this diversity isn't simply related to more representation from standard-brand religions: it has to do with the individualism that has been so much a part of the American character. More and more seem to want to add a hearty amen to Thomas Jefferson's creed, "I am a sect myself." In *Habits of the Heart,* Robert Bellah tells of Sheila Larson, a young nurse who describes her faith as "Sheilaism." She says, "I believe in God. I'm not a religious fanatic. I can't remember the last time I went to church. My faith has carried me a long way. It's Sheilaism. Just my own little voice."[2] So next to Judaism and Christianity, we need to set not only Islam and Buddhism, but also Sheilaism and Billism and Brendaism and Thomasism and Bettyism—and whatever religion you may have created for yourself.

The problem with this radical individualizing, it seems to me, is that we end up creating a bunch of little deities, none of whom is big enough to inspire wholehearted devotion. If you create your own god and I create mine, we may both be very sincere (a characteristic so highly praised in our culture that many confuse it with truth itself), but sincere in believing in nothing larger than our own imagination, nothing bigger than the exact proportions of our personal desires. In the end, a god like this is not only trivial but boring.

What this individualizing destroys, in other words, is any sense of transcendence—the very thing on which the major religions have always insisted. God, they have taught, is *other* than us. Even Christianity, which holds that God has become one with us in Jesus Christ, nevertheless maintains that this God is still *God,* the Creator, the "Holy One," the Being who though filled with love for us stands outside us. A God like this is big enough to be interesting, to say the least; big enough, actually, to turn our world upside down and turn our lives around and deliver us from the biggest problem we face—ourselves.

And if God really does transcend us, then whatever form our worship may take, it ought surely to be marked by a kind of spiritual courtesy. God deserves to be honored, to be treated with respect. Remember, we're talking about the One who brought all things into being, the One who holds in a single embrace butterflies and black holes, the One, as the spiritual says, who's "got the whole world in His hands." In what manner do you approach a God like this? With awe and great reverence.

A scene in Kenneth Grahame's *The Wind in the Willows* captures this sense of awe in the presence of the Holy: " 'This is the place of my song-dream, the place the music played to me,' whispered the Rat, as if in a trance. 'Here, in this holy place, here if anywhere, surely we shall find Him!'

"Then suddenly the Mole felt a great Awe fall upon him, an awe that turned his muscles to water, bowed his head, and rooted his feet to the ground. It was no panic terror—indeed he felt wonderfully at peace and happy—but it was an awe that smote and held him and, without seeing, he knew it could only mean that some august Presence was very, very near.

"Perhaps he would never have dared to raise his eyes, but that . . . the call and the summons seemed still dominant and imperious. He might not refuse, were Death himself waiting to strike him instantly, once he had looked with mortal eye on things rightly kept hidden. Trembling he obeyed, and raised his humble head; and then . . . he looked in the very eyes of the Friend and Helper . . .

" 'Rat!' he found breath to whisper, shaking. 'Are you afraid?'

" 'Afraid?' murmured the Rat, his eyes shining with unutterable love. 'Afraid! of Him? O, never, never! And yet—and yet—O, Mole, I am afraid!'

"Then the two animals, crouching to the earth bowed their heads and did worship."[2]

Courteous people cultivate this sense of reverence before the Wholly Other One. They pause, amidst all the distractions of life, and look up; they pause, even, amidst the distractions of worship services—with naked dancers or crying babies or giggling teenagers—and remember that they're entering the presence of God. What can follow is a wonderful blessing: awe in the presence of mystery. Albert Einstein said, "The most beautiful experience we can have is the mysterious. It is the fundamental emotion which stands at the cradle of true art and true science." This gift comes to the spiritually courteous.

———•———

Fifteen

Don't Wear Red
to a Chinese Funeral

Honoring Our Differences

IN MY FIRST YEAR AS A PASTOR, A LOCAL FUNERAL director would ask me to "do the service" for customers who had no church home. Grateful for both the experience and the honoraria, I helped out whenever I could. It wasn't easy to speak eloquently about people who, in my first encounter with them, were looking rather waxen and powdery and *very* still. I decided the less said the better, on the assumption that preachers rarely get criticized for being too short-winded. But with dear old George stretched out in front of you, you have to say *something*, and so you try to master the fine art of vague generalization so as not to offend with anything too specific. I wasn't worried about George's reaction, mind you, but I was concerned about inadvertently hurting the feelings of mourners.

I came close to doing that in a big way one afternoon, when I arrived at the mortuary to conduct the service of a Chinese man. I was wearing my "marrying-and-burying" suit, a white shirt, red tie, and shoes polished as shiny as the deceased's forehead. But the funeral director, an affable guy who loved to tell stories in the hearse on the way to the cemetery, most of which, I suspected, were more faithful to entertainment value than the truth, took one look at me and let out a horrified groan. The expression on his face was approximately what you'd expect had a corpse just sat up on the embalming table.

"What are you doing? Don't you know you never wear red to a Chinese funeral? Get that tie off!" And as he yelled at me, he whipped off his own tie and ordered me to put it on.

No, I didn't know you weren't supposed to wear red to a Chinese funeral, but I can tell you, I won't make that mistake again. In fact, I'll never again wear red to *anyone's* funeral. Unless I discover that for some group of people it's offensive *not* to wear red, which is entirely possible, of course, because there are a lot of traditions in this world and it's hard to keep track of them all.

And this seems a more and more difficult task. The diversity we encounter in our daily lives has grown dramatically. Immigration has brought the world into our communities, transforming them into an amazing mixture of cultural identities and religious loyalties. Drive across Los Angeles, and you go through neighborhoods of Mexicans, Guatemalans, Chinese, Taiwanese, Vietnamese, Armenians, Nigerians . . . and on and on the list goes. The Los Angeles public school system now serves thirty-three different language groups, with students who speak English as a first language in the minority.

Whereas at one time our national ideal was the "melting pot," the blending together of different ethnic strains into a unified cultural identity, now we celebrate the richness of the diversity. We prefer to think of ourselves as a tossed salad. (Or, as one of the students in the seminary I serve put it, a fruit salad—all the pieces sweet but different. His idealism is evident, but at least he got the part about differences right.) Arthur Schlesinger Jr. has written that "a cult of ethnicity has arisen both among non-Anglo whites and among nonwhite minorities to denounce the idea of a melting pot, to challenge the concept of 'one people,' and to protect, promote, and perpetuate separate ethnic and racial communities."[1]

Much good has come from this, if you ask me. Our children get a more well-rounded education when, for example, they consider the discovery of America not simply from the perspective of Columbus, but also from that of the Native Americans who were already here. It's about time we considered the achievements of African-Americans, Latin-Americans, and Asian-Americans, as well as Euro-Americans. And don't tell me it isn't more interesting to live in a neighborhood where you can walk around the corner and get, in addition to hamburgers and fries, burritos and kimchi and satay.

But this cult of ethnicity, to use Schlesinger's phrase, has had a downside: the vigorous assertion of the rights of one group over or against another, the movement from discovering ethnic roots to defending ethnic rights to demanding ethnic recognition, has threatened to rip apart the fabric of our society. One wonders whether we still have enough in common to hold us together, or whether we will fragment into a jumble of jostling advocacy groups.

Perhaps we could also speak of a cult of supersensitive feelings. As different groups—not simply ethnic but many, many others—discover self-identity and self-assertiveness, they're less inclined to take any sort of discrimination sitting down and more inclined to demand the justice due them. Their voices have sometimes risen to a loud cry and then descended to a whine. The results, on the whole, have been beneficial; we are, I think, moving—slowly, laboriously—toward greater recognition of the rights of some who have been overlooked and treated unfairly. But the blessings have not been unmixed. We have also become, to use Robert Hughes's phrase, a "culture of complaint." Almost everyone is a victim these days, ready to point the finger at those who have done them dirty. To be sure, a good many people are genuine victims of abuse. Yet a good many more have gotten swept up in the ethos of blame and found ready scapegoats to ease their own burden of responsibility.

Sensitive feelings may be like good wine: beneficial in moderation, but dangerous in excess. This is especially so when they're joined with a do-good earnestness that often slips into a political correctness that self-righteously polices everyone's words and actions to protect the feelings of those deemed oppressed. Robert Hughes comments that "where an administrator at the University of California in Santa Cruz could campaign against phrases like 'a nip in the air' and a 'chink in one's armor,' on the grounds that such words have expressed racial disparagement *in other contexts,* anything is possible; how about banning 'fruit tree' as disparaging to homosexuals?"[2]

All of which is to say that this diversity in which we find ourselves today can be mighty confusing and tiring. We have to worry about inadvertently stepping on ethnic toes or offending gender identities or overlooking the "differently abled" or committing "ageism." It can wear you out! It's enough to give you sensitivity overload, to make you want to quit trying. Why not just give up and retreat into the safety of your own little group?

Though this may be a tempting response, let me encourage you not to give in to it. First, even if some people are too sensitive, they still deserve your courtesy. The underlying assumption of this book is that all—even the thin-skinned—deserve respect. The truth is, often those who speak with particularly shrill voices have indeed been hurt by injustice in the past, and they may be facing subtle prejudices that go unnoticed by the rest of us. If their wounds have given an uncomfortable edge to their demands, well, it's easy to understand why. Those of us who have sometimes been insensitive, or even flagrantly guilty of injustice, ought to be willing to bear patiently with those who seem to come on with the intensity of a freight train; had we been in their situation, we would no doubt be roaring down the tracks with the throttle pushed to the wall.

Second, even though you can't make everyone happy all the time, that doesn't relieve you of the responsibility of extending kindness as often as you can. Of course you're going to blow it! Getting through life these days is like walking through a minefield; even those with the best intentions can have the ground explode under them. I'm reminded of Mother Teresa's response when someone asked why she bothered to care for a few suffering individuals with millions dying around her. Didn't she get discouraged? She replied that she was not called to be successful but faithful. We each must do what we can, in other words, and perhaps one kindness extended today to just one person will in some small measure make the world a more humane place. But whether it does or not, we know who we want to be—the sort of people who refuse to be shaped by intolerance and meanness, and who do our best to create islands of community in a diverse and often divisive world.

Third, you don't have to sacrifice your own cultural and religious identity to be respectful of others. There is a notion on the loose that ought to be caught and shot: the idea that tolerance demands silence about your own beliefs. In the area of religion, for example, we seem to think we must diminish distinctive convictions and settle for the lowest common denominator as neutral ground. We enthrone personal sincerity, but turn our backs over dogmas that divide; what matters, we think, is that we all have heartfelt beliefs, but please be sensitive enough not to mention any disagreements. So communities sponsor interfaith worship services where not even the word "God" can be mentioned (today even atheists claim to be "spiritual"), and the only thing that can be celebrated is peace and flowers and little children.

But an honest diversity in religion—as in ethnicity, say, or sexuality—demands that we each take our own traditions and commitments seriously. True interfaith dialogue can take place only if participants articulate their own deepest convictions. Otherwise, all you have is conversational mush and self-congratulatory sensitivity—pseudo-intellectual nonsense that leads no one closer to deeper understanding, let alone truth. When I, as a Christian, relate to a Jew, I expect him to take his Jewish identity and beliefs with utmost seriousness; when I speak with a Buddhist, I expect her to be a good Buddhist. And I expect them to allow me to be a Christian without apologies.

It's a sad moment when at a dinner party the host announces, "This evening we'll have no talk about religion or politics, because we want to have a good time." Don't anyone say anything about how we relate to God or one another; don't anyone dare bring up the most important and ultimately most interesting topics in life; let's keep this conversation as trivial as possible so we won't risk any embarrassing disagreements. Well, I'm not fond of conflict, but it seems to me we need to cultivate the art of civilized argument and learn ways to express our differences with respect for one another. Otherwise, we're likely to drown in a flood tide of banalities; we might as well stay home and watch TV.

Finally, you really can't stop worrying about wearing red to Chinese funerals and being sensitive to the diverse traditions around you, because you may still have a thing or two to learn. Unless you're certain that your culture's way of going about life is *superior in all ways* and that your understanding of God is *perfectly complete,* you just might pick up something of value from the traditions and beliefs of others. Even from those with whom you will ultimately disagree. Given the immensity of truth and the limitations of the human mind, we all need a large measure of humility—the humility that opens our eyes and ears and even our hearts to others who, perhaps at first, seem very different from us.

If almighty God can be humble enough for this sort of openness, we ought to be able to get down off the pedestal of self-sufficiency and start paying attention to the amazing diversity around us. God apparently gets quite a kick out of variety. Just look at creation: about a thousand insects would have been more than enough entertainment, if you ask me, even for the most curious mind, even for a God with an infinite capacity for concentration and delight. But no! God comes up with 300,000 species of beetles and weevils alone, not to mention the other little critters under our feet and buzzing around our heads. A God like this, it's safe to assume, finds at least as much pleasure in the diversity found amongst us humans. And if we can learn how to become connoisseurs of this variety, we just might move a little closer to the God-like image we have been created to reflect.

Robert Fulghum provides an appropriate image with which to end this chapter. The highlight of his summers, he says, was a week in Weiser, Idaho. I would not have included Weiser on my Top Ten list of vacation spots; I mean no disrespect to the fine people of this town; it simply doesn't pop into my mind along with Maui or Yosemite or for that matter, Timbuktu. But then I don't play a fiddle and Fulghum does, and that makes all the difference, because Weiser hosts the Grand National Old Time Fiddlers contest the last week in June.

This town of four thousand people swells to nine thousand, as fiddlers stream in from Texas and Oklahoma and Minnesota and even Japan. In the early years of the festival the pilgrims were pretty straight country folks, but then "long-haired hippie freaks" began to show up. It was hard to know what to do with these newcomers, because in spite of their looks, they knew how to fiddle. Really well. So one old gentleman had to put it this way: "Son, I don't care if you're stark nekkid and wear a bone in your nose. If you kin fiddle, you're all right with me. It's the music we make that counts."

"I was standing there in the middle of the night," Fulghum

said, "in the moonlight in Weiser, Idaho, with about a thousand other people who were picking and singing and fiddling together—some with bald heads, some with hair to their knees, some with a joint, some with a long-necked bottle of Budweiser, some with beads, some with Archie Bunker T-shirts, some eighteen and some eighty, some with corsets and some no bras, and the music rising like incense into the night toward whatever gods of peace and goodwill there may be. I was standing there, and this policeman—a real honest-to-god Weiser policeman who is standing next to me and *picking a banjo (really, I swear it)*—says to me, 'Sometimes the world seems like a fine place, don't it?' "[3]

It's the music we make that counts, and when that music is played with the harmony of human diversity, the world can indeed seem like a mighty fine place.

Sixteen

———•◆•———

Apologize When You've Blown It
Accepting Responsibility for Your Failures

At the end of Erich Segal's *LOVE STORY* is a
sentence of dialogue made famous by the movie based on the
book: "Love means not ever having to say you're sorry."[1] This
ought to be memorized: it provides a handy standard of stupidity. After saying something completely inane, you need
only remember this line and console yourself that what you
said wasn't nearly as dumb.

But it might be nice to pretend it's true. Apologizing can
be about as much fun as a root canal. The problem is that little addiction to which we—all right, to spare you embarrassment, I'll shift over to the first person and hope the
confessional tone gets me invited to some afternoon talk
shows—to which *I* seem prone: protecting and polishing my
ego. Any addiction I don't want to give up is little, of course;

nothing to be concerned about. I could quit anytime, but I haven't yet felt the need. Everything in moderation, as they say, and so I'm a user of self-centeredness in a way that is socially responsible and personally fulfilling. Do I worry about my image? Not a serious problem, really. No more serious than drinking for a bum who awakens in a skid road doorway trying to remember his name. In sober moments, though, between the hangover and the next swig of ego gratification, I know that saying I'm sorry is not only a significant part of the courteous life but sometimes a necessary step in the restoration of a broken relationship. It's important to learn to accept responsibility for failures.

Arturo Toscanini, the famed conductor of the Metropolitan Opera and the NBC Symphony Orchestra, was once directing a rehearsal and flew into a tantrum with a player. He angrily ordered him from the stage. As the man reached the exit, he turned and shouted, "Nuts to you!"

And Toscanini yelled back, "It's too late to apologize!"[2]

He was wrong: it's never too late to apologize. The offended person may have written you off, severing the relationship forever. But it's still not too late, because whether or not the one you wounded accepts your apology, you must accept responsibility for your behavior.

Which brings us back to that little problem of the ego. It's a master at shifting blame. The ego is like a basketball player who deserves an Oscar for his acting when the referee calls a foul on him: he points to himself in questioning disbelief, looking genuinely shocked, deeply wounded, as though the referee had accused him of spitting on his mother. Whatever happened, it can't be *my* fault. My parents messed up my potty training. My wife doesn't understand. My husband lacks sensitivity. My kids hang out with the wrong group. My boss makes Attila the Hun look gentle. It's always someone else's fault.

Did you hear about the guy who filed for divorce? When the judge asked him whether a third party was involved, the man replied, "No, my wife doesn't like to go to parties."

"Well," the judge asked, "Is she a spendthrift then?"

"You bet she is," the man said. "When it comes to spending she's very thrifty."

"Does she beat you up or something?"

"No, your honor, I'm the first one to get up in the morning."

"Why then do you want a divorce?"

"Because the lady can't communicate!"

Refusing to shift the load of your blame onto others can go a long way toward resolving a good many conflicts in life. But we need to expand on this idea a bit more; accepting responsibility is actually more complicated than disciplining a rambunctious ego. M. Scott Peck, in *The Road Less Traveled,* made an important distinction: "Most people who come to see a psychiatrist are suffering from what is called either a neurosis or a character disorder. Put most simply, these two conditions are disorders of responsibility, and as such they are opposite styles of relating to the world and its problems. The neurotic assumes too much responsibility; the person with a character disorder not enough. When neurotics are in conflict with the world they automatically assume that they are at fault. When those with character disorders are in conflict with the world they automatically assume that the world is at fault."[3]

It's possible to take too much responsibility for problems.

In my work as a pastor I've seen women abused by their husbands, physically beat up again and again, who refuse to seek help and instead take the blame upon themselves: if only I hadn't angered him; if only I were more understanding; if only I could meet his expectations. And I've seen men take responsibility for their wives' alcoholism: if only I hadn't spent so much time at work; if only I could have provided more for her financially; if only I could have helped more with the children. These are cases of assuming too much responsibility, taking the blame someone else deserves upon oneself.

The weight of my concern in this chapter, however, is with what Scott Peck calls a character disorder, the refusal to acknowledge the truth of our own failures. Instead of admitting we've blown it, we make excuses or find some way to squirm out from under the burden of truth. But unless we find a neurotic willing to take the blame, we're usually successful only in deceiving ourselves. I vividly remember a scene that was often repeated in my work as a counselor: a couple would come for help with their marriage, and the wife would soon point to the husband's drinking problem. He would deny it, saying he felt a man had a right to a drink after a hard day's work. She would point out how much he drank, how his children and friends have all expressed concern; she would tell about the night he spent in jail because of a D.U.I., and tell how he was about to lose his job; she would sometimes even threaten to leave him if he didn't go to AA. And what would be his response? He would always have an explanation for everything; it was always someone else's problem. I would be amazed and more than a little angry that the guy could be so self-deceptive. And then sometimes, by God's painful mercy, I would recall my own instincts at self-protection, my own tendency toward protecting my self-image, and I realized there was a person in me who was more than ready to pass the buck.

In Fyodor Dostoyevsky's *Crime and Punishment,* Raskolnikov murders a woman in cold blood for no good reason except to prove that he can live above the law of God. He knew exactly what he was doing; he is fully responsible. But he does not accept any blame. He did it, he says, "through some decree of blind fate." Even after Sonia, the woman he loves, insists he confess his crime to the police, he still finds excuses for himself. But his redemption comes about when, in prison, he enters a dark valley of agony and begins to see the falsehood in his life. One day he falls at the feet of Sonia, accepting her love, and in the strength of her forgiveness finds the courage to accept responsibility for his failures. This dedication to reality enables him to move forward into a new life.

To say I'm sorry—and mean it—is an act of courage by which we hold ourselves accountable to the truth. Our offense may be as small as disrupting an afternoon because we forgot to call home; it may be as large as destroying a life because we abused another person. Whatever the magnitude of our crime, we can't move through the rest of our days with integrity, we can't find our way toward redemption, until we say, "Yes, I'm guilty and I feel remorse for what I've done."

As a veteran of screwups and therefore as one who has had to offer more than his share of apologies, let me offer a few tips for saying, "I'm sorry." First, *don't do it too quickly.* A premature apology can be a cheap attempt to cut short the painful work of reconciliation with the person you've wounded. Because I'm uncomfortable with prolonged conflict, I'm generally pretty eager to apologize in order to put the ugly incident behind me. Sometimes, though, it takes a while for the other to acknowledge fully the pain of an offense; sometimes anger has to ferment before the cork blows. And sometimes I need to stay with my guilt a little longer, entering more completely into the stupidity or meanness of what I've done. Tossing off an "I'm sorry" might make *me* feel better, but the one who needs it most may not yet be ready to receive it.

Second, *stay committed to the truth*. When you're filled with remorse, especially over something serious, it's easy to allow guilt to bleed over your whole life. Again, I speak from experience. "I'm sorry for hurting your feelings by what I just said" becomes "I'm sorry for being such an insensitive slob who never does anything right." One delinquency, standing naked and exposed in the clear light of truth, seems to invite all my past failures to come out of hiding, and before I know it, I'm presiding over a convention of demons pointing fingers of accusation at me. Sorrow for wrongdoing can be like a drop of dye dropped in a tank of water: it doesn't take much for everything to be colored by it. But exaggerated apologies, though dressed in sackcloth and covered with ashes, are still lies, acts of dishonesty that cannot lead to a healthy restoration of a relationship. Any reconciliation that takes place on the basis of dishonesty is a time bomb waiting to go off, and when it does, an even worse rupture of the relationship will result.

Third, *"I'm sorry" has to be backed-up with behavior*. By themselves, words of apology can be hollow, meaningless. If you tell your daughter you're sorry for missing her soccer game, but never find the time to show up at her remaining games, she would have every right to question your sincerity. If you tell your boyfriend you're sorry for hurting his feelings with sarcastic put-downs, but keep the smart mouth motoring along at a nice clip when you get together, he would have every right to question what words mean to you. If you're really sorry, prove it.

This doesn't mean you need to grovel, endlessly wallowing in the mud of self-condemnation. An authentic apology should be an act of repentance, and this, according to the Bible, has very little to do with emotions and almost everything to do with behavior. It means turning around, going in a different direction. The word has a kind of no-nonsense, stop-the-sniveling sense to it: all right, so you dropped the ball; now pick it up and try not to let go of it again.

In 1963, George Wallace, then governor of Alabama, literally stood in the door of the University of Alabama, preventing Vivian Jones, a black woman, from enrolling as a student. Thirty-three years later he publicly apologized to Jones. And then, as proof that he meant it, he awarded her the first Lurleen B. Wallace Award for Courage—an award, named in honor of Wallace's wife, that recognizes women who have made outstanding contributions to the state of Alabama.[4]

Finally, *say "I'm sorry" as a way of going forward into the rest of your life.* However much you've blown it today, things can be different tomorrow. Some failures are mistakes, unintentional hurts caused because of limitations in being human; some failures, though, are calculated cussedness, intentional pain inflicted by perversity in the dark corners of the heart. Whatever you've done, though, can be a story about your past, not a prophecy of your future. So after accepting responsibility for your offense, accept something more, too: accept forgiveness. Whether or not it's offered by the person you've wounded, you can at least offer it to yourself. And most important, accept it from God.

The story is told of a monk who lived in a monastery high on a mountain. One day he descended to the village below, and a peasant ran up to him and said, "Oh Father, surely yours must be the best of all lives, living so close to God. Tell me, what do you do up there?" After a thoughtful pause, the monk replied, "What do we do? Well, I'll tell you. We fall down and we get up. We fall down and we get up."

We all fall down. The important thing is to get up and keep moving into the rest of life.

——•——

Seventeen

Use Nice Stationery

Attending to the Forms of Communication

I KNOW YOU'RE TEMPTED TO SKIP THIS CHAPTER. Why would anyone bother to read, let alone write, about using nice stationery? Who cares? Does anyone even remember what stationery *is*, for goodness sake? I understand your concern, but stay with me for a couple of pages, and then, if you think it's a lost cause, go to the next chapter with my blessing and no hard feelings.

At the outset, let me confess I've been called a Luddite. For those who majored in physics or basket weaving, or who have forgotten this bit of history, I should mention that the Luddites were a band of laborers who rioted in early nineteenth-century England, destroying textile machines to which they attributed high unemployment. The word thus came to refer to someone who opposes modern technology, who clings to the old ways. Reality is always more complex than labels. True, I still do not know how to use an ATM machine (see chapter 10), and yes, my favorite pens are a seventy-year-old Shaeffer and a twenty-year-old Montblanc—both fountain pens, of course, for I consider ball point pens an egregious affront to aesthetic sensibilities and felt tip pens a foul execration. But I'm writing these words on a laptop computer. All right, I'm not consistent, but didn't someone important say, "Consistency is the hobgoblin of little minds"? In some things, old ways are better; in others, new ways offer an improvement.

In this chapter I don't intend to try to bring back parchments and quill pens. I'm thinking of nice stationery as a kind of symbol of the form communication takes. It's worth thinking about this, because *how* we communicate influences *what* we communicate. The technological era—with its televisions, radios, telephones, faxes, VCRs, and computers—has changed not only the amount of information shared but the way we think and relate to one another.

The most obvious change has been the so-called "information explosion." The amount of information available boggles the mind; a kind of democratization of knowledge is taking place, with ordinary folks gaining access to things hitherto available only to a few. In chapter 9 I mentioned my broken arm; now they tell me I also have a partially torn rotator cuff. The evening after the doctor told me this, I logged onto the internet and in less than a minute I was reading articles written for surgeons, complete with pictures and advice about what *not* to tell patients! And I'm able to get weather forecasts on areas to which I will be traveling, order rare books, do research on products before purchasing, and so forth. There are many advantages.

Yet there is a downside, too. All this information speeds along an electronic superhighway—and where is it going? Where will it take us? To more data, certainly, and better networking. But will it lead us to more wisdom? I doubt it. Words and the disparate facts they communicate come at us faster than we know how to use them. "Like the Sorcerer's Apprentice," Neil Postman writes, "we are awash in information. And all the sorcerer has left us is a broom. Information has become a form of garbage, not only incapable of answering the most fundamental human questions but barely useful in providing coherent direction to the solution of even mundane problems."[1] Ted Koppel, in an acceptance speech for the Broadcaster of the Year Award in 1986, observed, "We have become so obsessed with facts that we have lost all touch with truth . . . Consider this paradox: Almost everything that is publicly said these days is recorded. Almost nothing of what is said is worth remembering."[2]

The result has been verbal inflation, with a consequent devaluing of words. To be sure, we still use them. We continue to have conversations, make and listen to speeches, read and write books, and depend upon the lingering power of words to create institutions like marriage (words of promise) and government (words of law). But currency in an inflationary economy stays in use, though it declines in value; words remain our primary unit of relational exchange, but their individual worth is declining.

And a bear market in the stock exchange of words will lead to a cheapening of humanity; a deterioration of language weakens the foundation of human dignity. This may seem like a big leap in logic, but it's really not: one of the things—the most important, probably—which sets us apart from animals is the capacity for discourse in language. I can already hear the howl raised by animal lovers protesting my humancentric arrogance; I can hear their lectures telling about the amazing ways animals communicate with one another. Granted, animals can convey certain things to one another. But don't tell me a hug from a chimpanzee is the same as a sonnet by Shakespeare. Go ahead and argue that one is not better than another, if you must, but please don't say they're the same. And because our species occasionally produces poetry by a Milton or fiction by a Tolstoy or hymns by a Wesley, we can and ought to claim this as our human distinctive. What sets us apart is verbal expression, this ability to convey ideas and feelings and hopes and fears into words, strung together in sentences and arranged in paragraphs. And this, I maintain, is something to which we must cling—even in a technological era.

In the movie *Dead Poets Society,* John Keating, played by Robin Williams, is an English teacher at a boys' school. He begins his class in poetry in a routine, boring way by asking his students to turn to the introduction in their textbook and having one of them read from the pedantic prose. But suddenly Keating interrupts and says, "Excrement. That's what I think of James Evans Pritchard, Ph.D.'s introduction to poetry. We are not laying pipe. We are understanding poetry. I want you to rip it out, and while you are at it, rip out the whole introduction. Rip it out!" Slowly, as their shock gives way to an awareness that he is serious, the students begin ripping pages from their hardback volumes of poetry. "This is a battle, a war," Keating declares, "and the casualties could be your hearts and souls. Armies of academics going forth, measuring poetry. But this will not happen in my class. You will learn to savor words and language."

You will learn to savor words and language. This spirit of savoring was captured in a letter Edwin Arlington Robinson wrote toward the end of his life to a friend, telling of his boyhood efforts to capture a line of poetry. Then he said, "Time had no special significance for a certain juvenile and incorrigible fisher of words who thought nothing of fishing for two weeks to catch a stanza, or even a line, that he would not throw back into a squirming sea of language where there was every word but the one he wanted. There were strange and iridescent and impossible words that would seize the bait and swallow the hook and all but drag the excited angler in after them, but like that famous catch of Hiawatha's, they were generally not the fish he wanted. He wanted fish that were smooth and shining and subtle, and very much alive, and not too strange, and presently, after a long patience and many rejections, they began to bite."[3]

I'm not suggesting we must craft every communication with the care of a poet fishing for just the right word. The forms will vary, depending on the purpose of the communication. A grocery list will be one thing and a letter to your lover something else. But here's the point: form counts, manner matters. Sure, it's great to telephone your daughter in college; nothing can replace the joy of hearing the voice of one you love. And sure, it's fine to send her E-mails during the week, keeping her posted on events in your life. But do you think these ways of communicating will mean the same to her as finding, at the student union post office, an envelope with your address in the upper left-hand corner? She knows it's a message you took the time to write, and she's tempted to rip into it right then and there even though Tom—*the* Tom you've been hearing about for weeks—is walking by, but she decides to save it for a little while, not simply to catch up with that gorgeous hunk but also to have something to look forward to. During Sociology class, she can almost *feel* it in her backpack; she's excited about it, but also a little worried, occasionally wondering what would be so important that you took the time to write rather than telephone.

And what if you *did* take the time to write, picking out nice stationery and thinking carefully about the words and phrases, trying your best to say something you've wanted to express for a long time, something like how much you love her and how proud you are of her? I will promise you something: she will not throw away the letter, but will hide it in some corner of her dorm room and read it again and again. By paying attention to the words and the way you sent them, you not only will have committed a little protest against the decline of language, joining John Keating in the battle for hearts and souls, you will have lifted the level of discourse with your daughter and thereby honored her, and you will have shown just how much you respect her.

A few weeks ago I was in an emotional pit, feeling lonely and depressed and wondering whether I had accomplished anything worthwhile with my life. I told myself I had allowed my perceptions to get distorted, and I soldiered on, doing my best to keep moving forward with my responsibilities. But a dark cloud was hanging over my head; better put, a dark cloud had settled in my soul. And then a letter came from Mike, a young man who had been a former parishioner. It was on stationery he had designed (he's a graphic artist), and it was two pages of single-space type. From the first sentence, I knew he had given thought to what he was going to say, so I read it carefully, slowly. He told me how much he had appreciated my pastoral ministry, and he gave me specific reasons why. By the end of the letter I had tears in my eyes. I offered a silent prayer of gratitude and promptly re-read it. Then I filed it with other letters I want to keep forever, because I get a lot of the other kind, too, and it's a fine thing to re-read the good ones once in a while.

Perhaps Mike could have said the same things over the telephone, but I doubt it; perhaps he could have sent me an E-mail, but I don't think I would have read it in the same way. What I know is that Mike took the time, chose stationery and words with care, and sent me a message from God.

I would guess that somewhere in the back of your closet, in a shoe box surrounded by dust balls, you've got a few letters you've had for some time. You wouldn't dream of tossing them into the garbage. In fact, if the fire alarm in your house went off, and for once it wasn't because of burned popcorn, that shoe box would probably be one of the first things you would try to save.

To tell the truth, as I come to the end of this chapter I'm feeling a little guilty. I telephone my daughters, who live thousands of miles away, at least once a week, and I send E-mails almost daily. But I think I'll quit this computer for a while, go down to the stationery store (I have in mind a pale blue, lightly textured paper), and spend some time trying to tell them, in a way they might want to remember, how much they mean to me.

Eighteen

Close Your Mouth
and Open Your Ears

Learning to Be a Good Listener

PRESIDENT FRANKLIN ROOSEVELT WAS ONCE AT A gala ball, shaking hands and smiling his big smile and saying the vacuous inanities customary on such occasions. But he grew tired of it all, and convinced that no one was listening anyway, greeted each person by saying, "I murdered my grandmother this morning." To which everyone said things such as "Wonderful!" "How lovely!" "Keep up the good work!" One diplomat was listening, however, and whispered in Roosevelt's ear, "I'm sure she had it coming to her!"[1]

I suppose we shouldn't be too hard on the folks who congratulated Roosevelt for committing a heinous crime. I have never met a president of the United States who was still in office, though I once spoke with Jimmy Carter as we both stood facing the wall in the men's room (what *do* you say at a time like that?), and I shook hands with Ronald Reagan after he politely endured one of my sermons. What I remember on both occasions was an overwhelming self-consciousness. So I imagine that if President Roosevelt had greeted me at a party, my major concerns would have been whether remnants of the spinach salad were sticking to my teeth and what I was going to say that would sound witty and profound and move him to seek my advice on the invasion of Europe.

Listening, though, is never easy, whether to the most powerful politician in government or the shyest kid in the nursery school. We're back to the problem of the ego, which has popped up periodically in this book because it pops up regularly in our lives. It can be more than a little distracting, causing us to worry constantly about buffing the shine on our image and staying in control of the situation. We must spout forth marvelously intelligent observations, and when someone else manages to slip in an occasional response, we must use the time to worry about bad breath and to discern what the other person really thinks about us and to plan what we're going to say as soon as we get the opportunity. All this leaves very little time for listening.

Listening is a whole lot more than not talking. It's easy to picture it as something passive, as pure receiving. Actually, it's hard work. I've realized this in a new way now that I have made the shift from being a pastor to becoming a seminary president. In the former role I preached and others listened (or so I hoped); now, I still preach but I also attend daily chapel services where others preach and I'm doing my best to listen. The whole experience has been sobering, and I think every preacher should have to go through it. I must confess only partial success in my attempts to be a good listener (this will not come as a shock to you who faithfully sit through sermons week after week). I've discovered that my attention has a mind of its own, often getting up and wandering around like a dog sniffing under every bush and blissfully ignoring his owner's commands. Fido, get back here this instant! The pooch may look up for a second or two, but then he's off to harass a cat and salute a hydrant. Keeping Fido at your side is no easy task; anyone who does it for any length of time deserves at least a nomination for the Nobel Prize.

This is why you'll never hear me complain that psychotherapists charge too much for their services. One hundred twenty-five dollars for a fifty-minute hour seems a lot, I know, and I've done my share of moaning. But have you ever tried to walk with Mr. Smith through the murky swamps of his inferiority complex at three o'clock in the afternoon as he tells you for the thirty-ninth time that his older brother was the favored child? Staying attentive under these conditions, not to mention artfully stifling yawns, is not for lightweights; it's hard work, right up there with going into the mines and playing linebacker for the Packers.

Listening is not the same as hearing. You listen in order to hear; it's the effort to open yourself and pay attention that sometimes, if you practice and stay at it, leads to hearing. And hearing leads to understanding, which can lead to tightening the bonds of human relationships. It's not insignificant that *communication* and *community* come from the same root. If we never heard one another, we'd be no more than isolated islands of egocentricity, never connecting, never building bridges by which we might escape from the isolation of self that inevitably ends in suffocating boredom. To put it bluntly, this is pretty much what the Bible has in mind when it speaks about hell—separation from one another and from God, and thus even from one's true self. On the other hand, a community in which alienation has been overcome and we live in reconciled love with one another and God isn't a bad way to picture heaven. Without putting too fine a theological point on it, any nailing down of a plank that builds a bridge of communication, takes one, if not all the way to the pearly gates, at least a good distance down the road in the right direction.

So how do we get good at it? If paying attention is the first step, the second is trying to figure out what's being said *beneath* what's being said. Communication always takes place on different levels, and the actual words spoken or written may bear scant relation to what's *really* being shared—if only we have ears, or maybe heart, to hear it.

Fiorello LaGuardia was mayor of New York during the worst days of the Great Depression and all of World War II. He was a colorful character who used to ride fire trucks, raid speakeasies with policemen, take entire orphanages to baseball games, and when the newspapers were on strike, he would go on the radio to read the Sunday comics.

I came across a story about him that took place one bitterly cold night in January of 1935. "The mayor turned up at a night court that served the poorest ward in the city. LaGuardia dismissed the judge for the evening and took over the bench himself. Within a few minutes, a tattered old woman was brought before him, charged with stealing a loaf of bread. She told LaGuardia that her daughter's husband had deserted her, her daughter was sick, and her two grandchildren were starving. But the shopkeeper, from whom the bread was stolen, refused to drop the charges. 'It's a bad neighborhood, your Honor,' the man told the mayor. 'She's got to be punished to teach old people around here a lesson.'

"LaGuardia sighed. He turned to the woman and said, 'I've got to punish you. The law makes no exceptions—ten dollars or ten days in jail.' But even as he pronounced the sentence, the mayor was already reaching into his pocket. He extracted a bill and tossed it into his famous sombrero saying: 'Here is the ten-dollar fine, which I now remit; and furthermore I am going to fine everyone in this courtroom fifty cents for living in a town where a person has to steal bread so that her grandchildren can eat. Mr. Bailiff, collect the fines and give them to the defendant.'

"So the following day the New York City newspapers reported that $47.50 was turned over to a bewildered old lady who had stolen a loaf of bread to feed her starving grandchildren, fifty cents of that amount being contributed by the red-faced grocery store owner, while some seventy petty criminals, people with traffic violations, and New York City policemen, each of whom had just paid fifty cents for the privilege of doing so, gave the mayor a standing ovation."[2]

Notice what Mayor LaGuardia heard that evening: he heard the charge of the shopkeeper; he heard the evidence; he heard the law. This was all obvious, apparent to anyone in the courtroom. But he also heard something else: he heard the desperation and broken heart of an old woman who loved her family; he heard the hammer of injustice as it pounded the weak; he heard the deeper intention of the law; and he heard the voice of his own compassion. Not everyone would have heard these things, but LaGuardia did, and that evening, if only briefly, an outpost of community was established in an earthly city and a light shined in the courtroom that had about it the particular splendor of the Heavenly City.

To listen well, then, means to listen deep down, to attend to what lies beneath or behind what's being said. A man comes home twenty minutes late from work, and his wife erupts with anger, "Why didn't you at least call me? Our dinner is ruined and we're going to be late for Jeremy's concert. You're so insensitive! The only thing that matters to you is your damn work!" The man thinks to himself, "Wow, this is pretty severe for being only twenty minutes late. She obviously doesn't know how hard I'm working and how many pressures I have—and all to support this family." But if he's smart and sensitive, he'll keep his mouth shut and open his ears, and he might well hear something else: "I'm upset because I've been alone all day and I'm a little jealous that you get to do exciting things, and I'm feeling boring and I'm wondering if you still love me the way you used to . . ." And then if he's *really* smart and sensitive, he won't try to explain anything but simply take her in his arms.

A teenager screams, "You're the worst mom who ever lived, and no, I will not go to church with you this morning. In fact, I will never go to church with you ever again, and you and your self-righteous friends can just go to hell!" Her mother dissolves into tears and feelings of failure. She worries she was too harsh in grounding her daughter the night before; she feels inadequate as a single mom, horribly alone. But before she falls completely apart in self-recrimination, she should pause long enough to hear something else in her daughter's anger: "Mom, I'm trying to figure out who I am, and I really don't like what I see, and last night I was for the first time feeling accepted by some of the other kids and so I stayed out after curfew. And it's not that I'm rejecting your God, but I'm struggling to find my own beliefs . . ."

Listening digs below the surface to hear intentions and not just words, to hear the heart and not just the tongue. It's "the silent shape of caring,"[3] as Lewis Smedes described it, an act of compassion. Granting this gift, we bestow a wonderful blessing—the blessing of our attention. And personal attention is like a magical wand waved through a conversation, empowering another person to feel valued, to feel that maybe her thoughts are worth something and that maybe, therefore, she is worth something. Dr. Karl Menninger said, "Listening is a magnetic and strange thing, a creative force. The friends who listen to us are the ones we move toward, and we want to sit in their radius. When we are listened to, it creates us, makes us unfold and expand. I discovered this a few years ago. Before that, when I went to a party I would think anxiously: 'Now try hard, be lively.' But now I tell myself to listen with affection to anyone who talks to me. The person is showing me his soul. It is a little dry and meager and full of grinding talk just now, but soon he will begin to think. He will show his true self, will be wonderfully alive."[4]

This quotation had in it an interesting turn in direction: Menninger first referred to the creative power of listening, to what it can do for the person who is heard; when he spoke of his own experience as a listener, however, he shifted his focus to what he would gain, to what he would learn about the person. Listening is a gift that rewards both the recipient and the giver.

The sunlight of your interest warms the petals of another person, enabling the rose to open, and by that same light you can see and enjoy the flower that has bloomed. If you shut your mouth and open your ears, in other words, you just might learn something worthwhile about another person. In fact, if you cultivate this art, you might even learn something about God.

In *Saint Joan,* George Bernard Shaw tells the story of a peasant maid from a small village who claims to have heard God calling her to inspire the French in their fight against the English. Her audacity gets her summoned before King Charles VII, who commands her to explain how an eighteen-year-old girl can take it upon herself to lead troops into battle. By what authority does she act? In the presence of courtiers, soldiers, nobles, and church officials, she tells the king how she has heard God compelling her to help her country. Charles interrupts, "O your voices, your voices! Why don't the voices come to me? *I* am the King of France, not you!"

Joan calmly replies: "They do come to you; but you do not hear them. You have not sat in the field in the evening listening for them. When the angelus rings you cross yourself and have done with it; but if you prayed from your heart, and listened to the thrilling of the bells in the air after they stop ringing, you would hear the voices as I do."[5]

You have to listen to hear some things. You can't be a self-important sovereign in your little world, pompously proclaiming your wisdom, and expect to hear the voices—from another person's soul or from the angels of heaven. It takes humble openness, careful attentiveness. You must do the hard work of quieting yourself long enough to hear the thrilling of the bells in the air after they stop ringing.

———•◦•———

Nineteen

Be First to Reach for the Tab

Developing a Generous Spirit

I'VE ALWAYS MAINTAINED THAT LITTLE DECISIONS in life, not big ones, create the most stress. Major choices—whether to marry a person or take a new job or have radiation therapy—generally have a history and a context that create a certain inevitability. But smaller ones leave you stranded with nothing but your own wits or character, and often demand an immediate decision. Toothpaste, for example. Do you opt for tartar control or whitening agents or baking soda freshness or sensitivity protection or one that somehow manages to keep your gum line from receding faster than your hairline? A decision like this can drive you nuts. Frankly, I think it's time for a Senate committee to hold hearings on this matter of toothpaste proliferation; we may even need the attorney general to appoint a special prosecutor.

The mental health of the country could be at stake, not to mention the GNP if we all take the time to read 562 labels whenever we need another tube of toothpaste.

And here's a little decision packing a big wallop of stress: you're at a nice restaurant, enjoying a great meal and conversation, and then comes the dreaded moment when the server places the bill on the table. What do you do? Pretend not to notice it? Go to the bathroom? Fake a coughing fit? Start moving your hand (very slowly) toward your wallet? Or do you boldly grab it before your friend picks it up? This is a complicated issue. How *good* a friend is she, anyway? Did you pay the last time you were together? And then, supposing she *does* pick it up, what do you do? Do you say, "Hey, let me help you with that"? And if so, what sort of tone do you use? The one that says, "I really would like to share the expense of this meal"? Or the one that says, "I'm just trying to be polite but we both know it's your turn to pay"? It's the accumulation of moments like these that make life difficult, if you ask me.

Let me relieve some stress. I can't solve the toothpaste problem, but I can help with meal tab anxiety: just pick it up. Maybe not every time (it's good, after all, to let others also experience the joy of giving), but most of the time. Be the first to reach for the bill; be the sort of person who does this instinctively, as a matter of habit.

In paying a bill, you pay a compliment. When you offer any gift—whether money or time or patience or forgiveness or anything else of value—you demonstrate respect for another person. You say, in effect, "I'm giving you something of value because *you* are of value." This is why courteous people—those who take seriously the dignity of others—tend to be generous people.

A generous spirit, though, probably doesn't come naturally to those of us who must persistently struggle with self-centeredness. Reaching for the tab probably won't be our first instinctive response; it will no doubt take some practice to develop this particular behavior. How, then, do we cultivate a spirit of generosity?

I've known some Great Givers, and let me pass on a few things I've noticed about them. First, they are *motivated by thanksgiving*. Generosity has nothing to do with means and everything to do with desire. Don't kid yourself by thinking, If I made an additional $10,000 a year, I would be more generous. No, you wouldn't. Actually, according to statistics on financial giving, you would probably give less. Another way to put it, the more money you have, the more money has you and the harder it is to break free from its grip. What makes people generous is something else, a particular attitude—an attitude of gratitude (see chapter 2). Thankful for what they have, they feel it's only right to share.

My friend Frank is on the all-star team of Great Givers. During the years I was his pastor, I wouldn't hesitate to call him if I knew a serious need in the congregation or community. "Don," he would say, "it's a done deal. Don't worry about it. I'll take care of it." And then he would call about a half dozen of his friends and say, "Listen, we've got a wonderful opportunity to help someone who really needs it. I've got us all down for five thousand dollars, and I knew you would want to be included." Well, as you might imagine, some have ambivalent feelings about being on Frank's "hit list." But one thing they know with certainty: they're happy to be counted as one of his friends because as sure as the sun rises every day they know if they were ever in trouble he would do his best to help. If you were lying wounded, the enemy had you in their sights, and the bombs were coming in, Frank would be the one to come back for you and carry you to safety; he walks with one leg today to prove it. And if you're having lunch with him, don't even think about reaching for the tab unless you're willing to risk a broken arm.

Why would generosity—with money, time, compassion, loyalty—be such a pattern of life for Frank? Here's a man who has suffered a great deal, living with a major disability, experiencing serious financial setbacks, going through times of great humiliation, facing the indescribable pain of losing a daughter in a car accident. What makes him tick? I've tried to figure this out, and here's what I think: he's one of the most grateful people I've ever met. I can't tell you how many times I've heard him say, "My dad used to say, 'Thank God we're rich! And some day we're going to have money!'" Frank always tells this story to witness to his own gratitude for blessings in his life—for God and family and friends and work and country and the opportunity to help people and, way down the list, for material prosperity. A thankful heart is an open heart, open to the needs of others.

And generous people tend to be *disciplined in the expression of gratitude*. The generosity of Great Givers isn't simply a spur-of-the-moment impulse. Anyone can feel an occasional pang of charity, a spasm of liberality brought on by the mood of the moment. But there's a big difference between doing a generous deed and being a generous person. The latter makes giving a way of life that transcends the vagaries of emotions. They know that sometimes, like anyone else, they'll be cranky with the human race in general and won't *feel* at all like giving; they know that some patterns of character require a disciplined commitment, that becoming a generous person takes promises and follow-through. So they carve out time in their schedules to volunteer with Big Brothers, or do rape crisis counseling with the YWCA or work at the food bank; and they make pledges to the United Way and their alma mater and their place of worship. They plan for giving, in other words, and keep their promises.

When I was sixteen and had just begun to drive, my father ordered a 1966 Chrysler Newport, the first brand new car he had purchased. Needless to say, the whole family awaited its delivery with eager anticipation, especially his son. And I, waiting for just the right moment, ventured a request to borrow the car for a special date with my girl-friend. I had the good sense to ask for an evening far in the future, many months away. My father, being a generous person, agreed.

Unfortunately, there were shipping problems, and the car was days late, and then weeks late, and then months late. Finally, it arrived—on the very evening my father had promised I could have it. It was a rainy Seattle night, and my girlfriend lived on the far side of town, many miles away. Had I been a more sensitive son, I would have released him from his pledge and let him enjoy a few days of peace with his shiny new car. But young love has its urgencies. To my father's credit, he believed a promise is a promise and there are some things more important than new cars. So I drove off, with my heart racing, and I can still see, in the rearview mirror, the tortured look on his face as I took his proud pos-session off into a stormy night. I should also report, to bring this story to a completely honest conclusion, that I can also still see the wincing of his face when, the next morning, I showed him a little dent, which, I swear, was not my fault but the result a bizarre accident. Honest!

Generous people, like my father, stick by their commitments, even when the emotional wave has petered out and they're in a trough where they don't much feel like sharing. They refuse to trust the emotions of the moment, and instead, they plan and promise and so develop a certain kind of character.

Finally, I'm pleased to report that Great Givers are *happy people*. The Good Book tells us God loves a cheerful giver, and that may be because they're the only ones left to love. Grumpy givers don't last; they always find too many expenses and other excuses to prevent them from helping out. You have to feel sorry for them: they're short-term investors blind to long-term gains. But those who give and discipline themselves to keep giving earn blue chip rewards. To put it bluntly, it pays to be generous.

Courtesy places an obligation upon us to be generous, to be sure, but there are different kinds of obligations. Lewis Smedes has made a wonderful distinction between an *obligation of ought* and an *obligation of opportunity*; some things we must do out of duty, but other things we must do because it's best for everyone—including ourselves. Giving is in the latter category.

I once visited a Presbyterian medical clinic in Ghana, which was a long Land Rover—ride away from my personal comfort zone. I was doing all right, really excited about the adventure I was having, until they told me they had just killed a black mamba (one of the deadliest snakes in the world) right outside the door of the house I would be using. I only mention this to illustrate that Donkorkrom Hospital wasn't exactly in the "high rent" district; those who lived there had to put up with daily difficulties most of us can't imagine. What shocked me, though, was how happy everyone seemed. No one seemed to be "sacrificing," though I knew they were doing exactly that. They appeared to be having a lot of fun.

The chief physician was Dr. Tim Hannah, an Australian who had left a successful medical practice in Europe. I said to him, "This is quite a change."

He replied, "Yes, I was making bundles of money, driving a new Porsche, and enjoying the comforts of affluence. But, frankly, it was boring compared to this." And then, with a big smile on his face, he said, "This is really living!"

One day Tim took me out to a big field and announced it was time for a little recreation. Out of a bag he pulled a boomerang. "I'm from Australia, you know, and now I'm going to show you how to use one of these things." He was a good teacher, and before long I was heaving that wooden wedge as hard as I could and it was coming back to me. I have no idea how boomerangs work; the physics are beyond me. All I know is, when I threw it hard away from me, it came flying back.

Which is exactly what Tim and other Great Givers experience. The more they throw away their lives, the more comes back to them. A long time ago Jesus said, "Give and it will be given to you . . . for the measure you give will be the measure you get back." And at another time he pointed to an even more fundamental truth, *the* great paradox in life: the ones who seek to save their lives will lose them, and the ones who sacrifice them will save them. Carefully hoard what you have and it will turn to dust in your hands; throw it away in generosity, and you gain far more than you lose.

When you give, what do you get? The answer can't be quantified (give five dollars and expect to get ten dollars back). I'm not sure it can even be explained, but let me take a shot at it. What you gain is a deep congruence with the way things ought to be; it's as though you finally hit the right note on the piano and the chord finds its harmony. Human beings, as I have said repeatedly in this book, have been created for community. Deep in our hearts is a desire—no, I'll put it stronger, a *need*—to connect with other people, to make music with others. But if we keep to ourselves, refusing to play our part and instead plunking out the tunes that strike the fancy of our self-centeredness, we create not music but a cacophonous confusion.

A generous act, even if only brief, hits the right note exactly and helps resolve the dissonance into a well-rounded harmony; a gesture of giving helps put things back together again, the way they were meant to be. And that will always feel right in the deep-down places, which is why, I think, only one word adequately describes what comes back to you when you throw the boomerang: joy.

I was once at lunch with my friend Frank, and I watched him take a twenty dollar bill out of his money clip and give it to the server as a tip. The young woman was almost paralyzed with astonishment. "This is for you because I want you to have a great day!" When she left our table, I said, "You gave her a twenty dollar tip for a fifteen dollar tab? Are you crazy?"

A big smile took over the whole landscape of his face, and he said, "Isn't it fun? Isn't it really *fun*?"

Twenty

———•———

Leave a Tip Worth Working For

Noticing Those Who Serve

Let's assume the previous chapter moved you deeply, and you have decided to become a more generous person. So the next time you're at a restaurant with a friend, you boldly reach for the tab. But you're still faced with a decision, aren't you? How much should you give for a tip? Fifteen percent? Twenty percent? Well, was the service good? Or did your server treat you as though you had a communicable disease? Should a tip be considered an automatic part of the cost of the meal? Or should it be seen as a reward for service well performed? This is one of life's complicated issues—and I haven't even mentioned taxi cab drivers, a subject deserving of a book by itself.

To help relieve your anxiety about tipping, let me offer some guidance: extend your generosity to those who are easy to overlook. Some people work in positions of service that others of us take for granted; they exist in the background, serving food, washing dishes, removing trash, cleaning hotel rooms, mowing lawns, and doing jobs that make our lives more pleasant. I think of them as "backdoor people"—those who come in the back doors of restaurants and hotels and stores and homes, who do work on which we depend but have not been accorded much status.

In this country we are blessed with a strong economy and a large middle class, and many of us enjoy a rising tide of prosperity. But this has blinded us, I fear, to sometimes subtle, yet nonetheless real, class distinctions. We pride ourselves on our American egalitarianism. No aristocratic pretensions for us! And certainly no Marxist blather about warfare between the proletariat and the bourgeoisie! We're all equal here, or so we like to think, and our self-congratulations drown out any dissenting voices. When the Fourth of July parade marches by, it's difficult to hear the cry of the street sweeper who's having a harder time making a living for his family than keeping our gutters clean.

Let's be honest: there are those on top and those on bottom. Those on top enjoy an affluence and power denied those on the bottom. It's not that privileged people are malicious, purposefully scheming to keep the disadvantaged on the bottom. Most, I'm sure, possess a genuine goodwill that would like to see all boats rise in the tide. It's just that it takes certain practical measures to get some boats unstuck from the mud, and some of these measures may seem to threaten boats that are already floating nicely. So when votes are cast, laws get enacted favoring those with advantages. Consequently, the tide eventually washes over some boats instead of lifting them, and some folks have a hard time keeping their heads above water.

Don't worry, I'm not going to expound an elaborate political or economic philosophy here. I'm simply making a plea that we notice those who come in the back door and extend our generosity to them. I'm aware that some who earn part of their income from tips do very well; some servers in classy restaurants probably make more than their tax accountants. But for the most part, tipping honors those who serve, and those who serve tend to serve with their hull resting on the bottom.

I'm convinced that one thing separating the generous from the stingy is the former have eyes opened wide enough to notice those in need. My friend Alan for example. One evening I stopped by his house to pick him up for dinner at a restaurant, but the telephone rang before we could get out the door. He answered it, and from his silence I knew that a salesperson was on the other end of the line. I should perhaps confess that my Christian faith has failed to change my character enough to love telemarketers; maybe someday I will learn to love them the way Christ told us to love our enemies, but at the moment I would like to have them rounded up and shot. Since the law frowns on this sort of thing, I am committed to slamming down the receiver the first second I realize I'm getting a sales spiel, and I wish the rest of you would follow my example instead of buying their stuff and encouraging them to invade my privacy. I mention my attitude on this modern scourge to underscore how surprised I was that Alan actually kept talking to the salesperson. He interjected an occasional "Oh" and even an "I see." He wasn't just being polite; he was making a new best friend. My irritation mounting, I was getting ready to pull the telephone line out of the wall. We had reservations and needed to hit the road.

When he finally hung up I said, "What were you doing, anyway? How could you possibly give so much time to a salesperson? Don't you know you're supposed to grunt something to indicate your disgust and then slam down the receiver?"

Alan replied, "Well, yes, it's annoying. But did you ever consider how desperate for work the callers must be? And can you imagine how awful it must be to face so much constant rejection?"

No, I hadn't considered these things. I hadn't even imagined them to be actual *people.* It never occurred to me that they might have feelings, that they might be working in a job they didn't like in order to make a living. And then and there, I breathed a prayer, asking God to help me some day grow up to be like my friend—a man with eyes open to the needs of others.

One day Gandhi stepped aboard a train as it started to move, and one of his shoes slipped off and dropped on the tracks. Unable to retrieve it, he calmly took off his other shoe and threw it back along the track to land close to the first. When an amazed passenger asked why he had done that, Gandhi smiled and said, "The poor man who finds the shoe lying on the track will now have a pair he can use."[1] With the eyes of his imagination, Gandhi saw a man with bare feet, saw him coming across a lone shoe and desperately searching for the other, and saw the disappointment on his face when he didn't find it; seeing these things, Gandhi did what he could to help.

Another friend of mind, Aubrey, has opened his eyes to

those in need; whenever I talk with him, I feel as blind as the proverbial bat. He lives in San Diego, and one day he let himself see the poor on the streets of nearby Tijuana, Mexico. It occurred to him that bakers might be willing to give away day-old bread for the hungry. He asked, and sure enough, they gave him plenty to fill his car. It then occurred to him that bakers might even enable him to fill a van. He first had to find a van, but once this minor problem was solved, the bakers gave him enough to fill it. It then occurred to him that if he could fill vans to feed the hungry in Tijuana, he might just as well fill 747 jets to take to famine-ravaged areas of Africa. And before long—I'm telling you the truth—Aubrey was organizing flights of jumbo jets to Africa and Eastern Europe filled with food and clothing and other things desperately needed by people there—people, it should be said, who were not just "backdoor people," but people who couldn't even get out of the alley to climb the steps on the back porch. Aubrey, you should know, is not a man with fancy degrees from prestigious universities, not a man of affluence or power; Aubrey has simply opened his eyes to people the rest of us find easy to overlook, and he believes in a God who helps those who help not themselves but others.

Now, you may be wondering what Alan and Gandhi and Aubrey have to do with tipping the woman who served you a ham and cheese sandwich or the man who drove you to within an inch of your life getting you across town. They are examples, it seems to me, of people who have chosen to see things the rest of us choose not to see. We all practice selective perception, of course, for no one can take it *all* in, no one can absorb the full weight of reality. From the vast array of stimuli coming at us, we allow some things to penetrate our consciousness even as we block out other things. And the question is this: What's in your line of sight?

The answer will say much about your values and even your character. Not everyone will be able to see the poor on the streets of Tijuana or masses dying of starvation in drought-stricken Africa; perhaps not everyone should even try to see these things all the time, for the burden of human suffering can crush you under a heavy load of despair. But courteous people at least make a practice of seeing those who serve, noticing those who come in the back door and stand in the shadows as they wait to provide for our needs. These servers, more often than not, are people who do their work from the bottom of our American class structure; they tend to be in jobs with very low salaries and depend on tips to make enough to meet the expenses of living.

So you're at a power lunch, enjoying grilled salmon and wooing a potential client, but you'd like another cup of coffee, and you're beginning to wonder if your server slipped on spaghetti and has been rushed to the emergency room. As impatience and irritation grow, time expands until even a few minutes seem like a very long time. When she finally appears, you tell her you wanted another cup of coffee but, now that you're too rushed, you'll have to settle for the bill. Then comes the moment of decision: how much will you tip? She kept you waiting five minutes for a refill, and you're not about to reward that sort of service. But did you notice some other things? Did you notice how full the restaurant was? Did you see the harried look on her face—a look that, to eyes of compassion, reveal a single mom doing her best to keep the household together and living with constant worry because her employer doesn't provide medical insurance and she doesn't know what will happen if one of the kids gets sick? Did you see how she *needs* your tip?

No one would blame you if you didn't. You had important things on your mind, important business to conduct. But had you given even a few seconds of thought to her and allowed your generosity to extend toward her needs, you might well have been rewarded for your sensitivity. Generosity pays, as I said in the last chapter. When we serve those who serve us, we're likely to get even better service the next time.

A number of years ago an English family journeyed to Scotland for a summer holiday. The mother and father were looking forward to the time away with their young son. But one day the son wandered off by himself, and he found an abandoned swimming hole. Naturally, he took off his clothes and jumped in.

He was immediately attacked by vicious cramps, and he cried out for help as he struggled to stay afloat. Luckily, a farm boy working in a nearby field heard him and came running. He dove into the water and pulled the nearly drowned boy to safety.

The next day the father went to meet the young Scot who had saved his son's life. As the two engaged in conversation, the Englishman asked the boy what he planned to do with his future. The lad answered, "Oh, I suppose I'll be a farmer like my father."

"Well, is there something else you would rather do?" asked the grateful father.

"Oh, yes!" he replied. "I've always wanted to be a doctor. But we are poor people and could never afford to pay for my education."

"You shall have your heart's desire," said the English gentleman. "Make your plans, and I'll take care of the costs." This was a generous tip for service rendered! And the farmer's son did indeed become a doctor.

Some years later, in December of 1943, Winston Churchill became dangerously ill with pneumonia in North Africa. Sir Alexander Fleming, who had discovered the new wonder drug penicillin, was summoned. Flying in from England, Dr. Fleming administered his drug to the ailing prime minister. And this was the second time he saved Churchill's life. Years before it was Fleming who dove into a swimming hole and rescued the boy Winston Churchill from drowning. The generous "tip" given by Churchill's father had reaped a generous return.[2]

I don't mean to imply that if you tip the cab driver well, he will one day save your kid from getting run over by an out-of-control bus, though stranger things have happened. I'm simply reinforcing the point I made in the last chapter: generosity pays handsome rewards. I can't say what the return payment might be. It may be better service the next time you're in need. Or it may simply be the joy of knowing you've given a hand to someone who could probably use it.

Twenty-one

———•—•———

Go Home Before
Your Host Falls Asleep
Not Abusing the Gift of Hospitality

MOST OF US PROBABLY HAVE CHILDHOOD MEMO-
ries of parents embarrassing us. For me, the worst moments
came not when Mom kissed me good-bye in front of my
classmates or when Dad, a preacher, tried to cram three sermons into one; these things caused only mild discomfort
compared with what happened when our family went out to
dinner with Aunt Florence. It was always fun to be with Aunt
Florence, and her daughters, Diana and Karen, were like sisters to my sister and me. The problem always came at the end
of the meal, when the server brought the bill. Let me put it
this way: neither Mom nor Aunt Florence needed to read
chapter 19, for each would *always* try to reach for the tab first.
There was a fierce competitiveness in their generosity, an
aggressiveness in their giving that's hard to exaggerate. About

halfway through the meal, the tension would mount. Each would be getting ready for action, watching the server's every move and preparing herself mentally, like a sprinter kneeling at the starting blocks or a prize fighter dancing in anticipation of the first round. I always felt sorry for the poor servers, who were oblivious to their true circumstances, never suspecting that setting the bill on the table would be like thrusting a handful of bloody meat into a tank of very hungry sharks.

Long before the bill actually reached the table, the fight would begin. "Here, please give it me." "No, give it to me!" And the poor server would look to the rest of us for help, with eyes reflecting the same amazement and terror as those of a deer paralyzed in the headlights of an oncoming truck. Eventually, one of them would get hold of it, and then things would really get nasty.

"Florence, give that to me. You know it's our turn to pay."

"No, you paid last time."

"Listen, Florence, I'm serious. Let us pay for it. . . . Florence, are you listening to me?"

"John, control your wife."

"Florence, *really* . . ."

"Ione, where did you get that stubbornness?"

"From my older sister. Now give me that bill!"

It could really be ugly, all this attempt to be nice. About three minutes into the mayhem of munificence, as other people began looking our way and little children began pointing, my father would decide it was time to go to the bathroom, and we cousins would roll our eyes in disgust and pray for the floor underneath us to open and deliver us from the embarrassment.

So be warned: if we're ever doing lunch, I'll probably reach for the tab, but if you beat me to it, don't expect an argument. When I was about twelve years old I made a solemn vow *never* to make a scene if someone wanted to give me a gift. I've learned many things from my mother, most of them through her good example. But in this case, I suppose, I learned that even a positive virtue—such as generosity—ought to be practiced with moderation. There comes a time when you have to surrender in the fight to give and learn how to receive. It's important to master the art of opening hands to accept gifts others want to bestow.

It may indeed be more blessed to give than to receive, as St. Paul says, but for many people it's also a lot easier. This is because when we give, we stay on top, in a position of "power." On the other hand, when we receive, we're actually in a position of "weakness," in a more vulnerable state. And many of us—perhaps *most* of us—prefer the sense of control that comes with giving. No, I'm not going to contradict what you just read in the last two chapters: we should definitely cultivate a spirit of generosity. But every bright trait has its shadow side; every good virtue brings with it a potentially bad vice. Generosity can subtly feed our hunger to dominate, and it can stroke our pride, giving us reasons, so we think, to offer ourselves hearty self-congratulations. The way to deal with this is not to give up being generous, but to learn how to balance it with being a good receiver.

My friend the bookie, to whom I introduced you in chapter 12, loved to talk, but he would always stand in the doorway. I could never get him to come into our apartment. "John," I would say, "come in and shut the door." And he would respond, "Naw, you kids don't want me here," as he then launched into another big story. I would keep inviting him in, wanting to offer hospitality, but he would consistently refuse, never wanting to be that vulnerable. It was sad.

These days I'm more blunt with people. Not long ago I was eating in a restaurant with a friend, a very generous man who always picked up the tab. But that day I wanted to have the opportunity, for once, to express my affection by paying for lunch. And so I said, "Look, you always pay. I'm not going to fight over this because of a childhood memory. But I *really* want to pay the bill today. I know you make far more money than I do; I know you like picking up the tab. But you need to learn how to receive from me. It's not fair for you always to be giving and not to let me have that joy." After a moment of stunned silence, he handed me the bill and said, "You're right. Thanks for the lunch."

Courtesy calls us to *accept* the gift of kindness. We should be careful, though, not to *abuse* it. The gift does not grant us the right to take advantage of the giver, to presume upon his or her kindness. Because we have been invited into someone's home for dinner, let's say, does not mean we've been adopted into the family and now have the run of the refrigerator. Relational boundaries vary, falling in one place for new acquaintances and in another for close friends, but we should strive to develop a kind of social radar that enables us to discern them and thus be able to honor them.

When I was a young pastor I visited a woman who had undergone surgery. We had a pleasant conversation, and I was in no hurry to leave. I was feeling pretty self-important in my new professional role; she seemed, moreover, to appreciate my presence. Then suddenly she said, "Would you please pray for me and go home? I'm tired and I can't take much more." I felt chagrin at not being more sensitive to her condition, yet I was grateful for her honesty. That day I made a mental note to remember to keep hospital calls brief. If a person acts pleased to see you, she may be doing just that—acting. She may be extending gracious hospitality to you, but that doesn't mean there aren't boundaries to respect. Trespassing can be very rude.

At the conclusion of World War II the Allies met at Yalta in the Ukraine. Winston Churchill and the British delegation were housed in the Alubka palace, on the grounds of which was a marble statue of a dozing lion, its head resting on its front paws. Churchill took a great liking to this statue, telling Stalin, "It's so like me." He also added that he understood there was a Russian tradition of presenting the best things in the country to important visitors. "Yes, indeed," Stalin responded. "The best thing we have now in Russia is socialism."[1]

I hate to side with Stalin, even in the smallest matters, but I have to admit I'm pleased to know the lion stayed put. Churchill had abused the hospitality extended to him, though probably in a perfectly charming way. Still, he stepped over a social line, it seems to me. Because a man gives you a bed doesn't mean you can walk off with his statuary. (Stalin himself violated other more important boundaries, of course, and walked off with a lot more than dozing lions, but that's another story.)

Not every host or hostess will be as blunt as my parishioner or Stalin. In fact, we ought to count on them lying to us. They will do their best, most of them, to make us feel welcome, even if it means telling a few whoppers as part of the obligation of entertaining. When Perle Mesta, the great Washington hostess, was asked the secret of her success in getting so many rich and famous people to attend her parties, she said it was all in the greetings and good-byes. As each guest arrived she would say, "At last you're here!" And as each left she expressed her regrets with, "I'm sorry you have to leave so soon!" Most of her guests, no doubt, were so flattered they never knew they had just walked through a pile of you-know-what so deep they should have wiped their shoes on the doormat.

So the next time you're at a dinner party and the date on your watch has already changed and you've lost track whether you're on the third or fourth glass of wine and you're *feeling* incredibly witty and your hostess is laughing at everything you say, and out of some belated attempt at courtesy you offer, "Well, I suppose I should probably be going," and she responds, "Oh no, already?" *don't believe her.* She's lying through her teeth. What she's *really* thinking is, "It's about time because you stopped being funny during the Carter administration and I've got to do the dishes tonight and get up early for work in the morning and if you reach for another glass of wine I'm going to break your arm."

Courteous people try to be sensitive to even the hidden costs behind another person's generosity. A folk tale from the Middle East tells of a man who owned the most beautiful thoroughbred in a country that valued fine horses above everything else. His stallion was coveted by his neighbors, and seldom did a day pass that he was not made a generous offer for the handsome animal.

But the owner fell on hard times, and hearing this, a horse dealer decided to visit. "If I make a generous offer now," he thought, "I will gain the horse and my friend's fortune will be restored."

As was the custom in that country, the men ate before any business was transacted, each enjoying a lavish meal. Finally, it came time for the dealer to make his offer. The owner listened carefully and eventually responded, "It is no longer possible for me to sell you the horse. Since I had nothing else to serve, we had to kill the horse, thus discharging my obligation as a host."[2]

I'm not suggesting that the meal you recently enjoyed at a friend's house might have been the thigh of his champion rottweiler, though I admit the thought of a human biting a rottweiler for a change may be attractive to some readers. I simply mean that, with some gifts, there may be more given than meets the eye. Your host, for example, may have just received notice of a downsizing that will leave him looking for work and searching for a new identity, or your friend may have listened attentively to your problems for the last two hours, never letting on that she had just found some marijuana in her son's room. The hidden costs of generosity can be anything—emotions, physical energy, time. And the respect we owe those who have given of themselves is not to abuse the gesture, not to step over the appropriate boundary.

When you're offered an expression of hospitality, in other words, accept it with gratitude. But for goodness sake, don't abuse it by taking more than you've been given.

Twenty-two

Hang Up the Phone During Dinner and at Bedtime
Avoiding Unnecessary Intrusions

Right up there with gravity and other major laws of the universe is the Law of Unintended Consequences. This basically says that things may or may not work out the way you intend, but you can bet your pension that they will work out in ways you don't intend, often with consequences that will sneak up from behind and bite you on the backside. As in the famous incident in which the World Health Organization once tried to help residents of Borneo exterminate houseflies. The insects were more than a nuisance; they were suspected of spreading disease. So with the best of motives, officials sprayed the inside of houses with DDT. They killed the flies, which made a nice feast for gecko lizards. But the DDT-poisoned flies killed the geckos, which made a nice feast for cats. But the DDT-poisoned geckos killed the cats, which made the rats very happy indeed. They were smart enough not to eat the cats, but ate everything else instead and passed on bubonic plague. Countries have governments to solve just this sort of problem, and so the bureaucrats came up with a solution: they arranged for large numbers of foreign cats to be parachuted into the area! This is true. You have to wonder how many illegal drugs were smoked to induce this level of creativity. I imagine guys walking out of bars just as thousands of cats dropped from the sky and forthwith taking a pledge of sobriety as they went straight to the nearest hospital. I never heard how the cats fared, but you can be sure they faced unexpected problems in a new culture.

This is what I mean by the Law of Unintended Consequences. You calculate one thing, you get something else. I don't know what Alexander Graham Bell had in mind when he invented the telephone in 1876, but I would guess his invention has had consequences he could never have imagined.

Some of the consequences have been good, very good. The telephone has made possible a revolution in communication that would have left our ancestors numb with amazement. With the push of a few buttons you can talk with your son in college, your mother on the other side of the country, and your stockbroker in Hong Kong—all before your morning coffee. It would be hard to overestimate the influence of Al Bell's invention in our daily living.

My first congregation had been going through difficult times when I arrived to begin my ministry. About twenty of us were present at my first worship service, and we were all filled with a strange combination of hope and uncertainty. The neighborhood had been "in transition," which means there was a growing African-American and Asian population, and a good deal of white flight. Most in the congregation knew they needed to reach out to their new neighbors, but not everyone felt that way. On that first Sunday a woman introduced herself to me and said, "I've been a member of this church all my life. I certainly hope you're not going to bring blacks into our church. I want you to know that if that's your plan I will fight you all the way." By the grace of God I kept my mouth shut, for a change, and simply smiled and told her I was glad to be her new pastor (see chapter 3, "Tell White Lies [Occasionally]").

A few weeks later I went to the public library, and with the help of a "reverse directory" I got the names and telephone numbers of everyone who lived in the area surrounding the church. I copied these off onto lists of about twenty per page, and on the following Sunday I said, "Now folks, I'm sure you'll agree we need to invite our neighbors to church. I'm asking you to do something very simple: just take one of these sheets and telephone the people listed, inviting them to worship with us." Everyone seemed happy to help with this project.

The next Sunday morning we were all stunned to have visitors—real, live visitors! And I was excited to see our first African-American family—until I noticed they were sitting right behind the woman who had expressed hostility to integrating the church. I was seized with nervous terror, worried about what she might say to them. It had been our custom to invite people to greet one another, but I seriously considered skipping that part of the service. It was printed in the

Order of Worship, though, and I'm enough of a Presbyterian
to be pretty leery of unplanned spontaneity. So I went ahead
with the greeting as usual, and to my horror, I saw my worst
fear coming true: after everyone else had moved on to the
next hymn, the racist woman I was beginning to loathe was
still talking to the visitors behind her. I just *knew* she was saying something rude, no doubt telling them they were not
welcome. Rivers of sweat cascaded underneath my robe as I
tried to get through the rest of the service. When finally I pronounced the Benediction and made my exit, I discovered
you-know-who right on my heels, spitting out her words
with a combination of shock and confusion, "Pastor, did you
see those people behind me?" (As if I could miss them, the
only African-Americans in the entire congregation.) "Well . . .
uh . . . You'll never believe this but . . . You know the telephone lists? . . . Well, *I* invited them!" Neither one of us
knew what to say and we stood there in stunned silence, but
I thought I heard in the distance a kind of low rumbling in
the heavens—the sound, maybe, of angels slapping their
thighs. Don't tell me God doesn't have a sense of humor.

I tell this story because it's one of the great ways the telephone has been used in my life, an example of how this technological marvel can be used to enhance human community.
At its best, the telephone does just that: spouses call from work
to apologize for being jerks at breakfast, parents listen to
homesick children, estranged friends decide to have lunch,
and brothers call sisters to say "I love you" and other things
that only took about forty years to get up the courage to say.
I'm not at all surprised the Almighty used the telephone to
help integrate my congregation; I'm quite sure the Almighty
has used it for many other good things as well.

But so has the Devil, I think. The telephone has had some unintended consequences, some pernicious, not the least of which was becoming a first-rate instrument of intrusion.

George Burns once explained the difference between irritation and aggravation: "The other day I was sitting by my pool getting a little sun when the phone rang. I ran into the house, picked up the phone and a voice on the other end said, 'Is Harry there?' So I said, 'You've got the wrong number,' and went back to the pool. Twenty minutes later the phone rang again. I ran in, grabbed the phone, again the same thing—'Is Harry there?' I said, 'Listen, you've got the wrong number!' A half hour later the same thing happened. 'Is Harry there?' That's irritation.

"Now the phone rings again. This time the voice on the other end says, 'This is Harry. Are there any messages for me?' That's aggravation."

Well, irritation or aggravation, the telephone can be mighty annoying. Consider an evening in a typical home. Mom drags her tired body through the front door, looking forward to hearing about Susie's tryout for cheerleader, but of course Susie is on the telephone talking with her best friend. After about a week, Susie hangs up and says, "Mom, I've got to run to Bill's house for study session . . . oh, and your sister called and wants you to call her back as soon as possible," which means Mom is on the telephone when Dad arrives home. When Mom and Dad finally sit down to dinner, the telephone rings, because salespeople, I'm convinced, have access to a satellite sensing device that reports the precise second every family in America sits down to eat. After saying four times he wasn't interested in pool cleaning service in January even if it did make him eligible for a

Caribbean cruise, Dad slams down the receiver in disgust. Ten minutes later, just as Mom starts sharing with Dad her frustrations with their relationship, feeling that they really could use a trip to the Caribbean, the telephone rings again. "Is Susie there?" the kid on the other end of the line asks. And so it goes through dinner, and into the evening when telephone activity really picks up. Both Dad and Mom need to make a few calls to follow up with some things from work, until they fall exhausted into bed. But Mom's comments about their relationship have been nagging at Dad, and so he decides it's time for some serious attention to at least one aspect of their relationship, and just as they've reached the point where pajamas have been shed and covers are being thrown back, the telephone rings yet again, and this time they have the good sense to let the answering machine deal with it, but the voice on the other end is Grandma, sounding agitated and so what could they do but answer it? When Grandma asks, "Are you busy?" Mom answers "No" because she could never — not in a thousand years, no matter how hot the passion — tell her mother she was just about to "do it." By the time she gets off the telephone, Dad has fallen asleep, dreaming of making love on the deck of a cruise ship.

Telephones not only intrude into home life, they now, thanks to advances in cellular technology, have the potential for intruding into *every single* aspect of the rest of our lives. Yes, you never have to worry about missing that important call, for you can now receive it on the freeway, in the restaurant, thirty thousand feet in the air, and even in the bathroom!

At this point in the chapter I must really work to control my emotions, because there are few things I find more annoying than watching someone drive by me, with one hand on the steering wheel and the other holding a telephone. This should be outlawed immediately, and I'm sure our legislators would have acted on this a long time ago if they hadn't been so busy fund-raising on their own telephones. Perhaps we should take matters into our own hands and organize vigilante groups to burn telephone-shaped patches in the lawns of offenders. But I don't really feel strongly about this, at least not compared with how I feel about having to listen to Mr. Big Shot call his people while seated next to me at a restaurant or in the airport. Am I the only one who finds it offensive to have to listen in on other people's private business? It's enough to make me want to step on his tasseled loafers and tell him the stock market is going to be just fine without him, so in the meantime, why doesn't he get a life.

Let me hasten to add, for the benefit of my dear friend who manufactures the finest cellular telephone in the world, this has been a wonderful technological advance. Parents thank God for it when children are driving alone at night, and if you happen to live in a remote village in India without the benefit of telephone wires, well, the advantages are obvious. So I'm in favor of cellular telephones. I'm even considering buying one. If I get one, though, I want to ask my friends and relatives to promise that if I ever begin to think I'm so important I need to conduct business in the middle of a fine meal, please have me committed immediately on the grounds of endangerment from the reckless use of an out-of-control ego.

I'm not, as I mentioned before, a Luddite (see chapter 17). I'm grateful for the good that has come from the telephone. I'm simply making a plea for awareness of its unintended consequences. It may be difficult to control the number of intrusions into our own lives, but we can do something about the intrusions we inflict on other people. The respect we owe one another requires us to think twice before picking up a telephone to place a call. Is it during the dinner hour? (If so, wait until later.) Is it possible the person you're calling may be in bed? (If so, drop the receiver immediately.) Is it really necessary to make a telephone call from the restaurant? (If so, go find a private corner to free others from minding your own business.) Courtesy calls us to be sensitive to the telephone's power for disruption.

And if you're selling something—anything whatsoever, but especially time-share condominiums—never at any time under any circumstances for any reason call my house during dinnertime.

———•◦•———

Twenty-three

Kneel Down to Speak with Children

Meeting Others at Their Own Level

ORIGINALLY, I TITLED THIS CHAPTER "BEND DOWN to Speak with Children," but when I visualize this I can see it's the wrong thing to do: if you bend down in the manner of keeping your legs straight and lowering your upper body, you will be bending *over* a child, which of course means staying above and in the dominant position. You may be thinking, So what? Isn't that exactly the position adults ought to assume when it comes to children? I would agree this is no doubt the best posture when speaking *at* children, the best form of communication for telling a child to quit hitting his sister, or to get off the pornographic web site, or to clean up her room before it's invaded by a squadron of cockroaches. But if you wish to speak *with* children, rising from the level of simple command to mutual communication, you need to kneel down.

If you ask, "How was your day at school?"—and you really want to know—get down low enough to look into her eyes.

Children, it seems to me, symbolically represent those who are in some way "weaker." A person in a wheelchair trying to get across the street is obviously weaker than those who have the full use of their legs; a person who sprints across the street because he's about to burst into tears, having just been fired from his job, is weaker in another sense; a pregnant woman who boards a crowded bus and appears ready to deliver yesterday is weaker in still another sense. Actually, when you think about it, everyone is weaker than others in one way or another.

But however weak you are, you will occasionally find yourself in circumstances in which your relative strength presents you an opportunity to help someone at his or her point of weakness. You're walking across the street and you notice a man in a wheelchair trying to get up a high curb, so you offer to help; or you're at a bar and you hear the guy next to you order his third drink and notice grief-laden eyes, so you say, "Tough day?" and you summon enough interest to listen as he spills his guts about losing his job; or you're sitting on a bus, grateful you found a seat two miles back when there were still some available, and a woman "great with child" boards, so you get up and insist she sit down. Doing these things won't get you on the cover of *Time,* but these little acts of kindness are footprints of courtesy in the sand of ordinary life.

Edna St. Vincent Millay, after receiving her degree from Vassar, headed for New York City, only to run into a cold wall of indifference. No one seemed aware of her existence; no one seemed to care. Her letters to her mother in Maine reflect great discouragement and loneliness. But one day she decided to go more than halfway to reach out to people. Things changed for her, as shown in this excerpt from a later letter: "It's such fun to treat people as if they were human beings just like yourself. They always like it and come right back at you with it. I picked up a spilled bundle for a woman the other day—her arms were so full she could hardly bend—and carried it for a couple of blocks. She blessed me as if I were an angel, kept saying how kind it was—and that it was things like this, happening once or twice in a lifetime, that made life worth living."[1]

Why would she have taken the time to help a stranger with a spilled bundle? My guess is this: she knelt down low enough to look into the woman's eyes. That is to say, she entered another world—even if only for a few seconds—by putting herself in the position of someone with too much to carry and needing help. And when she reached out to help, she lifted not only a bundle but a bit of the burden of living.

Joe Torre had been a catcher and announcer for the St. Louis Cardinals, and then was named manager of the Cardinals. Shortly after this, New York Yankees' announcer Phil Rizzuto suggested that managing could be done better from high above the baseball field—from the level of the broadcasting booth. Torre replied, "Upstairs, you can't look in their eyes."[2]

You've got to get downstairs, to eye level, to see another person's pain; you've got to enter that person's world to hear the often silent pleas for help. I once heard about a Young Life youth worker who was to lead a week-long high school camp. He knew one of his charges would be in a wheelchair and not wanting the boy to be alone, he got himself a wheelchair and spent the entire week in it, rolling right alongside the young man.

You can't always join another person at eye level in the literal sense, but you can enlist your imagination in the service of sensitivity. I don't know what it's like to be bound to a wheelchair, for example, and as long as I have the use of my legs, I will never know this in a complete sense. But once I happened to be on the same airplane as my friend Howard who despite confinement to a wheelchair because of multiple sclerosis manages an active speaking schedule, constantly flying by himself from one engagement to the next. I had no idea what a challenge this is for him until I watched flight attendants transfer him into a smaller wheelchair to get down the aisle of the plane and then lift him up and do their best to drop him into the seat. Unfortunately, they misjudged the angle, allowing his tailbone to crash down hard on the armrest. Howard, accustomed to these things, didn't even let out a mild whimper; he only thanked them for their help and settled in for the flight. Watching all this, I visualized myself in his condition: I imagined what it must be like to be so dependent on others, and I imagined the many, many flights he takes each year, and I imagined the countless trials he must have endured in the process—and imagining these things has made me a little more sensitive whenever I see a person in a wheelchair navigating through a busy airport.

Courteous people pause long enough to kneel down to eye level, using their imagination to enter another person's world, and then they extend a helping hand. Courteous people, in other words, assume the posture of sensitivity. It's usually not a big deal; most often, it takes only a few seconds of empathy. You kneel down, or maybe even sit on the floor, to listen to your child; you help the elderly woman upstairs get her laundry basket down to the washing room; you take some chicken soup next door when your neighbor has a cold; you offer to guide a person holding a white cane across the street.

And I think courteous people do something more: they're not only sensitive in the moment, they sometimes become active for the long run. Once in a while they assume the role of an advocate. After helping the guy in a wheelchair roll up the curb, they walk away from that moment of helping, but that moment of helping won't walk away from them. They keep thinking about it, wondering what might have happened had they not been crossing the street at the same time, wondering why the city hasn't put in wheelchair-accessible curbs, wondering why someone hasn't done something about it. They might try to put it all out of their minds, but it nags at them; every person in a wheelchair becomes a reminder. And so they write an editorial for the local paper, and before they know it, they're on a task force evaluating the accessibility of public places for persons in wheelchairs.

True, those who cope with some sort of weakness will most often need to raise their own voices to ask for help or demand the redress of injustices. But it shouldn't have to be so. Others of us ought to raise our voices on their behalf. Those who bear the burden of a personal battle with AIDS shouldn't have to be the ones who lobby for more federal funding for AIDS research; those who suffer racial discrimination shouldn't have to be the ones working for equal opportunities. Given human nature, though, and the gravitational pull of self-centered concerns, those who suffer will likely have to call our attention to their needs. But once we have heard their pleas for help, we ought to be willing to pick up our own sword and join the fight. No one can enter every fray; we must choose our battles carefully. If you're in the posture of sensitivity, though, you'll probably always be active with one cause or another.

One of my favorite moments in the 1992 Summer Olympics (Barcelona) took place in the 400 meter semi-final. Britain's Derek Redmond went down on the backstretch with a torn right hamstring. As medical attendants approached, Redmond fought to his feet. "It was animal instinct," he would later say. He set out hopping in a crazed attempt to finish the race.

A large man in a T-shirt came out of the stands, hurling aside security guards, and ran to Redmond. It was Jim Redmond, Derek's father. "You don't have to do this," he told his weeping son.

"Yes, I do," Derek said.

"Well, then," said Jim, "We're going to finish this together."

And so they did. With the son's head buried in the father's shoulder, they stayed in Derek's lane until the end, as the crowd rose and cheered and wept.

The race of life has its challenges, too. People fall for a lot of different reasons, whether a torn hamstring or a torn heartstring, and they're doing their best to hobble toward the finish line. Courteous people will occasionally get out of the stands to extend an arm and help make the run a little easier.

Unfortunately, the help we offer those in need can easily become patronizing. It's hard for the "strong" not to feel superior to the "weak." This is why we shouldn't *bend* down but *kneel* down; we shouldn't reach down from on high but enter into another's level of need. We do this most easily, I think, when we remember we're all strong in certain ways and we're all weak in other ways. No one is without need of help. If today I'm able to help my neighbor with a problem, tomorrow I'll need him to help me.

Outside my study window is a beautiful stand of redwood

trees. Raising my eyes from the computer, I'm overwhelmed by their majestic grandeur. Almost every day I thank God for them. It's not by chance that seven of them stand together; redwoods do not grow alone. They need each other. Most trees have roots roughly the same depth and width as their leaf pattern is high and broad, but redwoods have very shallow roots. So they grow together, intertwining and entangling their roots and thus supporting one another.

The only way for us to grow into majestic maturity is by entangling our lives, supporting one another. Otherwise, the first storm that blows our way will knock us flat. The roots of human community intertwine just one tendril at a time, very gradually, and almost always because someone has knelt down to look into the eyes of another; mutual support happens when someone willingly enters another person's world, accommodating himself or herself to that person's pressing need.

The Christian tradition tells of a God who, in love, has done precisely this. John Milton's *On the Morning of Christ's Nativity* describes well the divine humbling:

That glorious form, that light unsufferable,
And that far-beaming gaze of majesty . . .
Forsook the courts of everlasting day,
And chose with us a darksome house of mortal clay.

Which is why there is always a great paradox in kneeling down to another person's level: the act of lowering actually lifts us to God-like behavior. G. K. Chesterton tells us he learned about this strange reversal in his nursery: "My nurse once told me that if you start digging down toward the center of the earth and keep on going, after a certain point, you won't be digging downwards anymore but digging upwards."[3] Humility may at first seem like a movement downward but in reality it's a movement upward, a prelude to elevation.

In a book of luminous prose, Richard Selzer tells of his experience as a surgeon standing by the bed of a patient: "I stand by the bed where a young woman lies, her face postoperative, her mouth twisted in palsy, clownish. A tiny twig of the facial nerve, the one to the muscles of her mouth, has been severed. She will be thus from now on. The surgeon had followed with religious fervor the curve of her flesh; I promise you that. Nevertheless, to remove the tumor in her cheek, I had cut the little nerve.

"Her young husband is in the room. He stands on the opposite side of the bed, and together they seem to dwell in the evening lamplight, isolated from me, private. Who are they I ask myself, he and this wry-mouth I have made, who gaze at and touch each other so generously, greedily? The young woman speaks.

" 'Will my mouth always be like this?' she asks.

" 'Yes,' I say, 'it will. It is because the nerve was cut.'

"She nods and is silent. But the young man smiles.

" 'I like it,' he says. 'It is kind of cute.'

"All at once I *know* who he is. I understand, and I lower my gaze. One is not bold in an encounter with a god. Unmindful, he bends to kiss her crooked mouth, and I am so close I can see how he twists his own lips to accommodate to hers, to show her that their kiss still works."[4]

After a story like that, there's nothing much left to say. Get close enough to see the shape of the mouth and twist your own lips to accommodate it; the kiss will have its own rewards, I'm sure, and may even be the prelude to something else.

Twenty-four

———◆———

Respect Your Elders
Honoring Those Who Nurture and Lead

THE OTHER DAY I NOTICED A SOLITARY HAIR GROW-
ing out of my forehead. This was a mystifying development.
Can hairs just sprout up anywhere like this? Are there no biological rules against this sort of thing, no boundaries against
rogue hairs? Or could this possibly be a hair that somehow
got separated from the larger group on their way to my ears?
I imagined a lost, lonely follicle trying to find its way back to
the wagon train of homesteaders heading out for the new ter-
ritory that opens up as a body ages. I'm doing my best to push
back these trespassers, hacking away at them with the seriousness of Chief Sitting Bull going after General Custer. But
they're aggressive, and frankly, I'm losing the battle.

Anyway, after a few days I finally figured out what had happened. I didn't have a new hair growing in the wrong place.

I had a lone survivor! All the other hairs had retreated, leaving it the solitary outpost on a barren wasteland. And this had happened on *me*! On someone—if I may humbly say so—who has been known for great looking, though prematurely white, hair! So there it was, along with my reading glasses and "laugh lines," yet another proof that I'm getting older.

I'm a baby boomer, one of the group of post–World War II babies that has, by the force of its size, pretty much dragged American culture into its constantly changing orbit. When we were young, young was "in"; savvy media and business strategists targeted the youth culture. Now that we're into middle age, "easy fit" (baggy) jeans are in style and there are so many books on menopause that just trying to keep up with them can give a bookstore owner hot flashes. And I predict that, before long, we're going to redefine "beauty" to include a whole lot of wrinkles and "physically fit" to refer to any who can get to the end of the nursing home corridor without a walker.

I mention this to acknowledge that I'll no doubt be accused of looking out for my own best interests by writing a chapter on respect for elders. I can already hear baby busters sigh, "Yep, just like you boomers, who not that long ago tried to get the whole country to distrust anyone over thirty, now demanding respect of the aged." All right, *mea culpa*. But I can't help it that I had to get older to understand the virtues of advanced age! So, dude, get off your skateboard, turn your baseball cap around, and listen up. Someone on the front lines in the battle against ear hairs just may have learned something worth passing along.

What I've learned is this: elders ought to be respected. Now, by "elder" I'm thinking of more than those who are older. They're included, certainly, but I'm also referring to those who have nurtured us, who have in some way helped us stay on the road of life and have encouraged us to keep moving down it. I'm even referring to those in positions of authority over us and to whom we owe, by law or tradition, our submission. Parents and grandparents come to mind, and so do teachers and coaches and rabbis and pastors and bosses and policemen and elected officials and trustees—well, the list could probably extend from here to Pt. Barrow, and you can add the titles that come to your mind. Courteous people honor these elders; they extend to them the respect they deserve by virtue of their age, or their role in nurturing, or their position of responsibility.

Let's immediately acknowledge that not every elder, considered individually, deserves respect. Perhaps you have bitter memories of a father who abused you, or a policeman who beat you, or a teacher who belittled you; if so, I pray you've been able, by the grace of God and with the help of a good counselor, to find healing from the suffering you've endured. Some elders may well deserve to reap contempt for the pain they have sown. Even those who haven't been personally violated get weary from hearing about CEOs absconding with company money, priests molesting altar boys, government officials taking bribes, athletes throwing games. And we won't mention certain politicians, though I suppose they might be grateful for even this negative bit of publicity. In a world like this, is it any wonder we find it difficult to doff our hats in respect for those in positions of authority?

A friend of mine says we live in "perversely democratic times." He's not a closet totalitarian; when it comes to politics, he loves democracy. He simply means that today we turn

blind eyes to all distinctions of merit. We're radically egalitar-
ian, hesitant to recognize another person's superiority. No
one knows more, or is wiser, or has more skill, or works
harder, or bears more responsibility. We explain away any perceived distinctions by pointing to social convention or assert-
ing that someone was in the right place at the right time. A
Nobel Prize winner? Well, with the benefits of the same education and the time to sit around all day in a laboratory we
could probably do the same thing. A Wall Street billionaire?
Everyone knows the stock market is a crap shoot. A president
of the United States? Who among us hasn't thought we could
do that job better than any incumbent since Franklin
Roosevelt, if not Abraham Lincoln? We're all equal here in
America, so let's make sure no one gets too uppity!

And we're still living with the legacy of Vietnam. It's often
been pointed out that hearing leaders lie to us night after night
on the evening news, promising victory and peace while body
bags kept coming home and bombs kept falling, has made it
difficult for us to trust anyone in authority. We do seem to have
a terribly ambivalent attitude: we long for leadership but do
our best to shoot down actual leaders. We want people to
emerge to help us renew our country and its institutions, and
yet when we elect or appoint actual human beings we begin
almost immediately to search for flaws and chip away at
pedestals until they fall in humiliation. Soon after electing a
president, for example, we start talking about potential candidates for the next election, eventually investing huge hopes
in a person, telling ourselves we've finally found someone
worthy of the greatness of the American people. But almost
immediately after the inauguration, before street sweepers
have cleaned up Pennsylvania Avenue, we pull out chisel and

hammer and set to work with such efficiency that soon we wonder how in the world we could have elected such a person. Much of this is serious political debate, granted; much of it, though, is as uplifting as David Letterman mocking Bill Clinton night after night as "Tubby," not to mention having more fun with Clinton's sex life than Clinton had with it originally.

Of course pompous coconuts need to be knocked out of tall trees! By all means, bring on the court jesters to skewer all who have actually started believing their own sound bites! But let's be careful: in our eagerness to keep anyone from getting too uppity, we've flattened out all relationships until it's rare to find *appropriate* respect for our elders, *appropriate* deference for those in authority, *appropriate* honoring of those who deserve it.

My doctor recently asked me what I was writing, and I told him about this book on courtesy. He said, "Good! That's sure needed. Take my own kids—I can't seem to get them to call the neighbors 'Mr. and Mrs. Jones.' It's just 'John and Mary.' " Yes, it's now first names for everyone: pastors, doctors, professors, even the mayor we just met yesterday. Nowadays, about the only title we freely offer is "Your Honor," because it suddenly seems appropriate to show respect when the judge is about to throw the book at you. But all this earnest familiarity only creates a smog of phony affection that chokes the breath out of the genuine thing; promiscuous friendliness leaves no room for the gift of authentic friendship.

We need to recover the fine art of making appropriate distinctions. Some people are strangers, and there are rightful boundaries between strangers. Some people are acquaintances, and there are rightful forms of behavior between acquaintances. Some people are friends, and there are rightful liberties enjoyed between friends. And some people deserve special respect because of what they've invested in us or because of a position they hold. Courtesy notices these differences. It doesn't begrudge deference when it's due; it's not stingy in bestowing honor.

One of the Ten Commandments tells us, "Honor your father and mother," and considering what parents do for us, I believe we can remain faithful to the spirit of this commandment by broadening it to, "Honor those who nurture and lead."

There are good reasons for doing this. First, it's not easy being an elder, and anyone who survives it deserves respect. Those who are elders, in the literal sense of the word, generally have a good deal to cope with. Golda Meir wrote in her autobiography, "It is not a sin to be seventy but it is also no joke." Some of you could say a hearty "Amen!" to that, as you fight battles against osteoporosis or prostatitis or any of the other ailments that afflict us as our bodies begin to wear out. We're living longer now, thank God, and many of advanced age have decided they don't need to call the undertaker prematurely but instead can travel around the world or start writing the Great American Novel or even enter marathons. I know a man who recently turned eighty and started studying three things he had always wanted to learn—Spanish, swimming, and the piano. And he just published a book last year! Life can continue with great joy and productivity even in advanced age. Still, for most people, there are physical challenges to face. I saw a friend recently and asked how he was doing. "Great!" he replied, "except for my prostate gland and high blood pressure and some kidney problems. At this age it's just one damn thing after another!"

So I say, anyone who has struggled with the problems of declining health, and who has lived through the agonies of adolescence and the boredom of middle age and somehow survived sicknesses and betrayals and heartaches and family tensions and personal failures and the various trials that afflict most of us in one form or another—anyone still upright after all this, even with the aid of a walker or a wheelchair, deserves our respect.

There is another important reason for honoring those who have nurtured and led you—gratitude. Where would you be without those who have helped you scale some of the tough mountains you've had to climb? In the summer of 1989, a paraplegic named Mark Wellman gained national recognition by climbing the vertical granite face of El Capitan in Yosemite National Park. On the seventh and final day of his climb, the headlines of the *Fresno Bee* read "Showing a Will of Granite," and next to the headline was a photo of Wellman being carried on the shoulders of his climbing companion, Mike Corbett. Wellman's achievement was remarkable, but what most people didn't know was that Mike Corbett scaled the face of El Capitan three times in order to help Mark Wellman pull himself up once.[1] You have likely been helped up mountains of endurance and achievement by others who have carried you on their shoulders, perhaps scaling peaks two or three times to get you up once. Parents and teachers and others have invested a great deal in you, assisting you to become the person you are today.

Heading the list of influential elders in most of our lives are our parents. We know we should honor them, but truthfully, many of us have ambivalent feelings about them. For some, love has been commingled with other emotions: disappointment in not receiving enough affirmation or anger at being abandoned or deep sadness over still unresolved conflicts. What does it mean to honor parents—and yet own the various sentiments we have toward them? Years ago I came across an article by J. Wesley Brown that spoke honestly about our parents: "That they did not have total wisdom when they raised us, that they did not always know exactly what to tell us, what to let us do and what to prevent us from doing, does not mean they did not love us and intend to do well by us. Perhaps the greatest honor we can do our parents is to let them down off the pedestal of our imaginations, where we are inclined either to idolize them or to flog them as gods who failed (as indeed they must fail), and to accept them as people—people who need forgiveness as well as respect, who need honest relationships with their children perhaps more than anyone else."[2]

So yes, courtesy calls us to honor those who have nurtured us and to honor those who have authority over us. We won't be blind to their failings, but we can gratefully acknowledge their importance in our lives. And besides, before long we'll all be elders, literally if not metaphorically, and it might be nice to have set a good example of the way we'd like to be treated. Those pesky ear hairs won't let me forget what's just around the corner. Have you checked your ears lately?

Twenty-five

———•◦•———

Watch What You Say

Understanding the Power of Words

HUCK FINN COMMENTED THAT THE FARMER-preacher Mr. Phelps "never charged nothing for his preaching. And it was worth it, too." Most of us have probably heard sermons like that, as well as lectures, news commentaries, talk-radio banter, and of course free advice wafting over the back fence from a nosy neighbor.

Words, words, words. They come at us from all directions these days. It's as though we've been sitting on a curb in precisely the wrong place as a truck dumps a ton of them on top of us. There's no way, it seems, to dig out from under the load. A country-western song calls for "a little less talk and a lot more action," and though the singer has something else in mind his plea might well represent the cry of a culture going down for the third time in an ocean of words pouring forth from newspapers, magazines, telephones, televisions, radios, faxes, and computers. And yes, books.

We're suffering from verbal bloatedness (see chapter 17), but even in an inflationary economy the currency stays in use. Words still matter. If you doubt this, weigh the difference between hearing someone you care about say, "I love you" versus "I hate you." Imagine the difference between a judge saying, "Guilty!" or "Not guilty!" Words continue to have power.

The ancient Hebrews would never have said "a little less talk and a lot more action." They understood the power of words, especially God's. Genesis tells us that God *spoke* the universe into being. God said, "Let there be light," and nothing sat up and became something; darkness blazed into luminescent brilliance. "God said . . . God said . . . God said . . ."— the phrase is repeated again and again in the creation story, as if to leave no doubt that God's speaking brought all things into existence.

That account of creation reaches its climax with human beings, who, we are told, were made in the image of God. As a consequence, we have the God-like power of speech—a power with potential both to destroy and to create.

Mention the name Adolf Hitler and many will picture a man with a little mustache speaking to vast crowds of Germans, swaying them with demonic rhetoric. He was one of the greatest orators of this century, effectively using words to accumulate power, mobilize a nation for war, and lead the world into the darkest evil it has known. He used words to destroy.

Winston Churchill took up the weapon of his adversary and did battle. As Bill Hull described it, "From a concrete bomb shelter deep underground, he spoke to the people of Britain not of superiority but of sacrifice, not of conquest but of courage, not of revenge but of renewal. Slowly but surely, Winston Churchill talked England back to life. To beleaguered old men waiting on the rooftops with the buckets of water for the fire bombs to land, to frightened women and children huddled behind sand bags with sirens screaming overhead, to exhausted pilots dodging tracer bullets in the midnight sky, his words not only announced the new dawn but also conveyed the strength to bring it to pass." He used words to create.

Hitler and Churchill are dramatic examples, certainly. But we all make constant choices in our use of words. Do we use them destructively or creatively?

Those who understand the power of words watch what they say. They try to use words carefully. In the land of Babel they may sound like foreigners, talking and writing as though words still matter, guarding the sanctity of language and trying to be good stewards of its power.

One day John Henry Jowett, a famous British preacher of another era, was walking with a friend in a Birmingham park. His friend wanted to show him how the Holly Blue butterfly differed from the Common Blue. With the utmost caution he approached the resting insect so he could lift it off the leaf without injury to show the markings on the underside of the wings. Jowett watched in silence and then said, "That is just how I pick a word."

Do we need to be this cautious about *every* word? No, I don't think so. Let's be realistic: when arguing passionately or barking orders to save someone from a burning house, we won't worry much about linguistic style. Most of us just don't have the wits for it. I know I usually think of my best lines long after they're needed; after an intense dinner discussion, say, I spend the night tossing around and coming up with great zingers that could have zapped my opponents into silent awe before the logic and beauty of my ideas. But if we *could* think of just the right words and sentences, it would help. After all, as Mark Twain aptly put it, "The difference between the right word and the almost right word is the difference between lightning and the lightning bug." And lightning can dispel the darkness mighty effectively.

Often we'll have to settle for lightning bugs, I suppose. But that doesn't mean we shouldn't do our best to guard the gift of language. We ought at least to say what we mean and mean what we say. If we constantly obfuscate or hedge or exaggerate or minimize, we reveal our lack of confidence in another person; we show we don't think she can understand, or that he can't handle the implications of the truth. On the other hand, to speak candidly and clearly shows respect for others.

For this reason, not incidentally, we ought to enlist in the honorable and highly justified war against "doublespeak," a type of communication especially favored by the government. William Lutz has collected examples from the departments of Defense, State, and Agriculture. Military officers have referred to a pencil as a "portable handheld communications inscriber." A bullet hole has been defined as a "ballistically induced aperture in the subcutaneous environment." A tent is a "frame-supported tension structure." To kill is to "terminate with extreme prejudice." A parachute is an "aerodynamic personnel decelerator," and a toothpick is a "wood interdental stimulator."[1] Let's terminate with extreme prejudice this sort of foolishness!

We should choose words carefully, and we should use them to create, not destroy. Remember the playground rejoinder, "Sticks and stones can break my bones, but words can never hurt me"? Total nonsense. Whoever came up with this deserves to have a few sticks and stones tossed his way. Words can do far *more* than simply break bones; words can break hearts. I've had a broken finger, rib, and arm, and trust me, none of those hurt as badly as a broken heart, a crushed spirit, or a wounded soul. The words we use have the power either to build up or to tear down.

Some words are simply descriptive ("The red house is on the left"). Others are performative, causing something to happen by virtue of their utterance ("I declare you husband and wife"). Whether we're conscious of it or not, we use the latter all the time, or at least words that are close to it, words that do something to other people. Imagine a little girl hearing, "You have the most beautiful red hair!" Or that same girl hearing, "You have so many freckles, and I'll bet you can't wait to start wearing makeup to hide them." Both statements are descriptive, but they are also performative. The first will build confidence and self-esteem; the latter will drive a nail of self-doubt into her heart. "Words call forth emotions," Sigmund Freud wrote, "and are universally the means by which we influence our fellow creatures. By words one of us can give another the greatest happiness or bring about utter despair."

One Sunday near the beginning of the twentieth century, in a country church in a small village in Croatia, an altar boy named Josip Broz helped the priest at Mass. The boy accidentally dropped a glass cruet of wine, and it smashed to pieces. The village priest gruffly shouted, "Leave the altar and don't come back!" The boy never returned to the Church. He grew up to become Tito, the Communist leader of Yugoslavia after World War II.

About the same time, in St. Mary's Cathedral in Peoria, Illinois, an altar boy named Peter John helped the priest at Mass. He, too, dropped the wine cruet, and later in life he would write, "There is no atomic explosion that can equal in intensity of decibels the noise and explosive force of a wine cruet falling on the marble floor of a cathedral in the presence of the bishop. I was frightened to death." The celebrant at Mass that morning was Bishop John Spalding. With a warm twinkle in his eye, the bishop whispered, "Someday you will be just what I am." That altar boy grew up to be Archbishop Fulton J. Sheen, one of the most beloved and well-known pastors of the Roman Catholic Church.[2]

Most often, words that build up are expressions of encouragement. Look back at the turning points in your life: didn't someone say words that embraced you with affirmation, enabling you to think differently about yourself and empowering you with self-confidence?

I remember a dark season in my first church when I was feeling very discouraged. I was beginning to think being a pastor was about as much fun as a jab in the eye with a sharp stick. Then one day I saw on my desk a carved figure, a Moses with outstretched arm and pointing finger. Underneath it was a little note from Ash, a dear elder who was old enough to know his young pastor sorely needed some inspiration: "He is saying 'Let my people go.' You should be such a troublemaker. Go man go!" After reading this, my backbone straightened and I was ready to take on Pharaoh and his whole army for the sake of my people!

Never underestimate the power of encouragement. Joseph Priestly failed as a preacher, but Benjamin Franklin saw possibilities in him. "You have just the abilities to write a history of electricity," Franklin said, "and I will help you start by lending you my books and notes." Priestly went on to write the first history of electricity and to become a man of science, discovering oxygen and inventing the first fire extinguisher.

We've all heard of Isaac Newton. He discovered the laws of gravity in the 1600s, which revolutionized astronomical studies. But we might never have learned from Newton if it hadn't been for Edmund Halley. He challenged Newton to think through his original notions, quietly corrected his mathematical errors, and coaxed him to write his great work, *Mathematical Principles of Natural Philosophy*. His words of encouragement unleashed great potential.

And words can do something else: they can bless or profane; they can enhance faith, or mock it. Have you ever been so sick you thought you might die and were afraid you wouldn't? Were you blessed by hearing someone say, "I'm not sure what I can do to help, but I promise I will pray for you"? Maybe you didn't have much faith yourself and maybe you weren't so sure about the effectiveness of prayer, but those words did something to you, didn't they? They fanned smoldering coals of belief into a little flame of hope; they lifted your spirits.

On the other hand, I don't have to ask if you've heard profanity. These days you can't get through an hour without hearing it. At the risk of sounding like a cranky preacher, let me express my dismay at the constant stream of profanity coming from radio, television, and movies. The name of Jesus Christ, for example. For some of us, to hear this name used lightly, as an exclamation of anger or disgust or even as punctuation, grates against our sensibilities; it's like hearing fingernails scraping down a blackboard.

The writer Anne Lamott recently spoke at the commencement exercises of the seminary I serve. Near the end of her address, she told of being on vacation with Sam, her young son. They were on a beach and overheard a man who yelled, "Jesus Christ!" He was obviously swearing, not praying. So Sam said to him, "Please don't say that. It hurts us, because we love him."

Those who show respect for others are sensitive about these things. They don't take things that are deeply meaningful for others and stomp on them with the big, ugly boot of careless language. They watch what they say. They remember words have power; words do things. They employ words for blessing not cursing, for encouragement not discouragement, for creation not destruction.

———◆———

Twenty-six

Don't Leave a Messy Campsite
Cleaning Up After Yourself

WHEN YOU'RE A BABY, YOUR MAJOR RESPONSI-bilities are to eat and then throw up and poop. And you never have to worry about cleaning up after yourself. Someone will be there to wash your chin and wipe your bottom.

One of my memorable moments as a father came with my first experience in changing a diaper. My new daughter was such a *cute* little thing, so pretty and precious and precocious. Of course I would eagerly change her diaper! I was a modern father, after all, having been a star graduate (well, at least a passing graduate) of the Lamaze class, and I had stood by my wife's bedside counting minutes between contractions and coaching her breathing (well, all right, I took one break to go across the street for a steak, but she was taking *so* long and I was hungry, and I did hurry), and so I was eager to do my part in the raising of this child. As I laid Jennifer on the changing table I hummed and told her how beautiful she was, and I even took the opportunity to tell her, in a straightforward, unembarrassed way, all the "facts of life," adding that if she had any further questions she could ask her mother later, and with this sort of banter going on, feeling like the perfect father with the perfect child, I opened her diaper and said something very similar to "Oh shoot."

I had been an innocent, completely unprepared for this assault on my senses. Cute babies, I discovered, do not excrete cute fecal matter. There were days when her diapers should have been declared a disaster area so we could have applied for federal funding to help with the clean up. But I joined her mother in cleaning up after her, changing diapers and washing vomit out of her sleeper and wiping her runny nose. We did all this for one reason: we loved her.

It's no negative reflection on our love, however, to point out that we did not want this program of waste management to continue indefinitely. There came a time when our love eventually showed itself in teaching her how to use such things as toilets and wash cloths and handkerchiefs, for as she got older, she had to learn how to clean up after herself.

Any parent knows that's one of the challenges of rearing children. If they're to grow into mature adults, they have to accept responsibility for the mess their presence makes in this world. Unfortunately, it's not easy to get kids to cooperate with this plan of development. They generally prefer to head in another direction, one that leads to their room looking like a cross between a fraternity house after an all-night kegger and a dog run that hasn't been tended since the domestication of animals in 8000 B.C. Keeping a room in this condition becomes a matter of pride, an expression of adolescent assertiveness that psychologists might describe as "healthy individuation" but parents would describe as "disgusting disobedience." More pitched battles are fought over this, I would guess, than anything else, except the time to be home at night.

I have no helpful hints to offer parents who are currently on the battlefield. If I did, do you think I would be writing a book about courtesy? I would write one titled *How to Get Your Children to Clean Their Rooms Before the Environmental Protection Agency Files a Lawsuit Against You,* and it would be an immediate best-seller, being the only book in history promoted by both Dr. James Dobson and Oprah Winfrey. Solving this problem would be right up there with finding the formula for cold fusion or getting politicians to care more about the country than their own reelection. My only advice is to hang in there and remember that your child may be doing his or her best; it's just difficult to learn how to pick up after oneself.

This is one of the reasons for giving in to the 6,738th request for a pet. As your daughter learns to accept responsibility for a rat, so the theory goes, she will perhaps transfer that care over to herself and maybe even her room. She has to clean the cage, you tell her, or you'll get rid of Mickey. In her subconscious, Mickey's cage is associated with her own room, and if Mickey could get kicked out of the family . . . No, I'm making this part up. I long ago gave up trying to figure out what goes on inside the subconscious of children, or anyone else for that matter. But psychologists *do* say caring for pets teaches responsibility, and there is a *slight* possibility the experience might encourage your children to deal with their own cage, the one that has clothes strewn everywhere except the closet and posters of rock stars all over the walls.

Who knows what could happen if Johnny doesn't clean his room? It could become a breeding ground for bacteria, causing a rare disease, and the World Health Organization would quarantine your house in order to protect Africa and other underdeveloped countries from the contamination, and you would become front page fodder on supermarket tabloids and make embarrassing appearances on *Larry King Live.* "We tried our best with him, begging him to clean up his room, threatening him with grounding. We assume he's in his room somewhere, but we can't push open the door. The last we saw him was at Christmas. Where did we go wrong? We let him have a pet when he was little . . ."

So to stop the downward spiral into filth and humiliation, you reason and beg and threaten and punish and seek advice from your therapist, because you know it's important to get kids to learn how to clean up after themselves if they're to become reasonably mature human beings.

But what happens if they never learn this? Well, they become "adult" in many ways, most likely even parents who yell at their kids about messy bedrooms. Not far below the surface, though, remains that little brat who still expects someone to follow behind with a wash rag or vacuum or shovel, and who needs to learn to pull up his or her socks and accept the responsibility of being an *authentic* adult.

A mother, for example, has yet another quarrel with her daughter, telling her that if she can't find time to clean her room she will not be allowed time to visit her boyfriend. And as mother leaves the house, she's mad and more than a little worried about her daughter's obvious lack of maturity. When she gets to the supermarket, she buys enough groceries, she thinks, to feed the Chicago Bulls for at least a month. Then she loads them into a shopping cart, which she wheels out to her car. After getting all the bags in the trunk, she leaves the cart in the middle of the parking lot.

Let me put a question to all reasonable, rational readers: How is she any different, in principle, from the baby who's waiting for someone to change her diaper or the teenager who takes no responsibility for the mess in his room? (I may be a little touchy on this matter of shopping carts, because a few weeks ago I drove into the parking lot of a supermarket and watched a stray cart rolling directly toward me. I could neither back up nor turn, and had to sit there helplessly until it smashed into my car.)

The real problem, it seems to me, is not with babies or adolescents, but with "adults" who haven't yet grown up, who expect someone else to pick up the mess their presence makes in this world, who leave campsites unfit for even self-respecting bears, who leave roadsides strewn with litter, who—as long as I'm on a roll I might as well keep going to the big stuff—leave rivers polluted and oceans fouled and forests depleted and the atmosphere contaminated, and who—to mention a *really* big problem—leave their dog's poop sitting in a steaming pile on my front lawn.

When I was about four years old I had my first experience with someone else's litter. It was a Sunday morning, and so of course we were in church. After the last hymn I raced outside to get back to some serious playing. My eye caught sight of something bright in the gutter, and upon inspection, I saw a brown bottle that still had something in it. I did what seemed to me the perfectly reasonable thing to do, with the result that the congregation, emerging from the sanctuary, saw the pastor's kid standing in the gutter drinking beer!

This misadventure took place in 1953 in Kittitas, Washington. I mention this, in case some reader remembers tossing a beer bottle in front of a little church about that time. I hope your conscience is still troubling you, for your littering caused several things to happen: I received a major spanking in front of the congregation, which no doubt caused psychological damage, contributing to the formation of my basically shy personality, burdening me with a sense of guilt, making it a wonder I didn't turn my back on the church long ago, and giving me a permanently underdeveloped appreciation for beer.

If all these things happened with one beer bottle, imagine what could happen with a whole six pack lying around! So the next time you're tempted to toss something out your car window, remember my story, and think of a little kid who will reap the consequences of your careless behavior. Actually, think of all the little kids who will have to inherit the mess you leave behind. They will suffer much more than a spanking, if you—and all of us—don't learn how to get a grip on a consumerism that pours waste into an environment that is being rapidly depleted of its nonrenewable energy resources.

For fourteen years I had the pleasure of running along the beach in north San Diego County. For a couple of miles of my workout, I ran along a cliff that rose above the beach and offered a spectacular panorama of the Pacific Ocean. One day I noticed a man raking the trail along the cliff. It looked odd, his doing this on public property. So I stopped and asked, "What are you doing?"

"I'm raking the trail."

"I can see that, but *why* are you raking the trail?"

"Well," he said, "it's just so beautiful up here, and I thought somebody ought to take care of it."

I thanked him, on behalf of all who use the trail, and as I ran away I thanked God there was at least one person willing to accept responsibility for that little piece of God's creation.

Courteous people show respect not simply to those they encounter in the present but also to those who will come after them in the future. This is why they take empty popcorn tubs out of the theater and use holding tanks in boats and never throw junk out the car window and leave picnic sites cleaner than when they arrived and pause to pick up soda cans on the sidewalk. And this is why they do what they can in their little corner of the earth to be responsible stewards of the environment.

If we don't practice courtesy this way, the ones who will have to pick up the debris of our self-indulgent habits will be the next generation, our kids. And judging from the way they clean their rooms, the fate of this planet could be in serious jeopardy.

———

Twenty-seven

Keep a Secret

Earning the Trust of Others

AT FIRST YOU COULD SEE ONLY A LITTLE SPOT ON THE ceiling of my dining room. I thought nothing about it. But then, very slowly, it grew into a larger patch of ugly brown that seemed to announce itself whenever anyone entered the room. So I decided to look into this matter, following my usual method of handling household problems: I called someone to help me. (You could fit *all* my mechanical knowledge on the head of a nail, if not the point.) I was told that the discoloration was most likely the result of a leaky toilet in the bathroom upstairs.

Whereupon my imagination, with its usual unruliness, immediately began picturing different possible scenarios, among which was the one where I'm hosting a faculty dinner and sneak upstairs for a quick "bio-break," and just as I get myself comfortably situated on the relevant appliance, the rotted wood finally gives way, causing the president of the seminary, seated on his throne, to crash down upon the dining room table. Some faculty members would pretend not to be surprised, maintaining a steadfast liberalism, trying their best to affirm my particular form of self-expression; others, on the other hand, would see it as an example of presidential cheekiness, another case of the administration butting into their affairs. A debate would ensue, of course, for whenever two or more faculty get together a debate always breaks out, followed by ten-page memos proving their respective points. Students would inevitably get hold of one of the memos, and before long stories would be told about a wild faculty party where the president exposed himself. The gossip would spread, and I would lose my job and have to support myself by writing books about the dangers of leaky toilets.

Don't worry: I had the leak fixed before any of this happened. I only wish other kinds of leaks could be fixed as easily. I'm not referring to leaky plumbing but leaky people. Share a secret with some people, and you might as well put a full-page ad in the *New York Times*; give them confidential information, and they a become a human sieve. The urge to pass on "knowledge" (it matters not a whit whether it's factual) about others is so overpowering that any attempt to resist carries as much hope as a fruit fly's vow of chastity.

And that's bad news for all of us. Profane the sanctity of secrets, and gossip gets started; set gossip free, and all hell breaks loose.

There is something almost sacred about secrets. I began to see their importance after reading a book on this subject by Paul Tournier, the well-known Swiss physician. He maintains that secrecy is vital to our lives, enabling the maturation process. A small child, totally dependent on parents, must free himself little by little, and secrets can be instruments of that emancipation. A child says, with a mischievous grin, "I know something you don't know," and in a certain sense he is really saying, "I have my own identity; I exist apart from you."

Remember your child's messy room that we talked about in a previous chapter? You probably have been completely forbidden to look in certain drawers and closets, and you hyperventilate with agitation wondering what's in them. Pornography? Drug paraphernalia? Condoms? The urge to do a reconnaissance raid can be overpowering, and the arguments for it persuasive. But I believe an invasion like this can be justified only in the rarest of circumstances, if at all. If you suspect your son is doing drugs, for example, it would perhaps be better to take him to a clinic for a blood test rather than search his room. To invade his space by crossing the boundary of his privacy risks damage to his psychological health. To quote Dr. Tournier, "Every human being needs secrecy in order to become himself and no longer only a member of the tribe. . . . What grants secrecy its capital value is that individuality is at stake and every violation of secrecy is a violation of that individuality. . . . Respect for the individual is an absolute requirement. Either we have the sense of it and keep it scrupulously, or else we have started down the dangerous road of tyranny."[1]

It's not easy allowing our children to have secrets. I remember feeling hurt when my daughters kept something from me. Didn't they trust me? Didn't they know I could be their best friend? I felt threatened. And actually, my feelings were perfectly accurate. I *was* threatened; at least, my relationship as it had been was threatened. I was losing control of them, which had to happen if they were to mature into independent persons. Rationally I knew all this, but emotionally I fought it. My temptation was to seduce them into telling me their secrets by badgering them with questions or shaming them into a confession. Most of the time I resisted this, but not without a conscious effort.

This is why I refer to the sanctity of secrets. We need to allow our children and others to have them: it's part of their rights as human beings. Courteous people will honor the secrets of others.

What a wonderful thing it is to be told a secret. First, it's wonderful for the person who shares it. As Tournier points out, "If keeping a secret was the first step in the formation of the individual, telling it to a freely chosen confidant is going to constitute then the second step in this formation of the individual. Freedom is what makes the individual. Keeping a secret is an early assertion of freedom; telling it to someone that one chooses is going to be a later assertion of freedom, of even greater value."[2] When I know a secret and choose to share it with you, I exercise an act of personal freedom and power and generosity. That not only affirms my individuality, it feels good!

It feels even better, perhaps, to receive the gift. When you whisper a secret in my ear, you are saying, "I trust you. I want to share this part of me with you. You have worth." And this act of generosity forges a bond between us: I respond with a wink that says, "We know something the rest of the world doesn't know; we're in this together, you and I." A secret becomes a blessed icon pointing to the mystery of human fellowship.

But what an outrageous sacrilege to take an ax to this icon! To pass on a secret that is not yours to tell violates another person's trust, splintering his or her gift with a blow of contempt. This can happen accidentally, certainly, and most of us have probably inadvertently spilled the beans at one time or another. I never pass through a Christmas season without remembering a dinner conversation many, many years ago. My sister and I were old enough to be deemed trustworthy with the knowledge of what the other was getting from our parents, but young enough to be filled with restless anticipation, sure the Big Day would *never, never* arrive. Imagining the surprise my sister would enjoy, I got caught up in the excitement and forgot myself: I beamed a big smile over my meat loaf and potatoes as I blurted out, "Patti, you're sure going to love your new doll house!" She let out a cackle, and then, sensible of the severe transgression that had just occurred, looked up at our parents, who sat staring at me in shocked bewilderment. I felt like gutter slime, the worst son who had ever lived. I made the Prodigal Son look saintly.

It wasn't really that serious; my young conscience was too tender. Accidents happen. What's worse, what's way up the scale of despicable behavior, is to violate someone's trust willfully. To repeat a secret you have no right to tell takes another person's gift and throws it in the mud, trampling it under the heavy boot of callous disregard. It's an egregious betrayal, no matter how you justify it. And yes, you will probably try to cover it with the cloak of some justification, though it takes some creativity to drape treachery with fancy excuses and elegant rationalizations. But it can be done. "I wouldn't be telling you this, but I knew you would be concerned." "This is confidential, but I know you will not pass it on." "I'm telling you so you can join me in prayer." No matter how you dress it up, though, underneath it's still ugly.

One evening many years ago, when my daughter crawled up to the dinner table, I asked her, "Joy, did you wash your hands?" And she replied, "No, but I put some sweet smelly stuff on them." A good many people, I'm afraid, smear sweet "concern" and smelly pieties over very deadly germs. These germs, to name them, are *genus gossipus,* and they are passed from one person to the next by open mouth. As Morris Mandel wrote, "Gossip is the most deadly microbe. It has neither legs nor wings. It is composed entirely of tales, and most of them have stings."[3]

In one ear and out the other doesn't cause near the problems as in one ear and out the mouth, the preferred route information takes in too many people. Especially secondhand information. When we can tell ourselves we're not directly violating another person's confidence because we're simply repeating what we've heard that someone else heard, our tongues can really get loosened up for a nice piece of work. We might mention, as we pass on the news, that we're not really sure whether it's true, and even raise our eyebrows in judgment saying, "You know how people are with this sort of thing, so quick to gossip." This approach works really well, enabling us to rise above the cheap and tawdry behavior of others while self-righteously enjoying the cheap and tawdry behavior of our own.

A chaplain told the story of "an elderly, bedridden woman who was dying. Her overly anxious sister attended to her every physical need and persisted to ask the patient if she wanted anything—orange juice, tea, sherbet, ice? Finally, the dying patient took her sister's arm and brought her near so she could hear her speak, 'What I really need,' the patient told her, 'is a tender morsel of juicy gossip.' "[4] That would be a piece of nourishment, no doubt, to keep her going for days.

Gossip, frankly, is a great deal of fun. The brain's pleasure center gets a real jolt when we receive or pass on a tidbit about another person, especially if it's bad news, and *most* especially if it's about sex. I'm not sure why gossip is so much fun, but I suspect it has to do with several things: our anxieties may find momentary relief when focused on the misfortune of others; our guilt may ease slightly when we can rise in judgment over another person's failure; our loneliness may diminish briefly when, empowered with interesting news, we assume the center stage of someone's attention. Whatever the reason for its popularity, tattling is a universal sport.

Some time ago a professor at Princeton University conducted an experiment to demonstrate how quickly rumors spread. He invited six students to his office and in strict confidence informed them that the Duke and Duchess of Windsor were planning to attend a certain university dance. Within a week this completely fictitious story had reached nearly every student on campus. Town officials phoned the university, demanding to know why they had not been informed, and press agencies were frantically telephoning for details. The professor observed, "That was a *pleasant* rumor— a slanderous one travels even faster." Imagine the speed a rumor would travel if it was about the president of the university falling on the table at a faculty dinner.

Indeed, the more slanderous or salacious or scandalous, the

better. John Dryden, the seventeenth century British poet, commented on gossip: "There is a lust in man no charm can tame, / Of loudly publishing his neighbor's shame. / Hence, on eagles' wings immortal scandals fly, / While virtuous actions are but born to die."

The eagerness to publish a neighbor's shame would be bad enough, but what makes it worse is that it's rarely true. Given our natural limitations in knowledge (none of us is omniscient regarding all the facts and motivations surrounding an event), not to mention our propensity to edit stories, deleting and emphasizing for dramatic effect, the first casualty in gossip is truth. And this is why I said earlier that when gossip gets free all hell breaks loose. I was speaking theologically, at least from the standpoint of my Christian faith. The Bible calls the devil the "father of lies," meaning that evil breeds falsehood, and falsehood, in turn, demeans and isolates humans one from another, tearing apart human community. Nothing works better at destroying relationships than lies, and thus gossip is a handy ally in the battle for hell on earth.

So respectful people bite their tongue, resisting the urge to gossip. And they are especially careful to keep secrets, knowing there are few things worse than violating someone's trust. They do this because they know, with James Baldwin, "the moment we break faith with one another, the sea engulfs us and the light goes out."

Twenty-eight

Don't Let Your Dog Romance My Leg

Remembering Not Everyone Shares Your Interests

WHILE PLANS WERE BEING MADE FOR MY INAUGU-
ration as president of San Francisco Theological Seminary, the
chairwoman of the Board of Trustees confided in me that
students, to commemorate the occasion, were planning to
present me with a gift—a dog. My predecessor had had two
dogs, one of which was a yapping nuisance and the other an
affable golden retriever who became a kind of honorary student, sitting in classes soaking up the theology of John Calvin.
The students wanted to continue the tradition, and hearing
that I was dogless, came up with this way of expressing their
support. Any president of an educational institution knows
that all gestures of kindness, especially from students, should
be received gratefully and treated with as much conservatory
concern as the spotted owl or snail darter; the ecology of a

campus is a fragile thing, and any specie of presidential support ought to be protected.

But a dog? I wanted to be gracious; I wanted to demonstrate that I could be a good sport; I wanted to maintain continuity with the administration of my predecessor. *But a dog?* There comes a time when presidents need to draw the line, be tough, stand firm for certain principles. And my time had come even before I was inaugurated. I found a way to pass the word that this gift would not be received with pleasure, and consequently, I was not presented with a dog. Actually, now that I think about it, I was not presented with anything, which underscores my point about the fragility of student support.

I'm sure some readers will be disappointed I don't share their enthusiasm for pets. I wish I could: the *idea* of a dog, for instance, has always been appealing to me; I love the thought of man's best friend curled up at my feet while I'm reading a good book in front of the fireplace—the picture of wholesome domestic bliss. But I bring a certain history to this matter, and a painful one at that. The McCullough household does not have a good record with animals.

First, there was Fluffy, a kitten we acquired at the beach from someone trying to get rid of a litter. My daughters instantly fell in love with this little ball of white fur, and because she was free, I gave in to their pleas. I soon learned that "free pet" is an oxymoron, like "negative income" or "safe sex." My affection for Fluffy began to wane when she decided my leg would be a great place to sharpen her claws and practice tree climbing. I was not completely saddened, to tell the truth, when she disappeared. But being the caring father I am, I posted reward signs all around the neighborhood, never really expecting anything to come of it. About a month later someone called to ask if we were missing a cat. I confessed that yes, we were the likely owners, whereupon the caller said, "We'll be over in a few minutes." They brought us Fluffy in a body cast, along with a very large bill from the vet. It seems she had been in an accident, and thus her new owners thought it was a good time to return her. We nursed her back to health and were so happy when finally her cast was taken off and she could run about the yard, until she ran right into a possum who took a major hunk out of her newly recovered leg. The vet was happy to perform reconstructive surgery, of course, and the bill we paid put one of his kids through college. Just after her stitches were removed, Fluffy expressed her gratitude for our investment by running away once again. I did not post reward signs this time. But a few months later we discovered her at the neighbors', who had seduced her by giving her an entire room in their house and supplying her with gourmet meals. We had to acknowledge that Fluffy had chosen a better home, yet it was difficult explaining this rejection to my children.

We should have learned our lesson. But then there was Barney, a cocker spaniel who specialized in terrorizing skunks at two o'clock in the morning and thus waking up the entire neighborhood with the sounds and smells of his success. In his off hours he also terrorized my daughters. We got rid of him when a man bought him as an engagement present for his fiancee; I assume the marriage was called off or soon ended in divorce. And then there was Angie, a wonderful little cockapoo, who had a delightful personality, until it was permanently altered by her eating an entire bowl of chocolate-covered coffee beans, after which she spent her life bouncing off our ceiling and acting like she was auditioning for a part in *One Flew Over the Cuckoo's Nest*. And then there was Rascal, a pet hamster, who helped our children learn responsible behavior (see chapter 26) by allowing them to dip his feet in green paint so he could walk around the house impersonating a leprechaun. And then there was the school of goldfish who organized their deaths in such a way that every day for a week my daughters were tortured by a funeral and a flushing down the toilet to that Big Bowl in the Sky. And then there were a pair of finches, Low and Behold, who were eaten by Cruiser, the neighbor's cat. And speaking of birds, there was the parakeet my daughter Joy purchased with her own money. She took forever to come up with just the perfect name. Days went by, and then weeks. We all waited anxiously, feeling a bit sorry for the bird with no name. Then early one morning she ran through the house declaring she had finally decided on a name, and she summoned the family to gather around the cage. With a flair appropriate in a little girl who would eventually choose a career in theater, she took hold of the blanket that covered the cage at night and said, "His name is . . . ," paused for dramatic effect, and then flung off the blanket so we could all behold the bird at this auspicious occasion. But what we saw, just as she looked up and proudly proclaimed his name, was a dead parakeet. As dead as parakeets ever get. We stood in stunned silence, like a family around the grave of a loved one, not sure what to say. Eventually the tears of a hysterical little girl shocked us into action and we did our best to comfort the grieving.

After confessing all this, I expect to be investigated by the Society for the Prevention of Cruelty to Animals or perhaps face a class-action lawsuit on behalf of animal lovers everywhere, if not the animals themselves (given the litigious nature of our society, I'm assuming animals can now sue). But I share this sorry history to warn you: if your dog ever romances my leg, I will not like it. I will not think he's cute. Regardless of how much you love your pet, I will not share your enthusiasm.

I enjoy witnessing a person's passion for something—whether for pets or politics or a profession. I used to think of hobbies, to mention a common source of enthusiastic interest, as trivial and not very important, but I have since changed my mind, believing them a significant factor contributing to overall health. A person dedicated to a pursuit—raising schnauzers, say, or painting with watercolor or shooting skeet or collecting the baseball cards of every player in the American League in 1967—has a disinterested love, a child-like delight winsome to behold (don't forget, Jesus taught that we had to become like children to enter the Kingdom of God). So I like to hear someone instruct me on the four major types of Bordeaux grapes (or is it five?), or explain the difficulties of pruning bonsai trees, or share a secret recipe for killer cappuccino.

Up to a point. Beyond that point, I'm ready to bail out of the conversation. My initial interest feels pummeled by an assault of passion into an ordeal of patience; on the outside I may be smiling, but on the inside my attention flies away like swallows on their way to San Juan Capistrano.

One day opera singer Mary Brant went to a New York post office to pick up a package. When the clerk asked her for identification, she realized she hadn't brought any. "I can't give you a package without some identification," the clerk insisted.

"All right," she said, "I'll show you who I am." She began

to sing one of her arias. A crowd gathered to listen, and in a few moments the clerk said, "Okay, lady, you can have the package. Just be quiet."[1]

Unfortunately, some people don't know when to be quiet. You may be willing to take a few sips of information, but they sweep you down the street with a gushing fire hydrant. You have enough interest for a short story, but they give you *War and Peace.* Or at least it feels like that.

I try to remember this when I find someone willing to listen to me talk about sailing. I would be happy to spend the rest of the day and into the evening carrying on about everything from my latest adventures or misadventures on the bay to the torments of a diesel engine with a mind of its own to the problems of barnacles on my bottom (my boat's). But I watch their eyes as closely as the horizon for an approaching storm: they inevitably register an almost imperceptible shift in focus and an ever-so-slight lowering of the lids that signal an end to their interest. Sometimes, though, my passion for the sport sweeps me away until my listeners are ready to call the coast guard with a mayday warning.

It's a good idea to remember not everyone shares your interests, or you could have people jumping overboard and swimming away from you. Which brings me inescapably to a subject I've been trying to avoid throughout this book: smoking. I've been ignoring it because smokers, frankly, are easy targets and already beat up by a schizophrenic culture that abhors cigarettes and yet glorifies cigars, develops nationwide campaigns to convince teenagers of the gross filth of smoking and yet stuffs cigarettes in the mouths of its most glamorous screen stars and models, sues tobacco companies because they've hidden information that everyone has known from about the age of six, acts genuinely stunned by the news of the habit's gruesome consequences although everyone has witnessed, at least by the tenth grade, lungs blackened Cajun-style and then suspended in formaldehyde. I'm not a smoker; I can't stand smelling the stuff and I'm too much of a chicken to take the health risks; and I support all the new anti-smoking measures. But the self-righteous hypocrisy hanging in the air like smoke in a bar around midnight is enough to make me want to get a pack and join the folks slinking and puffing around the back doors of office buildings.

I mention smoking, please understand, not because I think smokers need to be told that not everyone shares their interest in this activity. I'm pretty sure they're very aware many people find their practice offensive; they've been hammered and shamed by sermons and lectures and laws telling them to take their butts outside. I mention this subject for another reason: to remind the rest of us that maybe not everyone shares our passion for pristine lungs. There's no convert quite as obnoxious as a convert to the new American religion of worshipping health. All power to those who have forsworn tobacco or started jogging fifty miles a week or eating broccoli six times a day; we can only rejoice in their new purity and hope for a long life. But really, after hearing some people carry on about the latest research on the devastating effects of fat, don't you just want to stuff a fourteen ounce New York cut steak down their healthy little throats? We'll soon get to the benefits of moderation in all things (see chapter 29), but for the time being let's acknowledge that courtesy calls us to cut down on an over-rich diet of forcing our latest convictions about health on other people, including smokers.

Not everyone shares our interests. It's wonderful to find

someone willing to hear about them; it's a moment of grace to be received with gratitude. But we should see it as just that—a *moment* of grace. The mercy of other people, unlike God's, has its limits. One way we show respect for others is by allowing them to be just people, with a finite amount of patience. They may be willing to take a few steps our way by granting the gift of attentiveness, but definitely unwilling to have us run over them with unbridled enthusiasm.

Twenty-nine

———•◦•———

Stop Drinking While You Can Still Remember Your Mother's Maiden Name

Bestowing the Benefits of Moderation

DURING PROHIBITION W. C. FIELDS AND A FRIEND heard that an acquaintance on Long Island had just acquired two cases of Irish Whiskey. They drove over to his house to help him drink part of the contraband treasure. About dawn they headed home, taking along several bottles from which they periodically refreshed themselves. After several hours they commented on the surprising length of Long Island. But they kept going. When they asked gas station attendants how far it was to the Queensboro Bridge, they received only blank stares or laughter. Eventually they found themselves in a hotel room, where Fields fell asleep. His friend noticed a palm tree outside the window and discovered they were in Ocala, Florida. He shook Fields awake, saying, "We're in Ocala, Florida!" And Fields responded, "I always said those Long Island roads were poorly marked."[1]

W. C. Fields' drinking was legendary, and stories of his love affair with the bottle make us laugh. Many people can tell their own stories, of course: the morning after an all-night fraternity party when Tom woke up stark naked in a tree house on the other side of town; the evening Betty carried on as though she were the wittiest, most beautiful woman in the world, but was too far gone to notice that her lipstick had smeared to such an extent she looked like a sad-faced Bozo the Clown; the shore leave escapade that somehow ended with two guys in jail and one at the altar.

But drunkenness has another side to it, and it's not very funny. Alcohol, for all the pleasure it offers, carries with it serious trouble for a good many people. About 43 percent of adults in America have been exposed to alcoholism in the family: they grew up with or married a problem drinker or had a blood relative that was one.[2] And the personal and social consequences of this are enormous, leaving individuals psychologically wounded, families torn apart, and society holding an economic bill of staggering proportions. Alcohol contributes to one hundred thousand deaths annually, making it the third leading cause of preventable mortality in the United States.[3] Having too much to drink is no laughing matter.

Please understand: I'm no teetotaler. I drink wine almost every evening, except for the occasional beer with my pizza. When the Hebrew poet praises God's love for people by saying, "They feast on the abundance of your house, and you give them drink from the river of your delights" (Psalms 36:8), I for one imagine at least a few swallows of that river tasting like a fine Cabernet Sauvignon.

But after many years as a pastor, sharing in the pain of lives devastated by the abuse of alcohol, I appreciate the case for abstinence. For some, turning away from alcohol is a very wise choice, and they should be applauded for their good sense and encouraged by the rest of us.

When hosting a party, for example, we ought to remember that not everyone drinks alcohol; this will mean having plenty of soft drinks on hand and helping nondrinkers feel comfortable and not "out of it." We'll work hard to make sure "boozing" isn't treated as a synonym for "fun." And if we have friends struggling with a drinking problem, we'll risk speaking the truth, with compassion and without judgment, and providing the support or even nagging necessary to help move them toward healing. This may likely mean getting them into a local group of Alcoholics Anonymous, probably the most effective means of treating this addiction.

For most of us, though, what's needed isn't abstinence but moderation. A drink or two with friends will be perfectly fine, one of the pleasures of life. But like many good things— sex and nuclear energy come to mind—drinking must be handled very carefully. It has the potential for both pleasure and pain, and the line between them is very thin and not easily recognized, especially after a drink or two.

This is why you should tell the bartender you're finished when you can still remember your mother's maiden name without a second's pause. (If you can't remember your mother's maiden name even when you're stone sober, try your spouse's birthday; if you can't remember that, set down this book immediately and make an appointment with a good family counselor.) The point is, you want to maximize happiness and minimize suffering, both for you and for everyone else. Moderation isn't really about saying no, but about saying yes to the greatest amount of joy.

Actually, moderation is an art that should be practiced in all areas of life, not simply drinking. Things that bring no real pleasure require no great efforts at restraint. Square dancing, for example, will never threaten to take over my life, necessitating my finding a twelve-step program to help cope with the temptations of too many do-si-dos; one evening of cutting in and out of a petticoat jungle provides enough of this sort of pleasure for an entire lifetime. But it's the things we like to do, the things we enjoy, that create the necessity of moderation. If a little is good, a whole lot is not necessarily better. I suppose there may be a few things in life that require full-throttle, pedal-to-the-metal, no-holds-barred immoderation, but aside from loving God, I can't think of what they might be. Most of what we enjoy doing actually improves with moderation, protecting us from the damaging effects of too much of a good thing.

My dad has been a pretty good cook for many years, though for a long time I was reluctant to admit this. He was always the first to extol the excellence of his creations, as in "Boy, when better spaghetti gets made, we know just who'll make it," and for some reason, this had a way of dampening my inclination to offer compliments. I'm not sure he has ever followed a recipe; at least I've never witnessed him bent over a book or using any sort of measuring device. His style possesses a certain free-flowing flair: a handful of this and a dash of that. But most of the time it has worked pretty well, except for when he went through his Cheese Phase. It started innocently enough, when he discovered that a little shredded cheese dresses up scrambled eggs. Someone made the mistake of complimenting him, and the next time we had even more cheese with our scrambled eggs, and before long we were fervently hoping for some eggs with our cheese. Cheese became for him the all-purpose additive, to be applied liberally to anything and everything. Recently my daughter and I reminisced about Grandpa's Cheese Phase, and she told me he'd confided in her that cheese was the secret to his great French toast! By the latter stages of this era things had gotten out of hand, so we employed some gentle teasing: "Hey everybody, I've discovered some food underneath all this cheese!"—and other equally subtle hints. He took our ribbing a little hard, and now he won't even *think* about adding cheese to his creations. His pendulum has swung to the Anti-Cheese Phase, which involves a good deal of pouting about how no one really appreciates his cooking. And his scrambled eggs seem a little dry.

Well, my point is that cheese is good, and a little more cheese may be even better, but a whole lot of cheese can definitely leave you gagging, not to mention make you a prime candidate for a heart attack. To enjoy cheese to its fullest, to allow it to serve as a tasty compliment to scrambled eggs, it must be used appropriately, without exceeding proper proportions. Moderation is the key to cheese use, as in so many things.

I belabor this story of cheese because it applies to many other areas. A glass of wine offers an array of pleasures; get smashed, and you won't be able to tell the difference between blackberry undertones and vanilla overtones. Exercise promotes physical vitality; become a workout fanatic, and you may very well damage your joints and undermine the health you so obsessively seek. Hard work enables you to provide many good things for your family; become a workaholic, and you may lose your family. Telling others about your religious faith is praiseworthy; preach constantly to all your friends and acquaintances, and you'll soon have no one left to convert. Moderation at first seems like a limitation on good things, but in fact it's the only way to protect them, the only way to maximize them.

Our desires simply can't be trusted. When something feels good or tastes good or sounds good or smells good or looks good—when our senses get a happy zap—our rational judgment faces a serious challenge that can push it over the edge of objectivity and start it sliding fast down the slope of fancy justifications toward the valley of moral impairment. When you hear of someone guilty of gross sexual misconduct, your first response may be, "How could he do such a thing? What was he *thinking*?" There was a brief moment when he was thinking, when he knew he had to be careful and keep things in their proper place, but it felt so good, so wonderful, that he was soon over the edge and racing through a slalom course of rationalizations until he wrapped himself around a tree at the bottom of the hill. It's easy to point the finger of judgment against someone being carried away on a stretcher, but truth to tell, we all do this to one degree or another. Our desires are powerful. Without the discipline of moderation, they will lead to imbalance and ultimately the destruction of the very pleasures we seek. Moderation sets a barrier around the good things in life, and not incidentally, protects us and the people we care about from the voracious hunger of our desires.

What helps us master moderation? Greater knowledge? Not likely, if you ask me. I believe in the benefits of knowledge, mind you; I spend a good deal of my life trying to educate myself and others. But in my experience, greater intellectual power usually provides more facility at highfalutin arguments to explain one's behavior. To speak personally: when I've failed, my prestigious degrees and advanced learning have simply given me more sophisticated tools for self-justification.

In the end, moderation is an act of the will—a gritty resolve to get a grip on our desires, a firm resolve to say no to one thing in order to say yes to something else. Moderation is the result of self-discipline, in other words. Unfortunately, for many people, self-discipline has about as much appeal as a blind date set up by your sister. It implies restraint, which in turn smacks of imprisonment.

But we must remember a great paradox: self-discipline leads to greater self-freedom. Only the figure skater who has sweated in the rink, hour after hour and year after year, has the freedom to do a triple axel. Only the pianist who has forced himself to practice when he would rather have been watching TV has the freedom to let his fingers fly through a Bach fugue. The great composer Igor Stravinsky put it this way: "My freedom will be so much the greater and more meaningful the more narrowly I limit my field of action and the more I surround myself with obstacles. Whatever diminishes constraint, diminishes strength. The more constraints one imposes, the more one frees oneself of the chains that shackle the spirit."[4]

With an image that evokes memories for some of us, M. Scott Peck writes of the need for balance in life: "I remember first being taught this one summer morning in my ninth year. I had recently learned to ride a bike and was joyously exploring the dimensions of my new skill. About a mile from our house the road went down a steep hill and turned sharply at the bottom. Coasting down the hill on my bike that morning I felt my gathering speed to be ecstatic. To give up this ecstasy by the application of brakes seemed an absurd self-punishment. So I resolved to simultaneously retain my speed and negotiate the corner at the bottom. My ecstasy ended seconds later when I was propelled a dozen feet off the road into the woods. I was badly scratched and bleeding and the front wheel of my new bike was twisted beyond use from its impact against a tree. I had lost my balance.

"Balancing is a discipline precisely because the act of giving something up is painful. In this instance I had been unwilling to suffer the pain of giving up my ecstatic speed in the interest of maintaining my balance around the corner. I learned, however, that the loss of balance is ultimately more painful than the giving up required to maintain balance. In one way or another it is a lesson I have continually had to relearn throughout my life. As must everyone, for as we negotiate the curves and corners of our lives, we must continually give up parts of ourselves."[5]

Moderation bestows benefits on us; we help ourselves move toward greater freedom and personal growth when we learn how to practice self-discipline. But our moderation also bestows benefits on others, and hence the reason for including this subject in a book on courtesy. For as I gain freedom over my selfish desires, I also create a sphere of freedom for other people. If I'm at a bar and take a third or fourth drink and can't remember even my mother's first name, I will likely become a nuisance—maybe even a *disgusting* one—and if the alcohol has so impaired my good sense that I try to get behind the wheel of a car, I may endanger the lives of other people. If I act from a warped sense of "freedom," drinking myself into a stupor, I only imprison myself and others behind the bars of my out-of-control desires. My friends will not feel very free as they try to get me home safely that night, perhaps having to apologize for me or even clean up after me. But if I practice self-discipline, I not only grant myself the freedom for more happiness (especially the following morning), I bestow on my friends the freedom to have a good time without having to baby-sit me.

So yes, moderation is an important way we express courtesy. Self-discipline demonstrates thoughtfulness; when we say no to some things, we say yes to the respect we have for ourselves and other people.

———— • ————

Thirty

Stay Out of the Bay Until You Know the Difference Between a Starboard and a Port Tack

Learning and Obeying the Rules of the Road

EVERY SAILOR IS FAMILIAR WITH THIS MOMENT OF tension: you're scudding along on a starboard tack (the wind blowing over the right side of the boat), and ahead you see another sailboat coming toward you on a port tack (the wind blowing over the left side of the boat). At first you try to judge whether you're really on a collision course, estimating the relative speed of the boats, the direction of the wind, and the strength of the current. If you conclude that the bow of one boat is likely to pay an unwelcome visit in the cabin of the other, you begin to hope the approaching boat's helmsman knows the rules of the road and intends to follow them — knows *you* have the right of way and are therefore supposed to hold your course. If the boat gets closer with no change of direction, you wonder whether the skipper has had a few too many beers, or has a bevy of distracting beauties on board, or is actually a motor boater who, in a fit of sanity, decided to rent a *real* boat but has no idea what to do with it (of course). If the boat gets even closer, your prayer life becomes fervent; if the boat gets closer yet, your language takes on a colorful hue as you shout suggestions about what the approaching skipper can do with his tiller.

I'm pleased to report that almost always the other boat turns, and the skipper, without fail, acts as though he really knew what he was doing all along, giving a slight wave that says, "Hey, we're cool and in control and have the right stuff." When the other boat doesn't turn, however, you have a *big problem* on your hands. A few months ago on San Francisco Bay, I heard one of these *big problems,* the sick sound of crunching and cracking, followed by distress calls on the radio.

If you want to take up sailing and have decided to rent a boat, *please* do not follow my example: when I was in college, I thought it would be fun to take a girl sailing, and so I looked up "sailing" in the encyclopedia, read the article thoroughly, and thus ventured forth with cocky and complete stupidity. I didn't even know there was such a thing as "rules of the road"; I was going out on water, for goodness sake, not pavement. I did manage to get the boat (and my date) back to the dock, but I won't tell you what the old Norwegian who rented me the boat said, in case this book gets into the hands of children. If you decide to sail, either go with someone who knows what she is doing or take a course from a certified instructor. And whatever you do, stay out of my bay until you learn the difference between a starboard tack and a port tack.

It's important to learn the rules of the road—and obey

them. In many areas of life there are agreed-upon patterns of behavior. These may be formal laws or informal customs, and their purpose is to keep us from killing one another. Whether sailing a boat or driving a car, racing horses or running a marathon, there are things you must do and avoid doing in order to protect yourself and others from harm.

You landlubbers need not worry about which boat has the right of way. But you probably *do* need to worry about which car has the right of way. To receive a driving license, you passed a test that assessed your knowledge of motor vehicle laws but not your willingness to obey them. Judging from the state of things on our streets and highways, a good many of you seem to think traffic laws are merely traffic suggestions. In the last few years I have driven in most of the major cities of this country and, believe me, too many of you are simply slowing down at stop signs, racing through red lights, not bothering to signal before turning, and running down anyone who's going the speed limit. A few weeks ago *Time* magazine ran a major article on "road rage," accurately describing your insane driving habits.

Yes, I do mean *you.* Not that *I* never break the law, you understand, but whenever I do, I have a really good reason and do so in a responsible way. Unlike the rest of you, who drive like you're on a bumper car at the state fair, who feel mightily empowered with your humongous "sport utility vehicle" and have watched too many commercials of it powering up steep mountains so that you naturally assume you can climb right over my lowly Buick, who are stressed by the increasing numbers of drivers like yourself packing our roads, and who need to go back and re-read chapter 4 ("Don't Let Your Fingers Do the Talking"). I'm almost afraid to leave my driveway with so many of you on the road who shift your brain into neutral whenever you put your car in gear. If I happen to break the law, it's only in the literal sense, without ever really violating its spirit; I'm careful not to leave my rationality in the garage. The problem is yours, as I said, and not mine.

Or at least that's what I like to think. In the matter of driving, as with a few other areas in life, I'm pretty quick to point the finger of blame at the rest of you. And so in that same spirit, let me point out that I'm probably not the only one with this self-defensive perspective on highway wrongdoing. In fact, I cannot remember ever, in my entire lifetime, hearing even one single person say, "You know, I have a problem with driving." Twelve-step groups support drinkers, overeaters, gamblers, sex addicts, and a host of compulsions that nowadays get readily confessed, but to my knowledge, you'll never find a group where people introduce themselves by saying, "Hi, my name is Kimberly, and I have a problem with running red lights." No! Because it's always the *other* drivers who are causing the problems out there in the concrete jungle. Whenever my daughter Jennifer and I are in the car and we see someone doing something stupid, we turn to each other and say in unison, "Aren't you glad we're normal?"

I can only imagine the excuses people offer cops when they get pulled over. You want a great idea for a book? Interview highway patrol officers on the best excuses they've heard through the years. It could become a best-seller: not only would it be funny, it could be a resource book for all of us. Come to think of it, maybe I'll call my agent. Or maybe it would be better to encourage the cops to write it, to get a few of them daydreaming when they should be keeping an eye on me.

Baseball may be the national pastime of nostalgia, and football the national pastime of the television age, but the national pastime of actuality, the one we *all* engage in one way or another, is the art and sport of making excuses for ourselves. Or occasionally for those we like. George F. Will told about the time Sugar Ray Robinson landed a punch after the bell had ended a round. Looking for an excuse for Robinson, the ringside broadcaster explained, "It's hard to hear the bell up here. There's a tremendous amount of smoke here in Boston Gardens." There seems to be a lot of smoke everywhere, getting in our eyes and obscuring a clear perspective.

Have you ever noticed how social problems always seem to be happening "out there" somewhere? They're always "national problems," or at least ones others are having. Take drugs, for example. As P. J. O'Rourke put it, "The only time I've ever been serious about drugs was back in college, when I seriously took a whole bunch of them. And I still take drugs now and then. Like most Americans I'm perfectly willing to tell the government where to go and then stand in the road to keep it from getting there. . . . We're Americans. These are modern times. Nothing bad is going to happen to us. If we get fired, it's not failure; it's a midlife vocational reassessment period. If we screw up a marriage, we can get another one. There's no shame in divorce. Day care will take care of the kids, and the ex-wife can go back to the career she was bitching about leaving. If we get convicted of a crime, we'll go to tennis prison and probably not even that. We'll just have to futz around doing community service for a while. Or maybe we can cheerfully confess everything, join a support group, and get off the hook by listening to shrinks tell us we don't like ourselves enough. Hell, play our cards right, and we can get a book contract out of it. We don't have to be serious about the drug problem—or anything else. . . . This is a democracy. We're free to change what our government does any time we want. All we have to do is vote on it. In the meantime, if people like me—rich, white, privileged, happy—cannot even bother to abide by the legal standards of their freely constituted society, of a society that has provided them with everything a civilization can be expected to provide, then those people deserve their drug problems and everybody else's drug problems, too."[1]

No one favors lawlessness, except perhaps professional criminals. We're all law-abiding citizens, at least theoretically. A good many of us vote for "law and order" candidates, by which we mean candidates who will put the *right kind* of criminals in the slammer, by which we mean criminals other than ourselves. Get those punks who steal stereos! But what about the slick broker who steals the life savings of the elderly? Crack down on gang violence! But what about those who abuse the rights of migrant workers? Do something about our cheating government! But what about the 18 percent of Americans who say it's not wrong to cheat on taxes because the government spends too much anyway? We have developed an enormous capacity for self-justification, for turning a blind eye toward our own fudging of the rules.

King Frederick II, an eighteenth-century Prussian monarch, was visiting a prison in Berlin where the inmates tried to prove to him how they had been unjustly imprisoned. All except one, who sat quietly in a corner while all the rest protested their innocence. Seeing him sitting there, the king asked him why he was imprisoned. "Armed robbery, Your Honor."

"Were you guilty?" the king asked.

"Yes, Sir. I entirely deserve my punishment."

The king then gave an order to the guard: "Release this guilty man. I don't want him corrupting all these innocent people."[2]

We're all innocent, and if we could just get rid of the real criminals this country would be a better place. Yet if we realize we're not completely, not strictly speaking, innocent, we nevertheless have learned how to arm ourselves with an arsenal of effective excuses to fight off any guilt that tries to ensnare us.

There is another problem, too, a well-kept secret, we might as well admit: most of us harbor an ornery character who actually enjoys breaking the rules. Or am I the only one with a little brat inside me who takes pleasure in launching spit wads at the teacher and walking through puddles after being given strict instructions to stay dry?

A railroad company made me face this tendency in myself. For many years I ran along the Pacific Ocean in Del Mar, California, where a particularly beautiful stretch was owned by the railroad. After a heavy rain eroded another big hunk of the cliff onto the beach below—or maybe it was an earthquake (I forget)—signs were posted exclaiming, WARNING! STAY BACK! UNSTABLE CLIFF! VIOLATORS WILL BE PROSECUTED. So of course I ran right by the sign, day after day, year after year. Tourists from Nebraska should certainly stay back, but I practically owned that cliff; I knew my way around that trail. And to be honest, the sign made the run seem even more beautiful and desirable and even necessary for my overall physical well-being. As the trail continued to erode, I imagined myself as the Last Man Across the Del

Mar Cliff, running with the trail falling away behind me, like in a cartoon.

I take some comfort in the fact that even St. Paul felt these rebellious feelings. He traced them to that little ornery character "sin," which fueled his desire to disobey: "I would not have known what it is to covet if the law had not said, 'You shall not covet.' But sin, seizing an opportunity in the commandment, produced in me all kinds of covetousness." In other words, when he heard God say, "Do not covet," he responded by coveting for all he was worth.

When you combine a tendency to make excuses for yourself with delight in anarchic defiance of rules, you get a very large pile of temptation, and it can get mighty difficult *not* to hold your course on a port tack, or sneak through red lights, or fudge a bit on your estimated annual income. But when you step back from your rebellious compulsions and take a deep breath, you know what you have to do: you have to obey the rules, for others' sake as well as your own.

Most of the laws and rules that govern our behavior are a good thing, and we should protect them because they protect us. We need to be able to count on other drivers staying on their side of the road and stopping when they're supposed to; and we need to obey these laws ourselves, if we don't want to become, in advance of our scheduled appearance, fuel for a mortician's crematorium. Oh, sure, anyone with the eyesight of a bat and the brain power of a slug can identify crazy laws that must have been passed by legislators sniffing illegal substances. In general, though, the laws and customs that govern our actions in relation to others help order life, make it more just and wholesome for the majority of people. We do both others and ourselves a favor when we respect them.

A TV news team was on assignment in southern Florida after Hurricane Andrew swept through with destructive force. In one televised scene, amid the terrible destruction and debris, stood one house on its foundation. The owner was cleaning up the yard when a reporter approached him and asked, "Sir, why is your house the only one still standing? How did you manage to escape the severe damage of the hurricane?"

"I built this house myself," the man replied. "I also built it according to the Florida state building code. When the code called for two-by-six roof trusses, I used two-by-six roof trusses. I was told that the house built according to code could withstand a hurricane. I did, and it did. I suppose no one else around here followed the code."[3]

Because you never know when the winds will pick up, it's a good idea to follow the code. It's a good idea to obey all the laws and customs that govern our lives, because for the most part, they help make our lives safer and more enjoyable. And with that, I should end this chapter. I have an appointment, and after what I've just written, I'd better not exceed the speed limit getting there.

Thirty-one

———•———

Don't Tell Jokes at the Expense of Others

Forbearing Humor that Demeans

"BY NOTHING DO MEN SHOW THEIR CHARACTER more than by the things they laugh at," wrote Johann Wolfgang Goethe. Aside from wanting to include women in the pronouncement, I would only question his use of the preposition at the end of the sentence, and this not out of a fussy concern for grammatical niceties (this is a translation from German, after all, and thus we should rejoice in its brevity), but because I would distinguish between laughing *at* and laughing *with*.

When my daughter Joy, as a little girl, inadvertently did something funny, we would respond with laughter she didn't find amusing. It was one thing if she had intended to get us going, in which case she would smile in a manner indicating she expected bouquets in honor of her comic genius. But when she said something with dead seriousness that sounded hilarious, say, or when she tried to pull a fast one on us, and we laughed, she would respond with a scowl announcing an approaching emotional storm. I would then say, "Joy, relax, we're not laughing *at* you. We're laughing *with* you." To which she would reply, "But I'm not laughing."

No one likes to be laughed *at*. To be the butt of someone's joke can be painful, as I discovered during my freshman year in college, when I came home from classes one day to find my closets and drawers completely empty. I wasn't upset at first; this didn't seem as bad as some of the things my "friends" had done to me, such as dumping large wastebaskets of cold water on me at two o'clock in the morning. I could be a good sport, know when to take a joke. So I didn't say much the first day, and I was even in a pretty good mood the next morning as I stepped into well-seasoned underwear. By that evening, though, I was ready for the little prank to be finished, and so I asked them to be good guys and tell me where they had hidden my things and there would be no hard feelings, etc. But they just smiled and said they couldn't help me.

By the third day, my mood was as nasty as the underwear I was wearing, so I decided it was time to act. I went down the hallway, burst into their room, and demanded my clothes or else.

"Or else what?" they wanted to know.

"Or else you'll be sorry," I said, lifting my towering mass of 5′ 8″ and 140 pounds as tall as possible and delivering my threat to four members of the football team—the quarterback, linebacker, and two members of the defensive line. I was not afraid. True, I had no idea what I was going to do, but I had the distinct advantage of twelve quarts of adrenaline pumping through my body, and I was at that moment willing to take on an entire regiment of Army Rangers if necessary.

At some point in our ensuing conversation, I became aware that I was leaning against a bookshelf that had been attached to the wall above a desk, and I noticed that I had been secretly slipping my fingers between it and the wall. "I am going to count to ten," I warned, "and if you don't tell me where my clothes are, you will be very, very sorry."

They laughed, of course, and asked what I thought I would do.

"Ten, nine, eight, seven . . ."

"We're *sooo* terrified . . . Look out guys, he's going to beat us up!"

"Six, five, four . . ."

"Oh, have mercy," they pleaded with expert mockery.

"Three, two, one . . ." And with the explosive power of rage I ripped the bookshelf out of the wall and sent it crashing down upon one of the bullies, with books and pictures and notebooks flying everywhere. The other three were in a paralysis of shock, which worked to my advantage as I lunged for the bunk bed on which they were sitting and with the strength of three days of pent-up anger pulled it over on top of them. As they were trying to get out from under it all, I advanced to the closet and sent clothes flying.

I was just starting to rip things when they said, "All right already! Enough! Your clothes are in the storeroom!" To tell the truth, by then I was having so much fun I was a little disappointed by their surrender. The next morning, though, I was happy to be able to salvage what was left of my social life by putting on some clean clothes.

Ever since then, I've been a little sensitive about practical jokes—at least the ones played on me. Like the Sunday morning several years ago when, a few minutes before the worship service, I raced to my closet to get my pulpit robe and found only a little pink tutu. Granted, it had my clerical collar and starched white preaching bands neatly tucked in its neck, thus it was manifestly a *Presbyterian* tutu. But even though we were in California I didn't think my congregation would go for it. About ten seconds before I was due to walk into the sanctuary, the secretaries appeared with my robe. In retrospect, their prank was kind of cute; at the time, though, it brought back unpleasant memories of three days when my closet was completely empty and I was being laughed *at* rather than laughed *with*.

Most of the time, laughter is one of the great blessings of being human. As Conrad Hyers has pointed out, "The ancient Greeks were not far from the truth in classifying human beings as 'laughing animals.' A fundamental difference between humans and donkeys, it was observed, was that donkeys can bray but only humans can laugh. If one has ventured to tell a joke, even the simplest of jokes, to one's dog or cat one senses the importance of the distinction. Animals take everything literally. They have no notion of double meaning, plays upon words, overstatement or understatement, incongruity or absurdity, irony or tongue in cheek. Animals take everything quite seriously. . . . In C. S. Lewis's *Chronicles of Narnia,* when Aslan creates talking animals, they discover laughter. At first they are ashamed by such 'queer noises' and try to repress them. But Aslan says to them: 'Laugh and fear not, creatures. Now that you are no longer dumb and witless, you need not always be grave. For jokes as well as justice come in with speech.' "[1]

As with any of God's good gifts, however, laughter can be warped, perverted from its original intent; instead of humanizing, it can demean. Most often, I think, the culprit is that little insecure person who resides in so many of us—the one who believes she is nothing but hamburger in a world of filet mignon, the one who's terrified that if others really knew who he was, he would become a fire hydrant in a world of dogs. This little monster of self-condemnation causes us to do some unpleasant things, not the least of which is to try to lower others in the mistaken notion it will elevate us. When we laugh *at* someone, we treat them with disrespect. This can happen through teasing with a mean edge, certainly, and through jokes and wisecracks about groups of people. We've all heard Polish jokes, and ones about blacks and Jews and women and men; we all tell them about lawyers. Often we chuckle, in spite of our liberal sentiments and professed love of humanity in general, but we're left with a guilty aftertaste, as though we've just swallowed some cheap wine with a particularly nasty finish.

Call me overly sensitive if you like, but as long as we're talking about stereotypes, let me vent my weariness with clergy jokes. I really wouldn't mind them, if they weren't so drearily uncreative. Have you noticed how they're almost always about Jewish rabbis going after money, Catholic priests struggling with drink, and Protestant ministers chasing women? And of course the setting for the jokes is always the golf course, because as everyone knows the clergy only work one day a week—a crack every rabbi and pastor has heard about, oh, twelve million times. I always seemed to hear it on Sundays following a week with two funerals, a wedding, five evening meetings, and four major crises to manage. It was hard to smile.

If we clergy find these jokes pretty lame, it's only because, like everyone else, we don't enjoy being laughed *at*. On the other hand, most of my colleagues are very quick to laugh about their mistakes, when they feel they're being laughed *with*. I recall the time a few of us were relaxing after a long day of business meetings, and Joyce recounted a memorable Christmas Eve when she was serving as a student pastor. She was running late that day, what with last minute preparations for her family, and so she was rushed getting dressed for the Candlelight Communion Service. When the elastic band on her pantyhose snapped, she knew she didn't have time to rummage around for another pair, and so she slipped a pair of panties over the pantyhose. We had to take her word that this was a rational solution to the problem, most of us being unfamiliar with pantyhose mechanics. But she was confident this would keep things in their designated places, and off she raced to the church.

At the beginning of the liturgy of the Communion, as she was standing behind the table offering a prayer, she felt the elastic band on her panties snap. Oh oh, she thought, still hoping for the best. Then she walked around the table to serve elders the bread, and the movement of her . . . ah . . . things . . . caused her undergarments to start sliding toward the chancel floor. As the congregation worshipped she calculated the risks, taking into account the relative speed of descent and the number of steps remaining in the service. It didn't look good.

When she walked around the table to serve elders the wine, the whole business slid down to her thighs. The narrowing of her legs, without going into too much anatomical detail, had a loosening effect, which left little resistance against the force of gravity. She knew she was in serious trouble. She had another walk to take—the longest yet. She needed to go around the table once more and down the steps to take her place on the floor in front of the congregation as they all sang "Silent night, Holy night." By the time she reached this destination, her panties and pantyhose had fallen around her ankles.

"Silent night, Holy night!" they sang, "Shepherds quake at the sight," and there might have been a few folks in the front row also quaking at the sight. It wasn't often they saw their pastor singing in cherubic earnestness with underwear around her ankles. What was she to do? There was no way she could walk out of the sanctuary in that condition, and so, lacking any alternatives, she stepped out of her panties and pantyhose and, with great pastoral dignity, kicked them aside—directly onto the feet of her parishioners.

"Silent night, Holy night," they continued to sing, and as Joyce walked down the aisle that evening it was for her also Embarrassing night, Breezy night.

When we heard that story, we didn't just laugh; we approached death. We laughed so hard we couldn't catch our breath and thought we would pass out from the hilarity. We weren't laughing *at* her, really; we were laughing *with* her. She had told the story on herself and was laughing as hard as any of us. And we were laughing not only at what had happened to her, but what has happened to all of us fallible human beings doing our best to represent the infallible Divine Being.

We were laughing because we've all been there—not necessarily with underwear around our ankles, but certainly with our dignity fallen to the floor. John could laugh with her because he had once recessed with a wedding party out of the sanctuary and had forgotten to turn off his wireless microphone and thus blasted over the speakers for the entire congregation, "I'm glad that's over! I'm sweating like a pig!" And Barry could laugh with her, remembering the meaningful baptism he had performed without a drop of water, faking it all the way. And Woody could laugh with her, remembering the wedding ceremony he had conducted with great style until he got to the vows and addressed the bride with the name of the groom's ex-wife. And I could laugh with her, remembering the wedding I had completely forgotten, until the best man arrived at my house about one minute before the ceremony was due to begin, asking if they could possibly have the key to the church, and there I was, standing unshaven, dressed in T-shirt and shorts, pretending I had everything under control.

Laughter liberates us from the self-important delusion that we have everything under control; it puts everything in a more balanced perspective. Have you ever tried to analyze laughter? It's not easy to figure out; there's a mystery to it. At least part of what it is, I think, is an instinctive response to a suddenly perceived contradiction. Charlie Chaplin walks along looking so dapper, and then slips on a banana peel: first we feel a moment of tension, because dapper men in control of life shouldn't be falling to the ground; but then the contradiction overwhelms us—a wonderful double take that liberates us to see we're none of us all that dapper or in control and we're pretty much falling to the ground in one way or another all the time. When we laugh we're saying to ourselves, It really doesn't matter as much as we thought, and so we can get up, dust ourselves off, and keep walking toward the next banana peel.

I have dear friends who worked for a number of years with Native Americans, and I have often heard them remark about the fine sense of humor in that culture. Recently they told me their theory about this: they have come to believe that humor is a coping mechanism, a way to keep things in perspective, and Native Americans, suffering more than their share of tragedies, have found liberation in laughter.

We all enjoy this liberation, discovering therapy for much of what ails us in a good, hard laugh. It can even be good medicine for physical maladies, according to Norman Cousins, who after being diagnosed with a painful, incurable disease, found more relief in old *Candid Camera* episodes and Marx Brothers movies than chemical painkillers. "I made the joyous discovery," he wrote, "that ten minutes of genuine belly laughter had an anesthetic effect and would give me at least two hours of pain-free sleep."[2]

Because laughter is such a good gift, so important to our well-being, we must be good stewards of it: we dare not misuse it for destructive purposes. To use humor as a weapon to put others down, or to steal snickers at the expense of others, or to pass on jokes that rely on stale and prejudiced stereotypes, might evoke a quick and cheap chuckle, but it won't be funny in the deep-down places where we could all use a little liberating mirth. On the other hand, when we laugh not *at* but *with* others, when we allow humor to help us all see the wonderful, crazy, and joy-filled predicament of being human, we not only show our respect toward others, we maybe even join with God in the heavenly mirth. As Frederick Buechner has written, "In the last analysis, the only one who gets much of a kick out of Satan's jokes is Satan himself. With God's, however, even the most hardened cynics and bitterest pessimists have a hard time repressing an occasional smile, and when he really gets going, he has pretty much the whole creation rolling in the aisles."[3]

———•◦•———

Thirty-two

Keep Card Companies in Business

Remembering Milestones

MY MOTHER, DAUGHTER, AND I HAD A MEMORABLE
adventure a few years ago when we chartered a boat in Seattle
and sailed it to the west side of Whidbey Island. Our destination was Mutiny Bay, where my parents have a home. Their
neighbor Bill had offered the use of his mooring. For you
landlubbers, a mooring is a large ball that floats on the water.
A chain connects it to something heavy, such as an old engine
block or a piece of concrete, and thus you can tie your boat
to it in the secure confidence it will stay put. At least that's
the theory.

The next morning in Mutiny Bay, we were eating breakfast when the doorbell rang. My father went to see who was
there and a few seconds later came running into the kitchen,

shouting, "Don, your boat has been spotted drifting out into the shipping channel!"

I bolted out of the house and ran down to the beach, wondering how I would explain to the charter company I had lost their twenty-eight foot sailboat. When I got to the beach, I saw nothing—no boat, no mooring. My heart pounded in terror as I surveyed the horizon. Eventually I saw it, or at least what I assumed to be it, floating off across Puget Sound. I looked around in panic, not sure what to do, and then I saw a man in a motor boat. I waved furiously, hoping that a stinkpotter (the official nautical term for a motor boater, at least in the sailors' lexicon) could be good for something. Indeed he was: he took me aboard and helped rescue the prodigal boat that had been running away to the far waters and the mooring it was dragging behind it.

When I told Bill that the chain on his mooring had apparently broken, he replied, "Oh, well, I knew it was getting a little thin, but I thought it would be good for a couple of days." Believe it or not, he was (and still is) a good friend.

I learned an important lesson that day: tie your boat to a mooring that will hold or you could find yourself in many fathoms of deep trouble. This principle can be applied to the rest of life, too. We all need to be tied down, securely fastened to something that will keep us from drifting. Convictions about religion or morality serve as moorings; so do commitments to other people, expressed in vows and promises. Without these ties, we can drift aimlessly into dangerous waters. The analogy has its limits, of course: sailboats are made to sail, not stay safely tied up. But even the sturdiest of boats will eventually need to find a harbor and drop sail. And then it pays to have a secure mooring you can trust.

I have come to believe that rituals—daily, weekly, annual—serve as moorings for us. Whatever adventures we're enjoying, whatever thrills of wind in the sails and water over the bow, periodically we need to tie our lines to moorings we've known and trusted, moorings that provide security for rest or repairs or re-provisioning. Rituals can serve this purpose.

As I've already acknowledged, the word *ritual* is not popular these days (see chapter 8); we prize freedom and spontaneity. But we need rituals to provide identity and structure to our lives. The rituals of remembrance, to name one kind, regularly remind us of who we are: birthdays, wedding anniversaries, class reunions, and religious festivals situate us in time and community, witnessing to our ties with other people. Life is not meaningless drifting, or at least it shouldn't be. We're historical creatures, existing through a succession of days from yesterday through today into tomorrow; we're going somewhere. Along the way milestones mark our journey, reminding us of where we've been, the company we're traveling with, and where we're headed.

If you commemorate a wedding anniversary, for example, you're pausing to remember a time in the past when you made vows and committed yourself to another person, you're celebrating your present life together as husband and wife, and you're renewing promises for the future. From one perspective your celebration may seem simply like a dinner in a fine restaurant, followed by a play at the theater and then some play in the bed. But it's much more than this: it's a significant ritual that honors your spouse and marriage, and in that honoring, tethers you, like a boat to a mooring, to an essential part of your identity.

For many years my family often vacationed in Seattle in order to visit relatives. We were living in San Diego at the time, and it was a very long way to drive. Hundreds of miles stretched on and on, punctuated only by stops at service stations, restaurants, and motels. For our children it seemed like two endless days of torture. Grandmas and grandpas and aunts and uncles and cousins were waiting for them, and their imaginations raced ahead to anticipated joys. Anyone with small children knows what happened along the way: we wouldn't be in the car thirty minutes, and a little voice in the back seat would say, "Daddy, are we there yet?"

"No," I would answer, "this is only San Clemente."

About an hour later: "Daddy, are we there yet?"

"No, this is only Los Angeles."

About an hour later: "Daddy, are we there yet?"

"No, we're not even in Bakersfield."

And on it would go through the day. The high points of the trip, which we held out before the girls like rewards, were when we stopped for breakfast, lunch, midafternoon snack, and dinner. These stops were always more fun than they had any right being, and the reason, I think, was that they became milestones of progress. After a few years, the girls learned what each stop meant. "Well, we're almost to Redding," I would say. "Oh, goodie," they would respond, "can we get a motel with a swimming pool?" After twelve hours in the car, the Holiday Inn seemed like the Ritz Carlton to them. The one time we departed from our usual routine was when we took a detour and stopped for lunch at the Pantyhose Junction Café, and the name is probably all you need to know to understand why, after twelve years, we're still talking about it.

Certain milestones in life signal that we're going somewhere, that we're on a journey that has been traveled by others and will take us to a destination that will make the long stretches of boredom worthwhile. These should be celebrated, I believe, and with great joy.

The only *bar mitzvah* I've attended was in Jerusalem, at the Wailing Wall. Now, let me tell you, if you're going to participate in only one *bar mitzvah,* it might as well be at the Wailing Wall, in the courtyard next to those ancient stones that mean so much to Jews. I wasn't exactly invited, I should confess, but I had been wandering around by myself, and the laughter and music drew me into the celebration. Joy has a kind of gravitational pull that I've never been able to resist. Before long I had joined the singing and dancing and prayers. I never bothered to mention that I was a Presbyterian minister, assuming it probably didn't matter. There seemed to be celebration enough to include even a spiritual descendent of John Calvin. A thirteen-year-old boy was being honored as a "son of the commandments," taking his place with other men in the community of faith. I've since wondered what happened to him. Has he tried to remain true to the commandments? Has he become a leader in the tradition that nurtured him and gave him his essential identity? Does he remember that day when he was the center of attention, when he was the reason for the celebration?

In my Christian tradition, water baptism signifies initiation into the community of faith. Christians disagree whether the children of believers should be baptized at infancy or when they are old enough to make a conscious commitment of faith in Jesus Christ. The usual pattern for Presbyterians is to baptize infants, and the first baby I baptized was my daughter Jennifer. It would take someone more gifted with words than I to describe my feelings when I sprinkled the water on her in the presence of the congregation that had called me to be its pastor. And the same feelings came rushing back again when, a few years later, I baptized my second daughter, Joy. Jennifer and Joy don't remember this important milestone in their lives, of course, and so I've tried to remind them as often as possible, describing it to them, making it a part of the family conversation through the years. It's *the* most important witness to who they are and to whom they belong, the fundamental fact of their existence, and I have wanted them to remember it always and to come back to it in their thinking during inevitable seasons of doubt and struggle for self-identity.

I worry that too often parents baptize their children and never say another word about it; it drops out of the family consciousness, as it were, with no trace of presence in the collection of family stories. For this reason, when I was a pastor, I told parents I would provide a professional-quality photograph of their child's baptism if they would promise to hang it on the wall of his or her bedroom. (I also wanted to assure them that a good picture would be taken, so they could tell Uncle George to leave his camera at home and stay seated so as not to ruin the ceremony for everybody else.) I encouraged them to point to the picture often, telling the story again and again, and even to celebrate the baptismal anniversary like a birthday, with presents and a party. I was always pleased when I heard of families following my advice, for I was hopeful the baptism would become for that child a mooring whose chain would hold.

Birthdays are milestones that many, especially as they pass quite a few, say they would like to forget. Not me. I think we've gotten it backward, making a big deal of birthdays of children but generally downplaying them as people get older, except for the fortieth or fiftieth that often get acknowledged with mourning dress and funeral music and sick jokes. The longer I live, though, the more I think we should celebrate the achievement of sheer survival. I'm not kidding! Life is difficult, and just getting through the challenges of living—the stress and boredom and anxiety and failures and infidelities and disease and grievous loss—ought to be reason enough to honor one another.

There are other important milestones: wedding anniversaries (marriages that survive these days ought surely to be celebrated!), religious festivals (Eid al-Fitr for Muslims, for example, and Yom Kippur and Hanukkah for Jews, and Christmas and Easter for Christians, etc.), and anniversaries of sobriety, friendship, employment, and the death of loved ones.

Perhaps we should even celebrate anniversaries of failure. The Ore-Ida frozen potato people make those mysterious little Tater Tots in your freezer and assorted kinds of french fries and hash browns; they also market frozen cauliflower, broccoli, onions, okra, and mushrooms. Ore-Ida has a reputation for creativity and innovation. What happens when one of those creative, innovative ideas flops? Do they assign blame? Do they fire some hapless manager? No. They throw a party. A cannon is fired, and everyone stops work to celebrate the "perfect failure." "They celebrate what they have learned; they celebrate knowing what will not work; they celebrate that no further time, money, and energy need be consumed in a thankless project; and they celebrate their freedom to go on."[1] And as some of my clergy friends would say, that will preach.

By now it should be clear that courtesy has to do with far more than saying "I'm sorry" when you accidentally bump into someone. It has an active side to it; it takes the initiative to express respect for others. The responsibilities of courtesy involve sensitizing ourselves to ways we can honor other people. It goes without saying that we should remember the birthdays of family members and close friends; however, those who excel at courtesy will do far more. They will keep track of other milestones, pressing a well-used calendar into the service of thoughtfulness: they will remember their parents' wedding anniversary; they will send a card to the neighbor on the anniversary of his wife's death; they will tell their godchildren, over and over again, about their baptism; they will mail a valentine to someone they know is in a dark cave of loneliness; they will throw a surprise party for a colleague on her retirement; they will write a note of congratulations to someone who completed a year of sobriety; they will send gifts to graduates. These things may not seem all that significant, but in truth, they are very significant. Through them a mooring is offered, and one with a chain that won't break.

As with so many acts of courtesy, it comes down to the respect we owe one another. To put it simply, people deserve to be honored. George Regas, former rector of All Saints Episcopal Church in Pasadena, tells a story about Desmond Tutu: "I remember something he said to me as we sat together, just sharing the deep things of the soul. 'George, you know I was raised in the Anglo-Catholic tradition of our church. We would have on the altar a tabernacle in which we would place the consecrated bread and wine—those elements made holy by God. And every time we would come by that tabernacle we would genuflect, we would bow our knee, in respect for God's presence at the altar. You know, I feel, George, like genuflecting every time a white person or a black person comes across my path. Bowing before them because they are vessels of the holy and living God.'

"I could hardly imagine that. In that cauldron of violence and bitterness and hatred, Archbishop Desmond Tutu sees in every person the worth they have because they are the children of God. That's why his life shines as a light to the world."[2]

The telephone call, or the card sent, or the party attended may be, in a very modest sense, a way of genuflecting before people. When we remember milestones in their lives, we tie them to a mooring worthy of respect.

Thirty-three

———•◦•———

Tell Your Buddy His Fly Is Open
Speaking the Truth in Love

DURING MY EIGHTEEN YEARS AS A PASTOR I PRE-
sided over many wedding ceremonies. They tended to follow
a similar sequence of events, beginning with me standing in
a side room with the groom and groomsmen as we waited to
file into the sanctuary to take our assigned places. Once we
each found the little X that had been taped onto the carpet
by the wedding coordinator, we turned our gaze to the door
at the back of the sanctuary, from which emerged brides-
maids, one by one, marching down the aisle. After the last one
had found her X, the organist would crank up the volume, I
would wink at the mother of the bride to signal her to stand,
the congregation would follow her lead, and the bride would
make her grand entrance, resplendent on her father's arm.

While we were standing in that side room, we passed the

time with a good deal of guy talk—silly banter and nervous jokes and asking the groom whether he really wanted to go through with it. And then, just as we had received the official cue to proceed into the sanctuary and I had started pushing the door open, someone would say, "Ah, wait, I need to find the men's room." If you've ever wondered why weddings always start late, now you know.

I've never really discussed with my clergy colleagues what they say during this waiting period; no doubt some use the time for inspirational edification, delivering mediations or leading in prayer. I always felt I should offer important last-minute advice, such as "Hey, everyone, check your fly."

They were surprised I would mention this, but I tried to offer full-service pastoral care. I knew there would probably be at least one guy—generally the one who had just raced back from the men's room—who, when he had taken his place in front of the congregation, would begin to fret about whether he had remembered to zip up (your mind can play tricks on you at a time like that). I had also been around the corner a time or two, and thus I knew that the best man would likely, at some point in the ceremony, lean over to the groom and whisper, "Pssst: your fly is open" (an unoriginal but widely practiced prank), whereupon the groom would look up at me in stark terror. I would then have to shake my head ever so slightly, indicating it wasn't so, but of course I had no idea whether it was true or not, because I could hardly survey the situation without causing three hundred people to wonder what I was looking at. So to save us all this embarrassment, I reminded the guys to check their zippers.

But what happens when your buddy has "left the barn door open," as we used to say in junior high school? You tell him! And if you're with other people, you wipe the smile off your face and assume a gravity implying something really serious has just happened, something like Alan Greenspan calling to ask your buddy's advice on the economy, and then the two of you go off by yourselves for a confidential huddle, from which he emerges to find the nearest pay telephone booth so he can zip his pants.

But what if the guy is not your buddy? What if he's just an acquaintance? What if you don't even know the poor fellow? Well, this becomes a more complicated matter. Sometimes you pretend not to notice, but sometimes you must, in the words of W. C. Fields, "take the bull by the tail and squarely face the situation." The situation may not be pleasant; staring at the backside of a bull has its drawbacks. Yet you do your best to speak the truth anyway, right? And do you know why? Because you want people to speak the truth to you.

Sure, we all tell the occasional white lie to spare the feelings of others, but even so, we ought to cringe a bit, knowing that this had better in fact be an *occasional* practice, because unless we tell the truth to one another we'll be nothing but isolated islands, left to fend for ourselves in a very untrustworthy and scary world. Only by speaking the truth can we build bridges to others—bridges that we ourselves will most certainly need someday.

Most people recognize the importance of upholding truth, yet we live in a world of falsehood. Truth regularly gets twisted beyond all possibility of recognition. Even when it's told, in the literal sense, it's often presented with such calculation and qualification we're left with the unmistakable feeling of a barbed hook tugging at our insides.

Which brings up politicians. I probably shouldn't mention

them. They're such easy targets, it's hardly sporting; it's as though they've painted bull's-eyes over their blue suits and red ties and are standing about three feet away from us. But since I brought up the subject, I will cite one of my all-time favorite speeches from the United States Senate. It took place about 130 years ago, and the issue was whether the sale of liquor should be legal in certain territories seeking state-hood. One notoriously anti-alcohol senator, who was "so dry he was a known fire hazard," challenged a colleague to stand and state his position. The senator rose and replied as follows: "You've asked me how I feel about whiskey. Well, here's how I stand on the question.

"If, when you say whiskey, you mean that devil's brew, the poison spirit, the bloody monster that defiles innocence, dethrones reason, destroys the home and creates misery and poverty—literally takes the bread from the mouths of little children; if you mean the evil drink that topples the Christian man from the pinnacle of righteousness and gracious living and causes him to descend to the pit of degradation, despair, shame and helplessness, then I am certainly against it with all my heart.

"But if, when you say whiskey, you mean the oil of conversation, the philosophic wine, the ale consumed when good fellows get together, that puts a song in their heart and laughter on their lips, the warm glow of contentment in their eyes; if you mean Christmas cheer; if you mean the stimulating drink that puts the spring in an old man's foot-steps on a frosty morning; if you mean the drink whose sale puts untold millions of dollars into our Treasury which are used to provide tender care for our little crippled children, our blind or deaf or dumb, our pitifully aged and infirm, to build highways and hospitals and schools, then I am certainly in favor of it.

"This is my stand, and I will not compromise."[1]

It's not for nothing the U. S. Senate is called the greatest deliberative body in the world. Not just anyone can straddle a fence like this; honing this skill takes a good deal of practice on campaign trails and in press conferences. Once in a while, though, a politician actually leaks out a little candor, and it's as welcome as a cold drink on a hot day. As when a member of the Texas State Legislature spoke in favor of a bill to outlaw certain kinds of sexual behavior: "There are three things wrong with this so-called new morality. It violates the laws of God. It violates the laws of Texas. And I am too old to take advantage of it."[2]

Hearing an honest admission like this makes me want to vote for the man, though I'm sure Texans wouldn't allow me to interfere with their political business (as I recall, their state motto is "Don't mess with Texas"). Hype and distortion and bald-faced lying are so prevalent in our culture that a simple statement of the truth is a wondrous, winsome thing to hear. But it can also be disturbing, especially if it's something I would rather not hear about myself.

In the middle of a conversation with a medical missionary from Africa, I complimented him on his facility with languages. "You're really amazing," I said to him. "I'm in awe of you. I really don't have a gift for languages." To which he responded, "That's nonsense. Out in the bush where I work, the uneducated people speak three or four languages. How many degrees do you have? A Ph.D.? Actually, Don, you're just lazy. You and your American friends just don't want to be bothered with learning other languages." Ouch. That was painful. I didn't like him slashing away at my self-justifications, which are among my most treasured possessions. As the late Carlyle Marney said, "You shall know the truth and the truth shall make you flinch before it makes you free."

Yes, it might make you flinch, but it will also make you free—free enough, maybe, to find your way on the terrain of life. Without commitment to the truth, the underbrush of falsehood quickly grows up and you become lost, unable to know where you are, let alone where you're going. M. Scott Peck has written that for psychological and spiritual health, we must be dedicated to reality, and he offered a helpful image: "The more clearly we see the reality of the world— the more our minds are befuddled by falsehood, mispercep- tions, and illusions—the less able we will be to determine correct courses of action and make wise decisions. Our view of reality is like a map with which to negotiate the terrain of life. If the map is true and accurate, we will generally know where we are, and if we have decided where we want to go, we will generally know how to get there. If the map is false and inaccurate, we generally will be lost."[3] By speaking the truth, we enable one another to chart accurate maps and thus get from here to wherever we're going with integrity and greater wholeness.

Our relationships, for example, depend on truth. Unless others speak truthfully to us, we never engage real people but only phony images; unless we speak truthfully to others, we never experience the exquisite joy of being known and accepted for who we really are. Any friendship worth the effort of cultivating demands honesty.

Tony Campolo told of a time his mother made him go to a funeral to show his respect for the deceased, Mr. Kilpatrick.

He drove to the funeral home, entered the chapel, and bowed his head. When he looked around, he noticed he was the only one there, and when he peered into the casket, he did not see Mr. Kilpatrick. He had gone to the wrong funeral. Campolo was about to leave when an elderly woman clutched his arm and pleaded, "You were his friend, weren't you?" Not knowing what to do, he lied and said, "Yeah, he was a good man. Everybody loved him." After the funeral, Campolo and the elderly woman went to the cemetery in a limousine. The casket was lowered into the grave, and both tossed a flower on it. But on the way back to the funeral home, Campolo confessed the truth: "Mrs. King, there's something I've got to tell you. I want to be your friend, and we can't have a friendship unless I tell you the truth. I'm afraid I have to tell you that I didn't really know your husband. I came to his funeral by accident." She squeezed his hand and said, "You'll never, ever, ever, know how much your being here with me today meant."[4]

I don't know whether Campolo and Mrs. King became friends; I only know they could not have become genuine friends without Campolo's honesty.

Does this mean we always blurt out the truth, no matter what? No, I don't think so. Let me suggest two guidelines. First, the truth must be pertinent to the situation. Lewis Smedes has beautifully summarized what this means: "A politician ought to speak the truth about public matters as he sees them; he does not need to tell us how he feels about his wife. A doctor ought to tell me the truth, as he understands it, about my health; he does not need to tell me his views on universal health insurance. A minister ought to preach the truth, as he sees it, about the gospel; he does not need to tell the congregation what he feels about the choir director. [Telling the truth] does not call us to be garrulous blabbermouths. Truthfulness is demanded from us about the things that we ought to speak about at all."[5] It is neither ethical nor courteous to dump all our feelings at all times on all people. When it is appropriate, though, we have an obligation to speak with honesty.

Second, the truth must be used to build up and not tear down. The truth can be used to ream out, beat up, and put down; it can be used to force someone into submission or to flatten into nonexistence another person's feelings of self-worth. But those who respect others will speak it with sensitivity, in ways that help others grow toward greater responsibility and maturity. This is part of what St. Paul had in mind, I think, when he wrote about "speaking the truth in love."

So Tom, after investing a lot of capital in his friendship with Mike—after much laughter and tears and Monday Night Football and jogging together—takes the risk to say, "Mike, by now you know how much I care about you. Because of my love, I need to level with you. I'm worried you're spending far too much time at work. To put it to you straight, buddy, you're neglecting your wife and kids, and I think you're headed for serious trouble. Now that I've spoken my piece, I won't keep bugging you (at least about this). But know that I want to help in any way I can."

Or Susan says to Andrea, "Well, my friend, before we get back to work, I want to share with you something I've been thinking about for a while. You know how much you've meant to me, not only as a friend but as my pastor. You know you're my spiritual mentor. I'm not a trained theologian or preacher, but I want to give you some feedback on a mannerism you have in the pulpit that's pretty annoying. . . ."

If you're blessed to have a friend like Tom or Susan, a friend who cares enough to speak the truth, even when it hurts, immediately get on your knees and thank God for this blessing. And if you want to be a courteous person, dedicate yourself to speaking the truth, when it's pertinent and with love, even when it's difficult. If we would all do this, we'd help one another chart maps that correspond to reality, and thus we just might have an easier time finding our way in life.

———•••———

Thirty-four

Pretend You Don't Notice When Your Dinner Partner Drools

Guarding the Dignity of Others

A T THAT AGE WHEN A CAR COULD RAISE AS MUCH
lust in me as women could in later years, when I was old
enough to think I knew how to drive but young enough not
to be able to drive, I happily volunteered to wash the family
car. The point was to be able to drive the car: the car was
never quite in the right place in relation to the hose, and so
I drove it back and forth over about fifteen feet of driveway.

I had the unhappy misfortune one day to have backed over
the bucket just as my father came out of the house. Neither
of us can remember what was on his mind. But now, after
spending many years as a pastor, I can guess: a member of the
church, probably, had been rushed to the hospital, or he had
been called to make peace in a family dispute, or a deacon
had just telephoned to criticize him about something—no

doubt something like this had filled and troubled his mind when he shot through the back door. *A man with a mission.*

I hadn't hurt the car and the bucket was only bent. No big deal, or so I thought. But at that moment my dad didn't need a squashed bucket under the axle. He erupted in uncharacteristic anger.

"Dumb kid! Why don't you watch what you're doing? Give me the keys!"

Then he jumped into the driver's seat, started the engine, and backed the car out of the driveway . . . right into the neighbor's car.

I did not laugh. Believe me, I wanted to laugh; I wanted to point my finger at him and cut loose with hilarity until tears ran down my cheeks and I fell into convulsions on the driveway. My dad had just yelled at me for running over a bucket and then smashed into the neighbor's Chevy. This was too good to be true, the stuff of legendary comedy. But I didn't even smile. I might have been careless with buckets but I wasn't careless with my life. About twenty years later, when I finally had gotten up enough courage to mention the incident, we both had a good laugh. At the time, though, it was better—*far* better—for everyone concerned to pretend I didn't notice.

There are times in life when it's better not to notice, to pretend you don't see something. Some situations call for selective blindness.

Life is not easy, as I've already pointed out several times in this book. This is usually not because of major crises, such as divorce or cancer, that are like tornadoes blowing through your picnic, forcing you to douse the fire, stash the potato salad, and run for cover. Most of the time, life is difficult for

much smaller reasons—because smoke from the fire is getting in your eyes, because yellow jackets are dive-bombing
the potato salad, and because mosquitoes are feasting on your
flesh. None of these things causes you to abandon the picnic;
you're in no serious danger and you're still having enough fun
to want to stay put. But these little annoyances keep you
pretty distracted. It's hard to bring the picnic off smoothly.

Take our bodies, for example. They require a good deal of
maintenance, and no matter how meticulously we watch our
diet and exercise and groom ourselves, something will go
wrong, and usually at the most inopportune moment.

You finally got up the nerve to ask her to lunch, and so
you spend a good deal of time that morning trying to make
yourself look like Mr. Major Stud, not only shaving with extra
care but taking the time to cut back the foliage in your ears
and nose. And at lunch, everything goes well, with the conversation more enjoyable than you had dared to hope. You're
sounding interesting and witty, if you do say so yourself, and
you're even feeling, well, quite attractive. Then she says something funny and you laugh with exaggerated enthusiasm, but
you weren't exactly calculating the effects of Diet Coke in
your mouth at the same time, which causes a major explosion you try to hold down, but something has to give and
what gives is your nose—all down your upper lip and chin.
With a movement faster than a lizard's tongue catching a fly,
you bring the napkin up to deal with the damage, smashing
your knuckles on the table but smiling as though nothing has
happened, wiping your face and praying for all you're worth
that if there's really a God in heaven a miracle will have just
occurred and she won't have noticed the eruption of Mt. St.
Helens. You carry on, of course, trying to appear cool and in

control, but all the time wondering if she's going to remember this date as "the lunch with Mr. Booger."

Bodies are wonderful things, but they can be hard to manage. After an interview for a job you've really wanted, you're smiling to yourself, knowing you didn't just hit the basket but dunked the ball with style, and then you notice something funny about your reflection in the sidewalk window, and so you pull the little mirror out of your purse and see a gargantuan piece of lettuce stuck between your two front teeth. For a moment, you contemplate stepping in front of an oncoming bus. Or you're at a fancy awards dinner, and you're the one to be honored, having brought in more sales than anyone in your entire region, and when everyone has finished eating and the master of ceremonies has finally come to the conclusion of his lame jokes, you start to feel a rumbling in your lower intestines, an ominous sound indicating big trouble in River City, and panic seizes you as you try to calculate whether you can make it through your acceptance speech or if you should run down to the restroom and hope you get back in time. Or you're in front of the class, giving a presentation you've worked hard preparing, and you're feeling pretty good about it all, until you catch an unmistakable whiff of body odor, and you're wondering who in the front row neglected to shower, and then, in the lower corner of your vision, you notice a patch of sweat under your arm about the size of the football field and it occurs to you that you are the one producing the foul atmosphere.

Well, I could go on with all sorts of illustrations, describing situations we've all been in at one time or another. But you get the idea: keeping unruly bodies in line can make life complicated. And this is only part of the problem. Things really get tricky when you add to the equation all the various social challenges we face as we struggle to keep from making complete fools of ourselves.

My father once attended a large conference for pastors, and part way through one of the lectures, a man seated quite a few chairs in from the aisle needed to make an exit. So he carefully stepped over people, whispering his apologies, doing the best he could not to be disruptive. A few minutes later he returned, and once again stepped over the same people, unaware that this time he was dragging out of the back of his pants a long trail of toilet paper, which gently swept across everyone's lap.

The poor guy: trying to be a good pastor and learn a few things, when he heard the imperious call of nature on his body, and so with due courtesy, he excused himself and then returned, only to embarrass himself and cause a complete social upheaval. As I said, life is no carefree picnic; if you survive the bees, watch out for the ants.

It's good to remember we're all in the same boat, or if not exactly in the same boat, we're all in leaky boats and bailing as fast as we can to stay afloat in very rough water. Let's agree to extend to one another the gift of merciful blindness: I'll promise not to notice your moments of mortification if you ignore mine. Let's create between us an invisible buffer zone of grace, a shield mercifully protecting us from the negative judgments of one another.

You say you wanted to crawl under the table when you saw a strand of spittle extending from your lip to your fork about the length of the Mississippi River? Relax, I never even saw it. Just as you were completely unaware of the zipper that had torn apart from my pants the day I was giving a lecture

in front of a very skinny lectern. Thanks for discreetly looking in other directions to save me from embarrassment.

I've been using examples drawn largely from the physical
realm, but I shouldn't end this chapter without extending its
horizon of application. Bodily problems make life difficult, to
be sure, but more serious challenges come with the inevitable
friction of relationships. People complicate things. I like to
say my work as a seminary president would be easy if it
weren't for the students, faculty, and staff. Perhaps you would
say something similar about your job. Other people sometimes have other ideas, other goals, other ways of doing
things. This tends to make a muddled mess at work, as well as
other places. Such as families. Families would always be wonderful, if it weren't for the actual people who make up families. If only they weren't so . . . or so . . . or so . . . !

Here's the problem: people are tired and have a lot on their
minds and therefore are not always as nice as they should be.
They don't always extend the courtesies we've been dis-
cussing in this book.

So what's our response? We *don't* forgive them. No way.
Forgiveness is too costly to squander on small offenses. We
need to save that for serious hurts, when we've been betrayed
or intentionally wounded. Forgiveness is like an antibiotic,
very rare and almost always effective, that saves relationships
from death. But you don't use antibiotics on every germ that
comes your way. Most of the relational germs that infect us
don't need anything as strong as forgiveness. They need simply to be overlooked, not noticed.

Yes, people do annoying things. They use obscene gestures,
they show up late, they speak before thinking, they forget to
say thanks, they spread discourtesy like a mean virus. Most of

the time, though, it's because life is difficult for them, too, and they're having a hard time keeping themselves together; they often feel bedraggled and beat up, and for this reason, they're not always as sensitive as they ought to be.

Just like you and me.

And so let's extend our agreement: let's surround one another with a buffer zone of grace that's large enough to cover all the day-to-day tensions between us. Do your best to be courteous in all circumstances, by all means, but when you blow it, I'll do my best not to notice. And when I blow it, I'll count on your gift of merciful blindness. That way, maybe we'll be able to keep the picnic going in spite of the annoyances.

Thirty-five

———•———

Wave to Motor Boaters
Strengthening the Bonds of Community

WHEN I'M ASKED WHAT I LIKE BEST ABOUT BEING a seminary president, I sometimes reply, with only half my tongue-in-cheek, "Sailing on San Francisco Bay." Other things about my job provide pleasure, of course, but it's hard to top being on a reach toward the city with a twenty-five knot wind blowing through the Gate, the lee rail under water, and two or three students on board. Keeping the boat on its feet takes concentration, to be sure, but we usually find time for conversation. They tell me about their classes and the ministries they hope to have, and I tell them about my experiences as a pastor. Sometimes I think it's the most important work I do.

But there are always some awkward moments as we set out from Sausalito. The students, most of whom have never been on a sailboat before, are ignorant of certain time-honored rules of the water. Their innocence, though, does not relieve my embarrassment when, in a spasm of goodwill, they commit the unpardonable sin of waving to motor boaters.

There is something mildly charming about this mushy liberalism, I admit, but nautical orthodoxy must be upheld. So my earnest lecture concerning the difference between halyards and sheets comes to an abrupt halt while I sermonize about a basic principle of life on the water: *sailors never wave to motor boaters.*

My mind flashes back to when my daughter was small, her face a little pink bump in the middle of the orange life jacket. "But Daddy," she would say, "are motor boaters bad people?"

"No, honey. They mean well. Their hearts are in the right place. They like to be on the water, after all. And anyway, God loves everybody, so we should be kind to them. But they're different from us. Their parents probably didn't give them wonderful experiences like we're having today—sitting here perfectly still, enjoying the peaceful calm, hearing the sound of water gently lapping against the hull. You hear it? You couldn't hear that in a motor boat. No, motor boaters aren't bad, but they're bereft of imagination; they have no poetry in their souls. If you want to go fast, get in a car; if you want to smell exhaust, stand behind a bus. But if you want to enjoy the beauty of God's creation . . ."

This is not a personal matter, mind you. Some of my best friends are motor boaters. It's just that certain standards should be maintained; there is an order to things that ought to be upheld. If today you wave at motor boaters, tomorrow you'll be waving at jet skiers, for goodness sake! And then where would we be? Anarchy on the water!

Recently, though, my convictions about this have been as troubled as the face of the water when an outgoing tide meets an incoming wind. It all started with a dream.

I had been working on my boat, applying yet another coat of oil to the teak, and felt a deep weariness seize me. So I stretched out on the V-berth for a few moments and suddenly found myself in a raging storm. The wind had ripped out my sails, and my diesel engine, straining to get me back to the marina, coughed with exhaustion before giving up the fight. Now I had no sails, no engine, and no hope. A fifty knot wind was blowing me toward the rocks of Angel Island and certain destruction.

Then I saw, through the spray of angry water, another boat—a big powerboat, with what must have been twin diesels working in perfect harmony, moving steadily through the storm. It was within hailing distance and it could rescue me, and so I hollered for help, waving furiously until my arms hit the top of the cabin and the pain mercifully delivered me from my nightmare.

Actually, the above dream was imaginary; I made it up. But it's a dream I *should* have had. For though I tease about sailors and motor boaters having nothing to do with each other, I really shouldn't. Sailors need motor boaters, and motor boaters need sailors; one thing my students had better learn is how to wave to motor boaters, for their lives will depend upon it. There are already too many groups at odds with each other: republicans and democrats, Christians and Jews, blacks and whites, boomers and busters, vegetarians and cattle ranchers, loggers and environmentalists, fishermen and Native Americans—these and many more avoid waving to one another.

What the world needs, in my judgment, is a lot more promiscuous wavers. These are people who wave to everyone; they are prodigal in cordiality, spendthrifts of good will. We would do well to learn from them.

Promiscuous wavers, first of all, *notice the individual*. Being aware of groups is certainly a fine thing; it's good to sensitize ourselves to prejudices and problems between races or religions or those of different economic levels. But we must remember that in one sense any group is only a generalized abstraction, an artificial category we use to impose order on the messiness of human life. This ordering can make some sense, to be sure; it no doubt helps us understand particular aspects of reality. But it's limited. In my daily life, for example, I don't really have a relationship with a group called "African-Americans"; I only have my friends James and Leon and Gayle and Christine, all of whom happen to have darker skin than mine. On the other hand, they all have lighter skin than others, even as I have darker skin than still others. I don't mean to diminish the significance of ethnic origins and cultural differences, but only to acknowledge that the matter is complicated, and we need leaders—intellectual and religious and political—to help us think deeper and better about some of these things. In the meantime, though, we encounter individuals, and how we treat them is no small matter.

Julia Ward Howe, who wrote "The Battle Hymn of the Republic," once asked Senator Charles Sumner to come to the aid of a needy citizen. Sumner turned her down with the excuse that he had grown too busy to concern himself with individuals. Howe replied, "Charles, that's remarkable. Even God hasn't reached that stage yet."[1]

Promiscuous wavers concern themselves with individuals.

They refuse to allow the stereotypes of a group to get between themselves and the actual persons they meet. They don't see a member of "the nautically challenged motor boaters" floating by, for instance, but an individual who, though in a different kind of boat, is still a human being and thus filled with the same feelings that bless and afflict us all. One of those feelings may very well be loneliness, a hunger to connect with others. So promiscuous wavers don't sit on their hands but flail them about in friendly greeting.

Second, promiscuous wavers *try not to do things that make individuals feel excluded*. They monitor their behavior so it doesn't, even inadvertently, assume the role of a bouncer, kicking others out and locking the door. Most often this happens through what's said or the way it's said. All the right words might be spoken, but in a patronizing manner. Or *almost* all the right words might be spoken, but the selective editing puts someone in his or her place. Or what's said might be whispered in front of others.

I suppose I'm especially sensitive about this matter of whispering in front of others because I grew up as a PK—a preacher's kid. This had many advantages, for which I'm thankful, but one serious disadvantage was that my buddies would frequently say, "Hey, let's not mention this in front of Don. We don't want his dad to know!" I missed out on a good many jokes and humorous comments; even worse, I was left wondering about the facts of life long after most of my friends had pretty much figured them out. I knew they liked me well enough, but I still felt excluded, an outsider, and this never feels good. The one person I could usually count on was Dan, my best friend, who knew I was just an ordinary kid and, when we were alone, would usually fill me in on the stuff the others had kept from me. He did what he could to include me, and I've never forgotten it.

Which leads me to my final point: promiscuous wavers *draw others into their circle with acts of kindness.* They do what they can—even if it seems small and insignificant—to strengthen the bonds of the human community.

"Warmth, warmth, warmth!" Miguel DeUnamuno wrote, "For we are dying of cold and not of darkness. It is not the night that kills, but the frost." Promiscuous wavers kindle a fire against the bitter chill of an individualistic society. It usually doesn't take much to warm things up; it only takes a spark to get a fire going. Even a little act of kindness can start the thaw.

There is a scene in Dostoyevsky's *The Brothers Karamazov* in which Dmitri has just been sentenced to imprisonment in Siberia. He is so exhausted he falls asleep on a courtroom bench, and when he awakens, he discovers that someone has placed a pillow under his head. He doesn't know who has done it, but he's elated. He believes it's a sign of the goodness of life. He will go to prison, he says, and keep God's name alive there, because he knows that God is in the world. A small act of kindness gives him courage to face his future.

Pablo Casals said, "The capacity to care is the thing which gives life its deepest meaning." Occasionally that care expresses itself in heroic sacrifices. I heard recently of a man who gave a lung to his sister who had been dying of a pulmonary disease, and I was moved by his self-giving. Few of us, however, are called upon to make sacrifices this large. Most of the time our caring must express itself in little acts of sensitivity.

You're hosting a party and remember that one of your guests is struggling to stay on a difficult diet, so before the big night, you call him to ask what you could serve that he would enjoy. You're at a worship service and notice someone you haven't seen before, a conspicuous newcomer, so you go out of your way to meet her and introduce her to others in your congregation. You're with a couple of friends and become aware that one person isn't saying much, for the obvious reason that he has no idea what you're talking about, so you steer the conversation in a different direction, toward a subject in which you all can participate. You wave at people, in other words, especially those on the edges or even outside; you invite them into the circle, or you draw the circle large enough to include them.

After World War I the Prince of Wales visited a military hospital that cared for thirty-six injured soldiers. In the first ward, he went from bed to bed thanking each soldier for his sacrifices for Great Britain. As he left the ward he said to his official host, "You told me there were thirty-six soldiers here, but I counted only twenty-nine. Where are the other seven?"

The official replied that the others were in very bad condition, so bad they would never be able to leave the hospital. "It would be better to leave them alone."

Undaunted, the prince found the ward and proceeded to visit with each soldier, just as he had in the previous ward. As he left, though, he counted the number of wounded and noticed there were only six. Outside, the prince asked the official, "Where is the missing soldier?"

"Ah, Your Majesty, that one is in a little dark room by himself. He is blind, dumb, deaf, and completely paralyzed by the injuries he suffered. He awaits release by death."

The prince quietly opened the door and entered the darkened room, finding the poor creature lying helpless upon his bed. The prince could not speak of his sympathy and his gratitude, for the man was deaf; he could not shake hands, for the man was paralyzed; he could not show how he felt, for the man was blind. So the prince slowly approached the bed, stooped over the wounded soldier, and kissed him on the forehead.[2]

Promiscuous wavers do their best to include everyone.

I always wave to a man in my small town, though he rarely responds. He spends his life wandering our streets in what appears to be a daze. Sometimes he stops and stands in place, staring vacantly for hours. He's disheveled, unkempt. If you weren't familiar with the sight, you might be somewhat afraid of him, for he seems out of place in our upper-middle class community. But we who live here are used to seeing him shuffle along. I wish I knew his story. What sort of blow did he suffer that caused this condition? Was it an experience in Vietnam? Was it drugs? Was it some sort of abuse? Was it an overwhelming grief from which he never recovered? I have no idea. But perhaps, had things been slightly different for both of us, he would be the seminary president and I would be wandering the streets. You never know. So I keep waving to him, trying, in a small way, to include him in my daily life. Every now and then he responds, and when he does, it makes my day. It's not much from either of us; it's a start, though, the first fragile threads in the bond of a relationship being tentatively woven together.

A couple of years ago some of our students did more than greet him on the street. They invited him to be their guest at Thanksgiving dinner. Maybe they remembered that the Jesus they were studying had the habit of eating with all sorts of people, some of whom were pretty unsavory characters. I don't know. Whatever their motivation, they drew their circle a little larger and included him that day. He didn't say much, I was told, but he was there, a part of the community. When I heard what these students had done, I was very proud of them. I was also grateful I had not yet taken them sailing and lectured them on waving to motor boaters. They were promiscuous wavers, thank God, and I'm hoping to learn from their example.

Thirty-six

———◆———

Once in a While, Be a Slob

Knowing When to Break the Rules

ONE ADVANTAGE OF WRITING THIS BOOK IS THE satisfying feeling of venting irritation with certain kinds of behavior. Even so, don't think it has been a nonstop party. I've also had to cope with a serious disadvantage: each of these chapters has followed me constantly, sometimes wagging a finger of accusation. When I ask my secretary to do something, I remember chapter 1 (did I say "please"?). When I'm deciding how much of a tip to leave on the table, I remember chapter 20 (was I generous?). When I'm finding it hard to admit a mistake, I remember chapter 16 (why not apologize?). Unfortunately, I don't always live up to my own standards. This is why I've been looking forward to writing this final chapter.

After thirty-five chapters of urging you to shape up and

treat others with respect, I'm happy to conclude this book with a simple message: *relax!* Once in a while it's worthwhile to say to that ever-so responsible person inside you, "At ease." Occasionally it's good to loosen your tie, kick off your shoes, and put your feet squarely in the center of the coffee table. And maybe burp while you're doing it.

I say this not because I think we're really a bunch of animals who can be caged only so long before the onset of deleterious consequences, though I suppose this ought to be considered. Garrison Keillor, in an article reflecting on the problems of male self-identity, commented that "this was not a great year for guys. . . . Guys are in trouble. Manhood, once an opportunity for achievement, now seems like a problem to be overcome. Plato, St. Francis, Leonardo da Vinci, Vince Lombardi—you don't find guys of that caliber today. What you find is terrible gender anxiety, guys trying to be Mr. Right, the man who can bake a cherry pie, go shoot skeet, come back, toss a salad, converse easily about intimate matters, cry if need be, laugh, hug, be vulnerable, perform passionately that night, and the next day go off and lift them bales on that barge and tote it. Being perfect is a terrible way to spend your life, and guys are not equipped for it anyway. It is like a bear riding a bicycle: He can be trained to do it for short periods, but he would rather be in the woods doing what bears do there."[1]

This may be why some men leave the womenfolk behind and head for the forest to beat drums, chant, and do other manly things in order to get in touch with their inner bear. I don't know. In any event, this is not what I have in mind when I maintain that we all—women as well as men—

should let ourselves be slobs once in a while. My motive for saying this isn't a low view of humanity, but just the opposite: human beings possess so much dignity, have such inherent value, they dare not allow themselves to be reduced to a set of rules.

This may sound odd, I know, coming at the end of a book listing various "rules" of courtesy. Are they necessary or not? If not, why did we both waste our time with this book?

Let me try to explain. We need rules, by all means; without them, we would be over our heads in a very deep pile of chaos. They may be legal laws imposed on us, or religious and ethical principles we choose to obey, or personal disciplines we adopt. They serve an important role in our lives by creating a kind of barrier to protect us from the worst part of ourselves. My ego is an unruly thing, getting me into all sorts of difficulties with spur-of-the-moment feelings and selfish desires. The rules keep its destructive potential under check, away from both my own best self and you; they help guard what is best within me and create a zone of freedom around you, preserving your dignity. So we pay attention to the rules, thinking about what sort of behavior works best to protect the interests of everyone, and as part of that process, we may even write or read books like this one.

Yet even while thinking about the rules—perhaps *especially* while thinking about the rules—we ought to pause to remind ourselves that they are only a means to an end and not the end itself. They are meant to serve our essential humanity, not define it.

When the rules become ends in themselves, they destroy the human dignity they were meant to protect by seducing us with two irresistible temptations. The first is to define ourselves by them, as though our lives ultimately consist of nothing but the accumulation of checked-off items on someone's to do list. The second is to use them to compare ourselves with others, patting ourselves on the back for the things we've done or not done, and pointing a finger in judgment toward everyone who hasn't reached our level of achievement. Succumbing to either of these temptations, it should be noted, provides considerable pleasure: it's handy to have the ambiguities and complexities of self-identity swept away by an easily measurable code of conduct, and it's deliciously enjoyable to know that while you may be no Mother Teresa, you're still a whole lot better than many others. The problem with giving rules this much power, though, is that they paradoxically set free the very force they were intended to check: they energize and embolden self-centeredness, thus further fragmenting human community. As ends in themselves, the rules trivialize the wonder of being human into a particular pattern of behavior. They blind us to a deeper mystery at the center of things.

To remind ourselves of this, to keep rules in their proper place—means to a greater end—we should practice (dare I say it?) a little selective rebellion. After reading this book you surely know I put a great deal of emphasis on the word *little* in the last sentence. I'm not suggesting anything major, anything that will hurt yourself or others; I'm simply acknowledging that we all need to loosen the girdles of restraint from time to time. Occasional expressions of freedom can remind us of the mystery rules were meant to protect.

One of my favorite insurrections involves eating. I believe that while I'm sailing, something magical happens so that calories and fat grams and sodium simply don't count. The sheer goodness of sailing makes these bad things disappear. (As for what happens on motor boats, I wouldn't presume to say; if you happen to be in such circumstances you'll have to take your chances [see chapter 35]). On my boat we take full advantage of this happy suspension of the rules. Lunch may consist entirely of potato chips, Chee•tos, and chocolate. Sometimes, though, we aim for nutritional balance by adding pastrami sandwiches. And we never worry about packing on fat or clogging up arteries. It's all perfectly safe.

How do I know this? I just made it up! Which is what you're supposed to do when you're playing. Making up things is at the heart of play, and if you've forgotten this, watch children: they're constantly suspending ordinary rules of reality to inhabit worlds of imaginary freedom. The refrigerator carton in the backyard is really a rocket on the way to Mars. The towel tied around the neck is really Superman's cape with power to defy leaden laws that keep adults on the ground. The solemn gathering in the attic is really a wedding ceremony or maybe a murder trial. Children know how to defy the canons of rationality and responsibility for the sake of a good time.

The older I get, the more I want to learn from children. One of the things they teach us is that play isn't simply a luxury but a necessary part of being human. In spite of what your parents taught you, play isn't something you earn as a reward for hard work. Hard work is something you do in gratitude for the gift of play. I learned this from an unlikely source— the great German theologian Karl Barth. He pointed out an interesting order in the creation story in Genesis: God climaxes creation by making man and woman on the sixth day. Then the seventh day dawns and you would expect Adam and Eve to get busy with naming the animals and taste-testing fruits and working up a good sweat by assuming their responsibilities for the earth. But no! Before they can get out of the house and catch the early commuter train, God says, "Let's take the day off." And they say, "But we haven't even put in a single day's work yet." To which God replies (my very loose paraphrase), "Yeah, I know, but I've just worked six days and am ready for a break, and so why don't you rest and play with me before you start worrying about weeds and mort-gages and college tuition. You must never forget, my dear creatures, that your very *being* is a gift."

And thus we are ready to name the mystery at the center of things: *grace*. I cannot explain this word with precision but only struggle for images. At the heart of reality is a torrent of unearned blessing headed our way, a crowning with dignity, a parent laughing with pride and pleasure because of us, a welcoming embrace. We have earned none of this; much of what we do makes us completely undeserving. But still it's ours, a gift. This is part of what I mean by grace.

If what I'm saying is true, then it's the best news we'll ever hear. For deep within most of us, I think, is a longing for an embrace—an embrace that somehow lasts after all other arms have tired and fallen away, an embrace that keeps holding in spite of the many times we break the rules, an embrace that confers a self-worth that overpowers our self-disgust, an embrace that finally and for all time takes up broken frag-ments of meaning and pieces them together in a way that makes sense, an embrace that sweeps away our loneliness and makes us part of a community in which we are known and affirmed and loved.

Greg Norman is a professional golfer known for his ice-cold stoicism. He says he learned his hard-nosed tactics from his father. "I used to see my father, getting off a plane or something, and I'd want to hug him. But he'd only shake my hand." Commenting on his aloofness going into the 1996 Masters golf tournament, Norman snorted, "Nobody really knows me out there."

After leading golf's most prestigious event from the start, Norman blew a six-shot lead in the last round, losing to rival Nick Faldo. An article in *Sports Illustrated* described what happened: "Now, as Faldo made one last thrust into Norman's heart with a 15-foot birdie putt on the 72nd hole, the two of them came toward each other, Norman trying to smile, looking for a handshake, and finding himself in the warmest embrace instead.

"As they held that hug, held it even as both of them cried, Norman changed just a little. 'I wasn't crying because I'd lost,' Norman said the next day. 'I've lost a lot of golf tournaments before. I'll lose a lot more. I cried because I'd never felt that from another man before. I've never had a hug like that in my life.' "[2]

Norman was surprised by the joy of a hug beyond anything he had experienced, a hug that touched a longing deep within him. A similar longing lives within each of us, I'm convinced, regardless of parents or spouses or lovers we've had, and when we feel an embrace so fulfilling it could only be from above our everyday relationships, or perhaps from deep within the heart of all things, well, we're likely to burst out singing, "Amazing grace, how sweet the sound . . ."

An embrace implies an embracer, of course. You can't be hugged by an idea or a principle or a theory, but only by a hugger. Many of us, therefore, would say that if grace describes the mystery at the center of things, it is because of a Grace Granter, a Divine Hugger, a Gracious Being whom we call God.

This is why I believe that rules of behavior, however wise and necessary, cannot be the final standard for what it means to be human. For if we are the product of overflowing grace, we have value *no matter what.* Our worth depends on something other than doing or not doing certain things; it rests wholly and for all time on an embrace that gives our life meaning.

So yes, we relax. We refuse to define ourselves by a list of laws; we remind ourselves—maybe even through an occasional, playful suspension of the rules—of the wonder that "we are wound / With mercy round and round" (Gerald Manley Hopkins).

And thus we come full circle, back to the beginning of this book. Not only are *you* a God-graced individual, so also is everyone else. The grace that pulled all things into being, also pulled into being the one who just cut you off in traffic, the one who waits on your table, the one who needs special assistance, the one you're tempted to laugh at, and even the one who prefers motor boats. These people, too, have a God-conferred worth, a glory that may be concealed but is nonetheless real. So out of gratitude for the grace offered us, we extend it to others, committing ourselves anew to the canons of courtesy; out of a desire to protect our own God-granted dignity, we act God-like, bestowing kindness on others as we offer the respect they deserve. "Rules" of courtesy don't create human worth, but they bear witness to it and help protect it.

The central figure in Christine Sparks's book, *The Elephant Man,* is a hideously deformed victim of neurofibromatosis.

John Merrick is so grotesque in outward form that he qualifies as a freak in a second-rate circus. Eventually a doctor rescues him and gives him decent lodging in a London hospital. Gradually the "it" becomes a person.

Contributing to this process was one of the leading actresses of the day, the beautiful Madge Kendall. She learned of the Elephant Man through a story in the *London Times,* and she went to the hospital to visit him, taking along an autographed picture of herself and a copy of the complete works of William Shakespeare. When he received these gifts, the Elephant Man opened the heavy volume to *Romeo and Juliet* and began to read aloud. She responded, reading Juliet's lines. The celebrated actress summoned all the gentleness and tenderness at her command and pressed her lips against the corner of his distorted mouth.

"Why Mr. Merrick," she said in a soft voice, "you're not an Elephant Man at all . . ."

"Oh . . . no?"

"Oh . . . no, no . . . you are Romeo."

The incivility of our time has caused many to grow an elephant hide that is hard and insensitive. But because we ourselves have been kissed and embraced by life-giving affirmation, we press our lips against distorted mouths, offering little acts of kindness, expressions of courtesy. We do this not to pile up merits on someone's scorecard of acceptable behavior; we do it in response to the grace extended to us and in recognition that really there are no Elephant Men or Elephant Women, but only Romeos and Juliets who are more worthy of respect than we imagine.

Notes

INTRODUCTION

1. Jill Lawrence, "Excuse Me, But . . . Whatever Happened to Manners," *USA Today,* December 16, 1996, p.1.

2. Brennan Manning, *The Wisdom of Accepted Tenderness: Going Deeper in the Abba Experience* (Denville, NJ: Dimension Books, 1978), pp. 50–52.

3. *Webster's Ninth New Collegiate Dictionary* (Springfield, MA: Merriam-Webster, 1984), p. 299.

4. C. S. Lewis, *The Weight of Glory* (New York: Macmillan, 1980), pp. 3–4.

CHAPTER ONE

1. Donald K. Campbell, *Nehemiah: Man in Charge* (Wheaton, IL: Victor, 1979), p. 19.

2. Diogenes Allen, *Temptation* (Cambridge: Cowley, 1986), pp. 62–63.

Notes

CHAPTER TWO

1. Clifton Fadiman, ed., *The Little, Brown Book of Anecdotes* (Boston: Little, Brown and Company, 1985), p. 544.

2. Rodney Clapp, "Why the Devil Takes Visa," *Christianity Today,* October 7, 1996, p. 20.

3. John Claypool, *Tracks of a Fellow Struggler* (Waco, TX: Word, 1974), pp. 76–77.

4. G. K. Chesterton, *St. Francis of Assisi* (New York: Image, 1957), pp. 74–75.

5. Gary L. Carver, "Joy in Suffering," *Preaching,* September/October 1990, p. 3.

CHAPTER THREE

1. As quoted in Lewis B. Smedes, *Mere Morality: What God Expects from Ordinary People* (Grand Rapids, MI: Eerdmans, 1983), p. 211.

2. Lewis B. Smedes, *A Pretty Good Person* (San Francisco: Harper & Row, 1990), p. 80.

CHAPTER FOUR

1. Robert Lipsyte, "Harassed Officials Fear 'Kill the Ump' Is No Longer a Joke," *New York Times,* January 19, 1997, pp. 1, 20.

2. David W. Major, *Princeton Living,* April 1995. This story has been told by Kathryn Watterson in *Not by the Sword: How the Love of a Cantor and His Family Transformed a Klansman* (New York: Simon & Schuster, 1995).

CHAPTER SIX

1. Clifton Fadiman, ed., *The Little, Brown Book of Anecdotes* (Boston: Little, Brown and Company, 1985), p. 186.

CHAPTER SEVEN

1. Donald Baillie, *God Was in Christ* (New York: Charles Scribner's Sons, 1948), p. 205.

CHAPTER EIGHT

1. Robert Farrar Capon, *The Supper of the Lamb—A Culinary Reflection* (New York: Farrar, Straus & Giroux, 1989), p. xiii.

2. Isak Dinesen, *Babette's Feast and Other Anecdotes of Destiny* (New York: Vintage Books, 1988), p. 27.

CHAPTER NINE

1. David Meyers, *Society in the Balance,* as quoted in Rodney Clapp, "Why the Devil Takes Visa," *Christianity Today,* October 7, 1996, p. 20.

2. George Bernard Shaw, *Man and Superman,* as quoted in Martin E. Marty, *Context,* December 15, 1991, p. 5.

3. Mark Sagoff, "Do We Consume Too Much?" *Atlantic Monthly,* June 1997, p. 94.

CHAPTER TEN

1. Ben Patterson, *Waiting* (Downers Grove, IL: InterVarsity Press, 1989), p. 10.

CHAPTER ELEVEN

1. Norbert Elias, *The History of Manners* (New York: Pantheon, 1978), p. 130.

2. Martin E. Marty, "Bulletiniana," *The Christian Century,* May 21–28, 1997, p. 543.

CHAPTER TWELVE

1. Clifton Fadiman, ed., *The Little, Brown Book of Anecdotes* (Boston: Little, Brown and Company, 1985), p. 43.

2. Ibid., p. 270.

3. "Money," *USA Today,* http://www.usatoday.com/money/consumer/budget/mdebt005.htm.

4. *The Hope Health Letter,* February 1996.

CHAPTER FOURTEEN

1. Douglas Coupland, *Life After God* (New York: Pocket Books, 1994), pp. 273, 359.

2. Robert Bellah, et. al., *Habits of the Heart: Individualism and Commitment in American Life* (Berkeley: University of California Press, 1985), pp. 232–33.

3. Kenneth Grahame, *The Wind in the Willows* (London: Methuen Children's Books, Ltd, Magnet Reprint Edition, 1978), pp. 134–36.

CHAPTER FIFTEEN

1. Arthur M. Schlesinger, Jr., *The Disuniting of America: Reflections on a Multicultural Society* (New York: Norton, 1992), p. 5.

2. Robert Hughes, *The Culture of Complaint* (New York: Warner, 1993), p. 30.

3. Robert Fulghum, *All I Really Need to Know I Learned in Kindergarten: Uncommon Thoughts on Common Things* (New York: Ivy Books, 1986), pp. 154–56.

CHAPTER SIXTEEN

1. Erich Segal, *Love Story* (New York: Signet, 1970), p. 131.

2. Clifton Fadiman, ed., *The Little, Brown Book of Anecdotes* (Boston: Little, Brown and Company, 1985), p. 547.

3. M. Scott Peck, *The Road Less Traveled: A New Psychology of Love, Traditional Values and Spiritual Growth* (New York: Simon & Schuster, 1978), p. 35.

4. As told by Edward J. Robinson in *Leadership,* Winter 1997, p. 73.

CHAPTER SEVENTEEN

1. Neil Postman, *Technopoly* (New York: Knopf, 1992), p. 69.

2. Ted Koppel, as quoted in *Harper's Magazine,* January 1986.

3. James J. Kilpatrick, *The Writer's Art* (Kansas City: Andrews, McMeel & Parker, 1984), p. 44.

CHAPTER EIGHTEEN

1. Ben Patterson, *Waiting* (Downers Grove, IL: InterVarsity Press, 1989), pp. 141–42.

2. Brennan Manning, *The Ragamuffin Gospel* (Sisters, OR: Multnomah, 1990), pp. 91–92.

3. Lewis Smedes, *Caring and Commitment* (Harper & Row, 1988), p. 151.

4. Karl Menninger, as quoted in *Bits and Pieces,* May 30, 1991, pp. 19–20.

5. Conrad Hyers, *And God Created Laughter* (Atlanta, GA: John Knox, 1987), pp. 79–80.

CHAPTER TWENTY

1. Clifton Fadiman, ed., *The Little, Brown Book of Anecdotes* (Boston: Little, Brown and Company, 1985), p. 231.

2. This story was originally told by Peter Marshall, the famed Chaplain of the United States Senate. See "A Baby's Cry," *Peter Marshall: New and Inspiring Messages* (Kansas City: Hallmark, 1969), pp. 54–55.

CHAPTER TWENTY-ONE

1. Clifton Fadiman, ed., *The Little, Brown Book of Anecdotes* (Boston: Little, Brown and Company, 1985), p. 520.

2. William R. White, *Stories for the Journey* (Minneapolis: Augsburg, 1988), pp. 69–70.

CHAPTER TWENTY-THREE

1. *Bits and Pieces,* September 1989, pp. 1–2.

2. As quoted by David R. Martin, *Leadership,* Spring 1992, p. 48.

3. Diogenes Allen, *Temptation* (Cambridge: Cowley, 1986), p. 72.

4. Richard Selzer, *Mortal Lessons: Notes on the Art of Surgery* (New York: Simon & Schuster, 1987), pp. 45–46.

CHAPTER TWENTY-FOUR

1. Greg Asimakoupoulos, "To Illustrate . . ." *Leadership,* Fall 1992, p. 47.

2. J. Wesley Brown, "Good News for Parents," *Christian Century,* May 6, 1981.

CHAPTER TWENTY-FIVE

1. William Lutz, as quoted by Lloyd Shearer, "Intelligence Report," *Parade Magazine,* January 10, 1988, p. 16.

2. Edward Chinn, *Preaching,* January/February 1991, p. 61.

CHAPTER TWENTY-SEVEN

1. Paul Tournier, *Secrets,* Joe Embry, trans. (Atlanta, GA: John Knox, 1963), pp. 22–26.

2. Ibid., p. 29.

3. As quoted by Arlin Schrock, *Leadership,* Winter 1985, p. 49.

4. Gary L. Thomas, "Deadly Compassion," *Christianity Today,* June 16, 1997, p. 21.

CHAPTER TWENTY-EIGHT

1. As told by Steve Brown in *Preaching,* November/December 1993, p. 78.

CHAPTER TWENTY-NINE

1. Clifton Fadiman, ed., *The Little, Brown Book of Anecdotes* (Boston: Little, Brown and Company, 1985), p. 207.

2. *National Center for Health Statistics, Advanced Data,* No. 205, September 30, 1991, p. 1.

3. J. McGinnis and W. Foege, "Actual Causes of Death in the United States," *Journal of the American Medical Association,* Vol. 270, No. 18, November 10, 1993, p. 2208.

4. Igor Stravinsky, *The Poetics of Music,* as quoted by Calvin Stapert, "The Statutes of Liberty: Freedom and Law in the Music of Bach," *Reformed Journal,* March 1985, pp. 11–14.

5. M. Scott Peck, *The Road Less Traveled: A New Psychology of Love, Traditional Values, and Spiritual Growth* (New York: Simon & Schuster, 1978), pp. 66–67.

CHAPTER THIRTY

1. P. J. O'Rourke, *Parliament of Whores: A Lone Humorist Attempts to Explain the Entire U. S. Government* (New York: Atlantic Monthly Press, 1991), pp. 120, 121, 122.

2. Donald W. Brenneman, *Leadership,* Spring 1991, p. 45.

3. As told by David R. Culver, *Leadership,* Winter 1993, p. 49.

CHAPTER THIRTY-ONE

1. Conrad Hyers, *And God Created Laughter* (Atlanta, GA: John Knox, 1987), pp. 16–18.

2. Norman Cousins, *Anatomy of an Illness* (New York: Bantam Books, 1981), p. 39.

3. Frederick Buechner, *Whistling in the Dark: An ABC Theologized* (San Francisco: Harper & Row, 1988), p. 68.

CHAPTER THIRTY-TWO

1. Patrick J. Wilson, "The Sacrament of Failure," *Pulpit Digest,* September/October 1993, p. 40.

2. George F. Regas, *The Living Pulpit,* July/September 1992, p. 11.

CHAPTER THIRTY-THREE

1. As told by Daniel Anderson and quoted by Barry Lorge, *The San Diego Union,* April 24, 1987.

2. Harold Kushner, *When All You've Ever Wanted Isn't Enough* (New York: Summit Books, 1986), p. 62.

3. M. Scott Peck, *The Road Less Traveled: A New Psychology of Love, Traditional Values and Spiritual Growth* (New York: Simon & Schuster, 1978).

4. Tony Campolo, *You Can Make a Difference* (Dallas: Word, 1984), p. 29.

5. Lewis B. Smedes, *Mere Morality: What God Expects from Ordinary People* (Grand Rapids, MI: Eerdmans, 1983), p. 216.

CHAPTER THIRTY-FIVE

1. As quoted by Martin Marty in *Context,* February 1, 1992, p. 1.

2. As told by Samuel M. Buick, *Parables,* October 1990, p. 4.

CHAPTER THIRTY-SIX

1. Stu Weber, *Tender Warrior* (Sisters, OR: Multnomah, 1993), p. 39.

2. Rick Reilly, *Sports Illustrated,* Dec. 30, 1996, as quoted in *Leadership,* Summer 1997, p. 64.

About the Author

Donald McCullough is President of San Francisco Theological Seminary (Presbyterian Church-USA) and Professor of Theology and Preaching. He has pastored congregations in Solana Beach, California, and Seattle. Dr. McCullough holds a Ph.D. from the University of Edinburgh and M.Div. from Fuller Theological Seminary. He is the author of several books, including *The Trivialization of God* and *Waking from the American Dream*.